NO FINISH LINE

My Life As I See It

Marla Runyan

with Sally Jenkins

G. P. PUTNAM'S SONS / NEW YORK

G. P. Putnam's Sons
Publishers Since 1838
a member of
Penguin Putnam Inc.
375 Hudson Street
New York, NY 10014

Library of Congress Cataloging-in-Publication Data

Runyan, Marla, date.
    No finish line : my life as I see it / Marla Runyan with Sally Jenkins.
        p.   cm.
    ISBN 0-399-14803-5
    1. Runyan, Marla.   2. Runners (Sports)—United States—Biography.   3. Women runners—United States—Biography.   4. Blind athletes—United States—Biography.   I. Jenkins, Sally.   II. Title.
    GV1061.15.R85 A3 2001   2001-43192
    796.42'4'092—dc21
    [B]

Printed in the United States of America

10   9   8   7   6   5   4   3   2   1

This book is printed on acid-free paper. ∞

Book design by Amanda Dewey

Frontispiece photo © Thomas Boyd/ The Register-Guard (Eugene, Oregon)

Acknowledgments

The authors would like to thank, first and foremost, Stacy Creamer of Putnam, who believed in the book from the outset and single-handedly brought it into being. Ray Flynn and Esther Newberg also deserve thanks for making it possible for us to do what we love for a living. Stuart Calderwood was a close, careful, and expert reader. And thanks to the many family members, coaches, friends, and doctors who provided insight and information that made the book more whole.

My mother, Valerie, who taught me never to allow the hurdles of life to stand in my way, and who took each one in stride as my advocate when I was too small to do so.

My dad, Gary, who taught me the values of hard work, perseverance, and commitment by demonstrating them every day of his life.

My brother, Grady, for his humor and music and logic.

Matt, "The Rock," my partner in life and best friend.

Summer, my other best friend.

John O'Looney, who made me laugh in the 8th grade when I forgot how and who told me to go out for the track team.

John Bailey, who taught me how to leap over a bar that I could barely see.

Rahn Sheffield, who taught me how to hurdle, literally, and who valued effort over victory.

Beth Scott, my "blind buddy," and her American flag.

Eugene, and the color green.

Dr. Richard Brown, who taught me the physiology of running in his loft in Coburg, Oregon.

Mike Manley, who trained me to experience running in a whole new way.

The Amazon Trail, the Rexius Trail, and Hayward Field.

Dr. Gary Wood, Dr. Mike Leahy, Dr. John LeGat, Dr. Ken Singer, Dr. Stanley James, Dr. Donald Jones, and Dr. Mark Scappaticci, who kept me moving forward on the track and off.

USABA

ASICS

Ray Flynn, for believing in me and for always having my best interests at heart.

Margo Jennings, for the future.

Sally Jenkins, because sometimes I swear you can read my mind and get to the bottom of things, and in doing so, teach me about myself. Thank you for making this book so true and real.

Jean Grendler of Northwest Orthotics, because I don't take one step without you.

Contents

NO FINISH LINE

1. A Matter of Perception

I run, seeing nothing but the open track just in front of me. Other feet keep a steady cadence alongside me. I don't know how many runners might be ahead of me, or behind. The pack is a creature of many colors, breathing and jostling around me. The pace quickens, and we bear down. Only then does the creature break apart, and string out. I feel the gentle curve that initiates the last 200-meter drive for home, and the final sprint down the straightaway. Now I am running against individuals, but who? Who was that who just passed me? Who am I gaining ground on ahead? Who cares, I say to myself. Knowing their names doesn't make it easier to beat them.

I can't see the finish line.

I cross it.

I lean over, gasping. I feel someone, a rival, take my hand. We jog around the track together, trying to get our wind back, and wait for the or-

der of finish to be posted. Suddenly, above my own labored breathing, I hear the crowd roar.

    "Who won?" I ask.

    "You did," she says.

I see sunlight, but I don't always like it. Light can illuminate, but too much light is blinding, and that's one of the more basic truths of this world. If life were a matter of sunny weather all the time, with not a cloud in the perfect blue sky; if there were only light, and more light, with never any rain or shade, you wouldn't see a thing but brightness itself. Light is no good without its opposite—you can't see a thing without a little dark.

What do I see? I've been asked that question, in one form or another, since I was small. I suppose the question is of importance now because I'm the first legally blind athlete to compete in the Olympic Games, and people think that if they can figure out exactly what I see, they'll know what is possible and what is not. They wonder how a woman who is only partially sighted can race at distances of 1500 and 5000 meters in world-class company, and I suppose it's not an unreasonable question, especially if you've seen me drag my nose across a printed page with a magnifying lens cradled in one eye, or watched me narrowly dodge a parking meter that's in plain sight. My answer is, when you run as fast as I do, things tend to be a blur anyway.

The first time I heard the question, I was a little girl, sitting on a white-tiled kitchen counter in my childhood home in Camarillo, California. The person speaking to me was my mother. "What do you see?" she asked. "Can you see that calendar on the wall?" My mother constantly tried to puzzle through my blind-ness, to define the boundaries of my vision, as if she could get to the bottom of it and, in doing so, fix it.

My answer was not so simple. Did I see the standard-sized cal-endar hanging just eight feet in front of me? I knew it existed. I could see the disruption in the wallpapered kitchen wall, a pattern of Crayola-like red and yellow flowers. But could I see the bold text that told me what month it was, or the small squares that rep-resented the days? The answer was no. I saw a white rectangle.

I couldn't see my teacher's writing on a chalkboard, either. Or street signs. Or the letters on a vision chart, with the exception of the big E.

"The doctor said you're legally blind," my mother explained. "If you can't see the letters below the big E, you're legally blind."

"No, I'm not," I said.

It was my initial knee-jerk response to blindness, and I still have it.

The problem here is one of perception: people confuse "dis-abled" with "inept." I am partly disabled, yes—but I am not in-competent. I have an edge of peripheral vision that, although cloudy, is enough to let me negotiate a world-class footrace. I can see people's feet. I can see the colors of my competitors' uniforms. I can see the red Mondo track surface, and the waving of flags—although I don't know which nations they represent.

I just can't see the finish line.

When I run a race, I don't always know whether I've won or lost. I can't see the clocks, or the lap counters, or the scoreboards. I only know that the finish is at the end of the straightaway. But you'd be wrong if you supposed that my vision loss impairs my

running, because I'm a 32-year-old woman, and I've been running for a very long time now, and I've come to understand that
there *is* no finish line.

In the summer between my third- and fourth-grade years, a
disease attacked my retinas and deprived me of most of my vision.
One spring, I could read my grade-school textbooks, and the next
autumn, I couldn't. After various misdiagnoses and other misad-
ventures in several optometrists' chairs, I learned that I had Stargardt's disease, a degenerative ailment that essentially leaves holes
in the delicate, light-sensitive membrane in the back of your eyes
that absorbs and translates images. Stargardt's had damaged the
central area of my retinas, called the macula. After it ran its course,
the details of the world had disappeared from my central view. I
was left with a slim band of peripheral vision, and even that sight
was flawed and needed correction.

I've lived with Stargardt's for so long now that my eyes seem
ordinary to me, and I can barely remember what it was like to
fully see. I only remember that things began to seem farther and
farther away. Such as print. A soccer ball at the other end of the
field. And the faces of the people I knew.

My answer was to run. I believed that when I was outdoors,
my vision was irrelevant. Indoors, in a classroom or a living room,
I was impaired, because I strained to read a book or see a television screen, or even to know whom I was talking to. But when I
was outdoors and running, I felt the same as everyone else.

And then I realized something extraordinary: I didn't just feel
the same as everyone else when I ran—I felt better.

I've been running ever since. I ran through high school in Camarillo, and through college and graduate school at San Diego
State University, where I graduated cum laude and earned a mas-

ter's degree in teaching children who are blind and deaf. I ran through a lot of setbacks and failure. I ran through bureaucratic hoops and red tape. I ran in obscurity, when all I earned was minimum wage from the local YMCA. I ran at the World Championships in Seville, Spain, and at the Sydney Olympic Games, where I finished eighth in the 1500 meters. I'm *still* running, and I'm now the top-ranked woman and the indoor record-holder in the United States in the 5000 meters, and a potential medal contender in that event. But through it all, I hope I've run for the right reasons: to value effort for its own sake, and to prove that impairment does not preclude excellence.

At times, people have not expected much from me, solely because I'm partially blind. I can feel them thinking, "Oh, you're visually impaired, just go sit on the couch." When I'm about to run a race, I can hear people whispering, "There's this blind girl running, isn't that great?"

But I believe that you can be more disabled by your attitude than by vision loss.

My vision is a relative thing: I don't really know how it compares to yours, because the only eyes I see through are my own. I'll tell you some of the things that I see, and some of the things that I don't. I can't see the numbers on a wristwatch, or the "Campbell's" on a can of soup in the grocery store. I can't see a menu, a newspaper, the address on an envelope, or the amount on a paycheck. I can't always see whether there's a curb in front of me, or a pothole, or a tree root.

I can't see my own writing. My printing is a kind of shorthand that resembles a child's writing, with missing letters and incomplete lines. My signature changes each time I sign a check or a credit-card receipt, and I've even been asked to produce other forms of ID to prove my identity.

Here's what I do see: a permanent blot in front of my eyes that almost has physical properties. It is a large oval that blinks and flickers like a strobe light. It has no particular color or definition, but it moves across walls and ceilings and blue skies like a gray stain. It is not something tangible, that's really in *front* of me. It's *inside* me—inside my eyes and retinas.

Imagine that someone took a flash picture, and the flash got in your eyes. For a few moments, you'd see a purplish or gray splotch, and no matter how hard you tried to look around it, it would still be there, right in the center. In a few minutes it would fade away, and the world around you would appear normal again.

For me, it stays.

That thing is always in the middle of my eyes—the indistinct blinking, like a sunspot. Sometimes I change my focus point, hoping to see around the obstructing mass and gain a clearer view of what's in front of me. But the blot moves just as quickly as my eyes, and blocks the view. The blot is the actual scar tissue in the retina, and each eye's scar tissue has its own shape.

But the will to see is primordial—the mind insists on trying to provide itself with some kind of image even when the eyes physically cannot comply. My eyes continually move and shift in an effort to compensate for my blindness. The good area of one eye tries to fill in for the bad area of the other. If we were talking, you might think it was rude of me to stare over your left shoulder— but actually, I see best out of the corners of my eyes, the area untouched by Stargardt's.

But no matter how my eyes compensate, there are some things

I simply can't do. I have trouble crossing streets, especially a street with more than two lanes.

The hardest thing for me to see is something directly in front of me. A parking meter, or a person standing alone, or anything stationary, seems to jump out at me. It appears out of thin air and I have to quickly dodge it.

Shortly before the 2000 Olympic Games in Sydney, my partner, Matt Lonergan, and I went for a run in Colorado Springs. We took a cement bike path that encircled a small lake. Like all distance runners, I'm attracted to soft surfaces, so I decided to veer off to the sand at the water's edge.

I didn't see a rope stretched across the sand, securing a boat. Matt glanced over his shoulder. Before he could say, "Watch out!" I tripped over it. It looked like my legs had been cut from under me. I face-planted.

I only run into objects that are perfectly still.

The truth is, running is the easiest thing I do. To run a race around a perfectly flat and smooth track, in a controlled environment, among a group of familiar people all moving at a similar pace, feels safe to me compared to the effort I have to put forth, and the menace I confront, in moving through an ordinary day in ordinary life.

How I run is a complicated and interesting question. I count heavily on my alternative senses: on the cadence of my stride and the sensations of the earth beneath my feet. I sometimes have no idea who my competitors are because I can't see their faces, but I do know some of them by the colors of their singlets, the shapes of their physiques, and the attitudes of their bodies. In a race, the uniform colors are particularly vivid because so many runners wear gear provided by their sponsors, such as ASICS, adidas, or Nike, and each company uses distinct palettes and patterns from season to season.

More often, I identify people by how they move and walk. In college I could always find my coach, Rahn Sheffield, because he had a certain strut across the track. Some runners are unique; their attributes are quickly identifiable even by me. In Sydney, I knew instantly when the Romanian world champion, Gabriela Szabo, jogged by me during our warmup, because of her size and idiosyncratic shuffle. Her feet turn over like little wheels, and her five-foot, 93-pound frame floated past me efficiently and quietly on the grass infield. The absence of sound was a dead giveaway.

Sometimes the specific identity of a runner is so indistinguishable to me that I don't know enough to be intimidated by who I'm running against. When I competed in the heptathlon, I lined up against Jackie Joyner-Kersee on more than one occasion and never knew that at my elbow was the greatest female athlete in history.

So, in an odd way, maybe my sight, or lack thereof rather, is a beneficial thing. I'm forced to run for the pure performance of it. I don't run for medals, although I've won my share. I run for the aesthetic and kinesthetic experience, the act of running itself. Running, to me, is freedom from confusion and obstacle. It is liberation from the medical technology that has slowed me down since I was a child. Running is freedom from the sedentary and the stagnant. It is movement, and it is simple.

I've come to believe that sight takes a multitude of forms. There is what I literally see, but also what I perceive, and that perception can be based on a variety of factors, from sound, to texture, to intuition.

Memory and recognition can provide a kind of sight too. When I first moved to Eugene and tried to run the soft, groomed wood-chip trails around town, I was constantly hesitant and unsure of where to put my feet. I ran like I was on eggshells. But now I've learned the trails like the back of my hand, and can run nineteen miles on a wood-chip trail, up hills, on and off curbs, without a glitch in my stride or a second of hesitation.

I know every little divot and incline of the Amazon trail from countless miles of interval workouts and four-to-five-mile tempo runs. I swear I have worn a groove right through the soggy soil from running so many loops. I can't see the detailed textural differences in my path, whether it's a raised root or a dip, but I know them from memory. It's only when I get down and tie my shoe, and my face is a foot from the ground, that I notice the components of the brown trail. It contains different colors, and an oatmeal texture, but the wood chips aren't distinctive. I don't always know when a leaf is a leaf and a wood chip is a wood chip, as opposed to something a dog left.

I rely on my other senses to do something as simple as catching the bus. If I stand at a bus stop at home in Eugene waiting for the bus, all I see is a plethora of lights coming toward me, the headlamps of cars intermingling with the flashing of stoplights and the flickering of caution lights. I count heavily on hearing the grunt of a bus engine, and it's so familiar to me that sometimes I really think I do *see* the bus.

I perceive via the temperature of the air, the grain of a running trail, the sounds around me, and the aromas—the piney smell that tells me I'm in the woods, or the car exhaust that tells me I'm nearing an intersection. My body finds a thousand alternate ways to fill in what is missing for me. I am most attuned when I run.

Perhaps to run is my way of becoming more sighted. Henry David Thoreau wrote, "We are all sculptors and painters, and our material is our flesh and blood and bones." Running is my way of regaining control over my body, and it is as much an interior act as exterior, an exercise in moving ever inward to meet myself. Emil Zátopek, the 1952 Olympic marathon champion, said, "Whoever wants to win something runs 100 meters. Whoever wants to experience something runs the marathon." I'm a distance runner, and I run for the experience. When I run smoothly, I feel in concert with the world, muscles rocking and limbs turning in rhythm with the globe.

That's why I run—because it's a way of experiencing the world through sound and touch and movement. I can stand not to *see* the world, but I can't stand not to move through it. The body was designed to move, and running is one of the basic building blocks of movement.

Movement is independence. In fact, the senses that I rely on most heavily have to do with my ability to move. Just being able to put my hands on something, or to feel whether I am standing on a hardwood floor or a wood-chip trail, is significant to me. If I want to see something, I must move toward it.

Moving through the world is my way of envisioning it.

I've become so practiced at moving through the world that often people don't realize I'm partially blind. I've consistently refused to conform to the definition of "legally blind," and I try to function more like a sighted person, sometimes even to the point of foolhardiness. This is a victory of sorts—and what I've been striving for, ever since I was diagnosed.

But it's also a form of denial. I think sometimes I've caused myself as many problems as I've solved.

I can compete for a medal in the 1500 meters in international competition, and yet I can't recognize someone five feet in front of me. This confuses people, and it hasn't fostered social acceptance, either. I set out to keep my blindness a secret in high school, and I mostly succeeded. But my pride came with a price. I set myself up for a lot of misunderstanding—I forgot that people could see me better than I could see them, and my face clearly displayed every mood I was in. How are other people supposed to know that I have no idea who the woman is ten feet away from me unless I can hear her voice?

How many times have I ventured outdoors only to learn that the long-sleeved shirt I've put on with "matching" shorts is really green and the shorts are purple? "Who's that girl with the green shirt and purple shorts?" others ask as I charge down the trail laughing at myself. "Oh, it's just Marla." As much as I rely on colors, I can't always see them. With Stargardt's, as you lose visual acuity, you also lose some ability to distinguish colors in dim light.

I could be an arm's length from Matt Lonergan, the man I live with, and not know he's there. What I do see is his familiar beige jacket, or his posture, or the way he crosses his legs, or the way he sits sipping his coffee while he reads *Track & Field News*. When I see those things, I know it's him. I can make out his face—his large nose, or a smile—when he's very close to me. But I still don't know the color of his eyes.

One of my former coaches, Mike Manley, shaved his beard

one day, and when he stood in front of me that afternoon, I didn't recognize him. A former training partner was always identifiable by her blond ponytail. But one afternoon she sat next to me on a bench and I had no idea who she was. She had cut her hair.

I don't see facial expressions. Very often I rely on what's said and how it is articulated, and not whether someone is smiling or grimacing. But no matter how tone-sensitive I am, I miss things.

In high school I memorized the colors of my friends' clothing so I could find them in the hallway between classes. But I couldn't tell male from female without the sound of a voice or some other clue to help me. There were countless times in high school when I walked right by people I knew, and I wasn't able to say hello because I wasn't sure who I was passing and I didn't want to embarrass myself by making a mistake.

The first time I really saw a face, I mean *really* saw it, was in a movie theatre. I was 17 years old and the movie was *Aliens.* My 12-year-old cousin Melody and I arrived late, and the only seats left were in the front row. I sat with a cricked neck, my head resting on the back of the theatre seat, but I saw every pore and bead of sweat on Sigourney Weaver's face. It was fascinating. *Aliens* quickly became my favorite horror movie, not just because Sigourney Weaver was a designated bad-ass, but because I could see the details of human expression.

To go into the world blindly is to play a game of trust. Every day, you plunge into a swirl of confusion—and sometimes fear and frustration. The rest of the world has all the information, while you do not. This requires you to strike a delicate and constant balance between wariness and faith. Sometimes no amount of self-sufficiency can help you, and when that happens, you have a choice: You can get angry, or you can trust in the basic benevolence of the universe and the essential goodwill of people, and hope you don't get hurt.

Don't we all live that way, really? Blind or not?

If the alternative is to remain at home and never hazard anything, to allow wariness to overcome faith, I consistently choose the opposite. It's not always a comfortable choice, and on occasion I've felt that I live in two different worlds. Sometimes I feel very, very visually impaired, and at other times I feel almost fully sighted. I live in a no-man's land.

I feel most blind when I have to read something in a public place. Every printed thing is unreadable and inaccessible to me—unless I have a powerful aid, like an eight-power magnifier or a closed-circuit television, which you can't exactly carry on errands. Think of all the times in a day when you look at print, from reading the newspapers in the morning, to scanning a computer screen, to filling out a job application, to ordering a coffee off the menu at Starbucks. Now try to go an entire day without reading anything.

I'll go to a grocery store or a coffee shop and feel completely impaired. I feel most blind when I'm in a rush to get something done, like find the right gate number in an airport. I have to ask someone to help me, explaining my situation. It's only recently that I've made my peace with asking for that help.

But there are very few things I haven't been able to master, once I've applied myself to overcoming the obstacle.

People can become caught up in that term "legally blind." They make sweeping assumptions based on the definition. But there are subtle degrees and whole ranges of sight and countless terms to describe them: there is low vision, partially sighted, visually impaired. Back in the '70s there was much debate about whether "visually impaired" was a more proper term than "visually handicapped."

These days, "person first" language is the politically correct descriptor. So I'm defined as a "person with a vision impairment." The terminology has become more important than the particulars of each individual's range of vision and ability to adapt. And that, to me, is silly. You can use any term you like, but it doesn't define me. In the end, it's my responsibility to ensure that the attributes by which I would prefer to be defined are more visible to you than my blindness.

I can't see well, and I run. So let's get on with it.

What I find most ironic is that if there is interest in this story, it is based partly on that term "legally blind." People say, "She's not supposed to run that fast. She's blind." But perhaps we should ask whether our definition of legally blind should be changed.

I've met visually impaired people with doctorates, and I've met some who are content to sit on the sofa and say, "I'm blind." It all comes down to perception—how do *you* perceive your vision loss? That perception, to me, is far more significant than how you perform on the vision test. It's up to the individual to determine what she can and can't do.

My own perception of vision loss is that it's a challenge, like a long-distance race. It requires perseverance and patience and a positive attitude. It's a race—with no end in sight. Perhaps that's why the longer track events are what I'm best at. In an event requiring perseverance and patience and the surmounting of obstacles, I'm in my element. Just as I talk myself through each lap of the 400-meter track, I talk myself through each year of my life, and remind myself that fatigue and frustration are only temporary, and I must keep moving forward.

My blindness is a positive thing. It provides a sharp contrast between the easy and the difficult. It not only has forced me to prove my competence but also has pushed me to achieve. It has given me gifts, such as will and commitment, that I use every day.

This book is just another kind of endeavor to see. It's my attempt to put images together into a complete picture, to find the gaps in my vision and to fill them in with something more whole.

2. The Big E

I didn't have a Barbie-and-Ken childhood. What for other kids was a time of untroubled playfulness, of slides and ladders, kites, puppets, hoops, and candy wrappers, was hard work for me. My chief memories are of exhaustion, pounding headaches, and a seemingly endless succession of doctor's offices. I remember white coats and cold steel medical equipment and other adult torture devices—tongue depressors and pin lights and eye charts.

The onset of sudden partial blindness doesn't sit well with any child, but I was particularly ill suited for it, because I didn't deal well with obstacles. Even in the crib, I was serious-minded and achievement-oriented. I hated anything that held me back. Put me in a playpen or confront me with any other kind of restriction from a stroller to a bib, and I would scream and cry, and try to climb out of it. My parents claim that the first words out of my mouth were, "I wanna do . . ."

Whatever it was, I wanted to do it. There's a picture of me as a little girl, a grade-school snapshot that was taken when I could still fully see. It shows the face of a child with an almost empress-like confidence, chin upraised and eyes full of certainty in her own abilities—and it raises the question of what she would have done if she hadn't been stricken by Stargardt's. I was a gymnastics prospect by the age of 5, competing with girls already in junior high. I was a little diva who loved Olga Korbut, the Russian gold medalist. I studied her every move: I would stick my arm straight up in the air as if I were ready to do my routine in front of a world audience, and I'd announce my scores to my mother. Our living room was the Olympic Arena. I was good enough that a local coach suggested to my mother that I be sent away to a school for prodigies, but she didn't want to break up the family and subject me to that kind of pressure. Instead, she enrolled me in soccer, tap dancing, violin, and anything else that I showed an interest in. I did everything. I was a doer.

My parents couldn't figure me out. My father, Gary Runyan, was a self-made bank executive who had arrived in California from Iowa on his own when he was 17, after he almost lost his life in a bad car accident. He fell asleep behind the wheel one night and demolished his car. He broke almost every bone in his body. When the police arrived, they couldn't find him at first. He'd flown into a ditch. Somehow, he managed to crawl back to the road and then haul himself into one of the squad cars. That's where they finally found him, unconscious in the backseat. He'd broken all his ribs and both his legs. When he recovered enough to travel, he moved to southern California, where he got a job in the San Fernando Valley as a bank teller, and he worked his way up from there.

My mother, Valerie, was the daughter of a milkman. She was born and raised in southern California, and as a young woman she looked like a classic California girl, with a cascade of very blond hair, a trait that I did not inherit. She had a touch of the showgirl in her; she was animated and musical, and her favorite thing in the world was to sit at a piano and play show tunes. One afternoon when she was in high school, her mother came home and said, "Valerie, there's a cute new bank teller at the bank. You should go down there and meet him." My mother put on her newest outfit, strolled into the bank, and wandered up to the window where my father was working. Pretty soon they were a couple. My grand-father, Bob Rankin, insisted that they couldn't get married until my mother had finished college, so they waited until she had graduated with a degree in music—and gotten her teaching cer-tificate as well. They were married, at last, in 1962. My brother, Grady, was born in 1966, and I was born in 1969.

For the first few years of my life, a period of which I have only a few faint images, we lived in Salinas. I remember a large red rug in the living room under the piano. The hue was so vivid that my brother and I would pretend the rug was hot lava; we'd put cush-ions on the floor, pretending they were rocks, and hop from one to the next. I remember sometimes falling asleep on that rug un-der the piano while my mother was playing or giving lessons to local children.

Not only did I want to do everything; I wanted to know everything. My mother spent a lot of time at the piano, singing to us, and I would demand to know what the lyrics meant. She would sing and play TV themes, commercials, Scott Joplin's "The Entertainer," or show tunes from *Annie* or *Oliver!*

She would sing "God Bless America," a song I found especially puzzling. *"Stand beside her and guide her through the night from the light up above . . ."* she'd intone.

"Guide who?" I'd ask.

"From the mountains, through the prairie, to the oceans, white with foam . . ."

"What's the foam?"

Unlike most children that age, I had a strong sense of order. I preferred quiet, and dimness; too much light and noise and commotion unnerved me and made me headachy and queasy. I wonder now if that was because I was struggling to see properly; if those were the first signs of the onset of Stargardt's.

I was 9 years old when the blot crawled across my eyes. Although I first noticed my vision impairment in the fourth grade, in retrospect I may have experienced some of the symptoms much sooner than that. On long afternoons in the sun, I would often feel faintly ill.

What other people thought of as a California paradise, I found to be the source of a torturous glare and a pounding in my temples. Camarillo is an upper-class town of white stucco strip-malls and white concrete sidewalks and cloudless 75-degree weather every day of the year. The brightness and the whiteness together resulted in an unrelenting glare, and there were days when I would have given anything for some clouds. That sun was constant and monotonous, and day after day I would come home from school or the playground and retreat to my room, crying from the headaches.

I hated any sort of tumult. Kids screaming on the school bus, an unruly classroom, any lack of control made me uncomfortable. I needed intense focus—and it seems to me that it must have been because my eyes were betraying me.

In the early 1970s, the progressive-education trend made its way to Camarillo, and an experimental school was launched. My mother enrolled me for the second grade. It was supposed to be child-centered, with an emphasis on creativity—but what it amounted to was total chaos. I despised it. There was no discipline and no achievement standard. It was a free-for-all.

I didn't know what was expected of me. There was nothing to succeed at. I was accustomed to having goals, and meeting them—to winning gymnastics ribbons and soccer trophies. The only thing I liked about this formless kind of school was recess, when our second-grade teacher would take us out to the playground and let us run around an oval field.

I wanted to be noticed for being exceptional, and I wanted adult praise—and when I couldn't earn it, I tried to get it by being different. One day a little boy came to school with special eyeglasses. They had flip-up lenses for the sun, because his eyes were light-sensitive. They intrigued me, and he also got special attention from the teacher, which I envied.

That afternoon, the class was particularly out-of-control. Kids were climbing the walls and screaming, until finally even our permissive teacher had had enough, and she declared that as punishment we would have to sit in total silence and copy words out of the dictionary. It struck me as a useless task—senseless and boring and a typically inadequate punishment. As we began to copy words into our notebooks, the little boy began to cry because he was having trouble adjusting to his new glasses. The teacher put him on her lap and said, "You have glasses, just like me." Not only did she excuse him from the assignment, but he got to sit on the teacher's lap. I sat behind my desk and stewed.

I envied him so much that when I got home I fished around in a drawer full of odds and ends and found an old pair of silver-framed granny glasses. I asked my mother if I could have them, and she said sure, because they had very little magnification in them.

The next day, I wore the granny glasses to school. One of my classmates said, "Oh, you got glasses?"

"Well, no," I said.

"If you wear those, your eyes really *will* get bad."

I didn't care. I wanted the attention. More than anything, however, I wanted some kind of success. I only wore the glasses for a couple of days before losing them on the playground.

My brother, Grady, was enrolled in the more traditional local school, Camarillo Heights. He had regular textbooks, and maps that pulled down from the wall, and globes. "We never look at maps," I complained to my mother. "We never read books. We just sing songs and make puppets." That was all we did, make sock puppets. We would sit at our tables and roll up socks and pin arms and legs on them, and add yarn for hair. Day after day. I was halfway through third grade before my mother finally gave up and withdrew me.

She put me in the local public school, El Descanso—and I loved it. Everything was orderly. We had structure. We had books. We actually did lessons. We could achieve things. But at the end of that third-grade year, my teacher called my mother. "Marla is holding her books closer to her face," she reported. "Maybe you should have her eyes checked."

I didn't know what she was talking about. My desk was at the back of the room, and I distinctly remember being able to see the blackboard during a lesson on the use of parentheses.

"I can see fine," I said.

But there were other small signs that my vision wasn't what it should be. Glitches, lapses, things that I should have seen, that other people saw, but that I didn't.

We took a trip into the Sierra mountains because Grady and I had never seen snow, and my mother and father wanted to show it to us. When we got into the peaks, we pulled the car to the side of the road, and my father pointed out a ski resort, where a chairlift was traveling up the mountainside. We stood beside the car. My father said, "Look, it goes all the way to the top." Grady marveled at it. I couldn't make it out. While the rest of my family watched the chair as it moved up the valley, I searched the hillside for it. "Where is it?" I said. "Where? I don't see it."

My father didn't say anything about it, but years later he confessed that that was the first time he wondered if I might have a problem.

One afternoon I had a headache so severe that I couldn't stand up. My mother took me to the emergency room, where I was diagnosed with food poisoning from eating an old can of Spanish rice. The doctor said, "Later tonight, check her vision by holding up three fingers." My mom thought the food poisoning might cause permanent vision problems.

It seemed like I had headaches all the time. My parents were puzzled by them; after any kind of hard exercise I always seemed to take to my bed.

Every Friday afternoon, the local grade school offered extra-curricular activities, and my mother enrolled me in the tap-dancing program. I stayed in it for one year, and I was miserable. I used to leave that place with a pounding headache every afternoon, after listening to all those kids in their tap shoes making that racket. Back then I thought the headaches were from too much noise, or from being in the hot sun for too long, but now I think it was from spending a long day simply trying to focus.

On my first day of school in the fourth grade, my deteriorating vision became a crisis that would take over all of our lives. That day, I sat at my new desk, halfway back in the sixth row of the class, as my new teacher, Mrs. Wagner, began to write spelling words on the board. My pencil was poised to take them down. I stared up at the board, waiting for the words to distinguish themselves and make some sense to me.

I couldn't read them.

I continued to peer at the board. I could see some marks, but hadn't she written words up there? Numbers? I couldn't tell. I could only see vague shapes.

I began to cry.

My teacher stopped what she was doing and took me outside.

I thought I was in trouble. I would be in trouble because I couldn't read.

"What's wrong?" she asked.

"I can't see the board," I said, tremulously.

I was devastated. To me, fourth grade was going to be a paradise of discipline and achievements. Fourth grade meant I was an older kid now, no longer in primary school. My classroom was everything you could want, with maps and globes, and my aunt had made me a new outfit, and instead of play tables I had my own individual desk, which I felt was more academic. But now my confidence was destroyed.

The teacher took me back into the classroom and moved me into the front row. "Can you see it now?" she asked. I could see the lesson, a series of words to test our spelling, and I started writing them down. Before very long, however, I wouldn't be able to see the board even from that close.

After school, Mrs. Wagner walked me to my mother's car and told her what had happened. "I suggest that you have Marla's eyes checked," she said. For the time being, she would either move me to the front of the room during board lessons, or she would copy the lesson down on a piece of paper and hand it to me. That afternoon, my mother made an appointment for me with a local optometrist.

I sat in an office with a large piece of metal machinery in front of my face and looked at an eye chart on the opposite wall. The doctor clicked various lenses in front of my eyes.

"Does this look better?" he asked.

"No," I said.

Click. He slid another lens in front of me. "What about this?"

"No."

Click. "And this?"

"No."

The doctor turned on the lights and shrugged. Even though I could only make out the second row of letters, he announced, "Nothing seems to be wrong with her. Her eyes appear to be fine." The doctor explained that since I didn't respond to any of the lenses he'd tried, my vision must be intact.

I returned to school—and continued squinting at the board. Two weeks later, Mrs. Wagner called my mother again.

"Look, this is very severe," she said. "She's two inches away from her books when she reads."

My mother made an appointment with another optometrist. Again, he found nothing wrong. That's when our search for an answer began in earnest. It would take eight months, and three different doctors, to arrive at a correct explanation for what had happened to my eyes in the space of a single summer.

In the meantime, I embarked on my own interior search, and it took me into the dark in more ways than one.

I developed a peculiar way of dealing with my vision problem: I became obsessed with blindness. I was hooked on the TV show *Little House on the Prairie*, in which a main character, Mary, was going blind. Next, I announced that I wanted to learn Braille.

My mother, by now increasingly anxious, drove me for an hour to Los Angeles for another eye appointment, this time to see an ophthalmologist. He performed the same basic vision test that the optometrist had, and, once again, there was no lens to which my eyes would respond. But this doctor wasn't satisfied with that result.

He placed a pair of 3-D glasses on me, put a book in front of me, and asked me to point out things that popped up from the pages. After a while, he removed the glasses and asked me to follow him into another room.

At one end of the room was a large square black curtain with a dot in the middle of it. I stared at it curiously. It looked like something you would use in a puppet show. The doctor sat me on a stool in front of the curtain. He held a stick with a light-colored tip in front of me.

"I want you to stare straight ahead at this white dot, and I'm going to move the stick out to the side," the doctor said. "When it is no longer in your view, when you can't see it, you tell me."

In his other hand he had a little piece of chalk. The idea, he explained, was to determine my field of vision. By making chalk marks on the black curtain, he would determine how far my vision extended. Eventually, the chalk marks should form a neat oval shape on the curtain, around the central white dot.

I couldn't do the test.

Every time I tried to fixate on the white dot, it disappeared.

The doctor couldn't get a consistent reading of my field of vision, because I couldn't find the central point of orientation. There was no making sense of what I saw and didn't see—his marks changed every time.

I stared straight ahead, and he pulled the stick out to the right, until I said, "Okay, it's gone." He made a white chalk "X" to mark the spot. But when he moved the stick outward again, I gave a different answer. Now the mark was further out to the right. The test was completely invalid, because I couldn't fixate centrally.

I didn't know why I couldn't see it—and he didn't know, either.

Finally, after about fifteen minutes of this, he asked me to wait outside, and he called my mother into his office. This was their conversation, as I learned later:

"I think it's psychosomatic," he said.

"But that can't be," my mother said. "Why would you think that?"

He began asking my mother some questions.

"What's Marla's favorite TV show?"

"*Little House on the Prairie.*"

What was happening on *Little House on the Prairie*? Mary was going blind, that's what. Then my mother told him about the episode with the granny glasses. It only further validated his diagnosis.

"It's called emotional myopia," he said.

My mother didn't want to believe it, but he was a doctor. He couldn't be wrong, could he? Not with all that expensive equipment in his office, and the degrees on his wall. She had no choice but to believe in him. And perhaps, in her mind, emotional myopia was a preferable diagnosis to being told that her child was handicapped. That word, "handicapped," was still a stigma in the '70s—you didn't dare say that your child was impaired, especially not in a "perfect" white-collar community like Camarillo. It was simply too hard to confront.

We went home, and she called my teacher for a conference. "Well it seems Marla has this thing, it's psychosomatic," my mother said. "They say she's going to grow out of it, and until then we have to kind of go along with it."

My teacher agreed to accommodate me in class. She would copy down all the assignments in advance and hand them to me, instead of forcing me to try to read the board.

My mother maintained her composure outwardly, but she wasn't at all calm on the inside. I found out later that she and my father stayed up that night talking, and trying to figure out where they might have gone wrong, why would their child have such a psychological problem? They just sat there, perplexed.

"We're an average family," my mother said. "We don't beat our kids with a belt. We're just typical. Why is this happening?"

It took my mother a day or so before she could tackle the subject with me. Finally, one afternoon she said, "You know, Marla, the doctor says you're making this up."

I felt shock, and disbelief. It never occurred to me that my mother would believe him over me. I could hear the confusion in her tone of voice; she wanted to be sympathetic, but she was angry, too. I couldn't tell exactly who or what she was angry at. Was she angry at me? Was she angry at the doctor because she knew he was wrong? The truth is, she was as angry and confused as I was. A part of her was thinking "How can she do this to us?" And yet, in her heart, she didn't believe the doctor.

I felt the same mixed emotions emanating from my teacher: I was forcing her to go out of her way and accommodate me when I didn't really need special attention—even a doctor had said so.

My parents and my teacher searched and searched for a reason for my behavior. I was searching, too. Why didn't anybody believe me when I insisted that I couldn't see the television? I would sit huddled in front of it, just a few feet from the screen.

"I can't see it," I wailed. "I can't *see* it!"

"Honey, you're just tired," my mother said. "All you need is more rest."

I was frightened. Could I really be making all this up?

I continued to insist that I wanted to learn Braille. I found a children's book at the school library about the life of Louis Braille, and on the back cover was the Braille alphabet. I studied the pattern of raised dots in each Braille cell and memorized it.

One afternoon my mother came to pick me up from grade school, and the teacher walked out to our car with me.

"Marla, show your mom what you just turned in," she said.

I handed my mother a piece of notebook paper. Underneath

all the words on each page was a series of dots that I had filled in with my pencil.

"Marla just did her entire book report in Braille," the teacher said.

My mother was stunned. She said, "Oh . . . isn't that wonderful."

But inside, she thought, *Oh, my God, she really does have emotional myopia.*

My mother couldn't hide her lack of enthusiasm for that report. I was quite impressed with myself, but she was obviously not pleased. No one else was, either; not my teacher, not my father.

Not long afterward, I was watching television when a preview aired for a movie called *Ice Castles.* It was the story of a blind ice-skater. I was thrilled by the commercial, so much so that as soon as it ended, I jumped up and ran down the hall to the kitchen, and I began babbling excitedly to my mother.

"Mom, Mom—there's a movie about a girl who ice-skates and she's blind, and I have to watch it."

My mother stared at me. She decided to confront me.

"Marla, why do you like shows about blind people?" she asked.

I didn't have an answer for her.

If the people around me were growing angrier by the day, so was I. Everything in school began to seem stupid to me—especially the things I couldn't do. But worse, *everything* began to seem hard. I was barely getting by. I could read my books—if I virtually pressed them to my face.

My teacher still tried to accommodate me, but she had no way of understanding my very real limitations. For instance, she constantly used an overhead projector instead of the chalkboard—and it happened to be the worst thing for my condition. That blank white field with faint writing across it drove me crazy. She couldn't know that the peculiar nature of my vision loss was that things very bright and very white were hardest for me to perceive. A piece of paper. A mirror.

She would write a sentence on the overhead projector, and we were supposed to copy it down. I would have to sit on the floor underneath the projector screen and squint up at it until my neck and eyes ached. It had very low, limited contrast, and what I saw was an indistinct white domain with scratches on it. Even a dark green chalkboard was easier for me to deal with.

I began to develop a strong sense of the ridiculous, and of what I believed to be right and wrong. With about four weeks of school left, I finally rebelled. It was a spring day, and we had a substitute teacher. All the kids were wild for school to be out; the classroom was in chaos, and the substitute couldn't get control. Our lovely, wonderful, controlled, quiet, disciplined room was a madhouse. Kids were yelling and throwing papers, and my head hurt, and I was frustrated with my vision.

So I just walked out.

I got up from my chair, walked out to the playground, and sat on the monkey bars. Nobody came to get me or to discipline me. They just let me sit there.

Outside, it didn't matter what I could or couldn't see.

At last, summer vacation came. With the sun and the heat, my headaches intensified, and so did my vision gap. We took our annual family camping trip to Lake Meade, and I water-skied—something I loved to do—but now I couldn't see the other boats around us, or the shore. Whenever I heard the noise of another boat, I would drop the line and sink into the water, terrified by the sound of a propeller I couldn't see. Finally my father said, "Marla, you have to trust me. I wouldn't let you ski if another boat was anywhere near you."

On that trip, my parents began to suspect that my vision problem was more than just an imagined one; that something was seriously wrong with my eyes. Finally, one incident convinced them of it. We had an eight-hour drive from Lake Meade back to Camarillo, and as we drove through the night, I lay in the back of our family van, watching the headlights of the oncoming cars. We were on a dark, isolated two-way highway through the desert, and the headlights seemed very, very bright to me, almost painfully so. What's more, the lights seemed to be surrounded by clouds.

After a few hours, we decided to stop in some small town for dinner. We stopped at an intersection with a red and green signal and then pulled in to a diner. Inside, the waitress seated us and gave us our menus.

I blinked. And I kept blinking, trying to adjust to the fluorescent lights of the diner. But behind my eyes I could still see the oncoming headlights, and the red and green of the stoplight, throbbing.

"I can still see the signals," I said. "It's like they're burned into my eyes."

My parents looked at each other. And at that moment they decided that my vision simply wasn't right. Something was very wrong.

What we didn't know was that Stargardt's caused me to see artificial light ten times brighter than normal. Because the disease had damaged my retinas, light wasn't being properly absorbed. I didn't really notice during the day—unless I had to look at something like an overhead-projector screen. Artificial lights at night were more intense to me, and they were diffused, more or less surrounded by a kind of haze.

By the time we got back to Camarillo, my mother was determined to have me properly diagnosed. She grimly began making doctor's appointments, one after the other. But we still followed one wrong path after the other, too.

I had a CAT scan, to check for a brain tumor. Next, I saw a nutritionist. I had to write down everything I had eaten over a two-week period, from a bowl of Rice Krispies in the morning to a 7-Up at recess.

The nutritionist said, "Well, first of all, she shouldn't be having Rice Krispies or 7-Up."

The nutritionist was into the no-sugar movement—after all, it was southern California in 1978, when the health-food craze was taking off—and he went so far as to suggest that sweeteners could be affecting my eyes. Thanks to him, my mother went on a health binge. No more sodas. Or ice cream. Or sugar on our cereal.

She started buying strange whole-grain cereals, and breads that you had to keep in the refrigerator or they would get moldy in a day. The only peanut butter she would keep in the house was all-natural and organic, the kind you had to stir with a spoon to make the oil disappear. I thought it was gross. I wanted Skippy. We couldn't even have regular applesauce. She had heard a nutritionist on television say, "Applesauce is like candy, and apple pie might as well be poison."

It lasted for weeks and weeks. Finally, it was my father who broke. One evening he came home from work with a six-pack of Pepsi and a gallon of ice cream under his arm. He didn't even like ice cream or soda very much, but he was tired of watching Grady and me suffer.

My mother continued to make appointments with various doctors, who hazarded all kinds of theories. But no one could give us a concrete answer as to what was wrong with me. Meanwhile, with each misdiagnosis, I reinterpreted myself as a failure. All I knew was that I couldn't do my homework, and if you couldn't do your homework, you were dumb.

By now my parents had worked themselves up to a fever pitch. All they could think was, *somebody tell us what's wrong.* Everything became so serious. We became totally immersed in my problem, and we forgot how to laugh. At times, it may have been as hard on my brother, Grady, as on anyone in the family. He was the perfect boy. You never had to tell him to do homework, and he did his own laundry, and he set the table, or did some other chore no one asked him to. It was the only way that he knew to help. My parents unintentionally excluded him because they tried to spare him the worry they felt. I can't recall the four of us ever sitting around the table discussing this situation; it was such a tender subject that no one wanted to bring it up. But the result was that Grady was left out. He became more and more passive, withdrawn, and unresponsive.

Finally, my mother called an acquaintance of hers who was a nurse and told her what was happening to me. The nurse recommended a local pediatric ophthalmologist, who agreed to see me. I sat through yet another series of tests, and when they were done, the doctor said, like all the others had, "Well, there is something wrong here, but I don't know what." In turn, he recommended that I see a retina specialist named Dr. David Boyer.

Dr. Boyer worked at a hospital in Los Angeles, a full hour's drive away, but by this point my parents were so desperate for an answer they would have gone anywhere.

A single large black chair sat in a dimly lit room. I climbed into the chair. I was so small that when I put my hands on the armrests, my shoulders shrugged up to my ears. I tried to get comfortable and leaned back, but the chair swallowed me. My head nestled beneath the headrest; everything was too big for me.

I squirmed, feeling overwhelmed by the size of the adult chair. I felt . . . on view. There was just one light in the room, a small spot, and it shone directly on me, blinding me and reducing everything else in the room to grays and darks. It was as if I were on my very own stage, and the spotlight was shining down on me, blinding me further and preventing me from making out any details in the rest of the room. My vision was made worse because I had been given drops to dilate my eyes.

My parents sat quietly and uncomfortably on a small sofa to my right, lost in the shadows. I peered into the darkness and tried to make out their faces. It frightened me that my father was present. Always before, it had been my mother who had taken me to my various eye appointments. My father now worked for a bank in Los Angeles; he had been promoted to an executive position, but it meant a two-hour daily commute for him. I rarely saw him during the day, because he would get up at six and be out the door, and not get home until 8 P.M. after fighting rush-hour traffic. He worked all the time. He seemed stern and formal in his work attire, and that made me even more apprehensive. For him to miss a day at the office meant serious business.

I knew why I was there: to see a retina specialist. My parents had explained the term to me. No other doctor had been able to diagnose a specific reason for my failing eyesight; to explain the deterioration. Some of them had been unwilling to say that I had a problem, much less suggest how to fix it. My 9-year-old mind concluded that this doctor would know the answer. He was a *specialist*. That's what specialists did.

Something caught my eye, something small and colorful sitting on a tray, the one thing that was appropriate for a child in a room full of other things that clearly weren't: the heavy pieces of equipment and the charts. I reached over and grabbed the object. Rubbing it back and forth in my hands, I felt that it was rubber. I held what I had found close to my face and examined it. Of course: I recognized the orange and yellow stripes and the black hair. It was Ernie from "Sesame Street." A finger puppet. Bending and straightening my index finger, I brought Ernie to life.

The specialist entered. I held my hand up to block the beam of light, trying to see him. He shook hands with my parents and introduced himself as Dr. Boyer. He walked toward me, into the light, and as he did so, he became colorful and clear. He spoke with a soft voice.

"I see you found Ernie," he said.

"Yes," I whispered, and quickly put Ernie back on the tray.

Dr. Boyer touched a switch on the wall and extinguished the beam. Instead, a much weaker beam hit the opposing wall, and it illuminated a projector image of the all-too-familiar eye chart.

Dr. Boyer handed me a spoon-shaped device and asked me to cover one eye.

"Which one?" I asked.

"It doesn't matter. You pick."

I covered my left eye and focused straight ahead on the poster-shape of the eye chart. I could see the lighted square of the chart itself, but I couldn't see the contents inside the square. I knew they were letters, from my long experience, but I couldn't distinguish them or count how many.

Dr. Boyer began turning a knob on his projector, which changed the magnification on the chart. Click. They got larger. Click. And larger again. Finally, after three or four clicks, the murky figures began to resemble letters to me. He turned the knob once more, click. Now just two images remained on the screen. I could see their rectangular shapes, but I couldn't make out exactly which letters they were. "M" or "B" or "H" or "F"? They were all possibilities.

Finally, Dr. Boyer turned the knob again. Click. A larger single letter appeared. It was the first and the largest letter on the chart.

This letter I could see.

"E," I said, proudly.

All that just for an E.

The doctor asked me to move the black spoon to my other eye, and we went through the procedure all over again. And once more, I couldn't tell the doctor what letters I was looking at. He clicked the knob until the big "E" appeared.

Finally, Dr. Boyer clicked off the projector and turned on the overhead lights. He conducted a series of smaller tests, peering at my eyes using a variety of magnifying devices and pin lights pressed close to my face. Finally, he folded up and pocketed his apparatus and asked me to leave the room.

I didn't like that at all. But I went into the hallway, while my parents remained closeted with Dr. Boyer in his office. I studied the carpet, which was an industrial gray with some kind of pattern to it. I played hopscotch on the pattern, but I wasn't having all that much fun. Everything seemed strange and out-of-sequence. My eyes, dilated for the test, made what vision I had even more blurry and distorting than usual. Then there was my father's presence, and his uneasiness, and, finally, the fact that I had been left out of the meeting in the doctor's office. Here I was, finally getting all the attention that any child could want, but now I didn't want it anymore. I thought again of my father inside, and how uncomfortable he had looked sitting there on the couch.

After a few minutes, the door opened and my parents came out. They looked at me expressionlessly, and together we walked down the hallway in a perturbed silence. Nobody said a word. *Why isn't anyone talking to me?* I wondered. Tension continued to build until we were out of the building and into the bright sunlight. I recoiled, my eyes still fully dilated from the vision tests. The light hit me like a blow in the face. I put on a pair of cardboard temporary sunglasses the nurse had given me. Suddenly, I was exhausted. I could feel yet another headache coming on.

I climbed into the backseat of our blue Ford van. Still, nobody said a word to me. I wanted something, anything, out of my parents. I knew if I said something harsh, I might at least get a reaction. At that point I would have done anything to break the tension.

"I'm probably just going to go blind," I announced.

"No, you're not!" my father answered immediately. "You are *not* going blind."

What I couldn't have known was that Dr. Boyer had just told my parents that I was, in fact, going blind.

Inside the room, the doctor had said to my parents, "I feel terrible to have to tell you this. But it appears that your daughter has butterfly dystrophy, and she will go blind."

There was dead silence in the room.

"It's a form of retinal degeneration," he continued. "We need to do more tests to confirm it, but that's what I believe she has."

My parents were speechless when the doctor finished. They didn't say a word. "She needs to come back in two weeks for more comprehensive testing," Boyer said, apologetically, rising.

This was why my parents had remained speechless all the way to the car.

They were in shock all the way home. They remained in shock for the next two weeks. At some point they gently explained the doctor's diagnosis. Coincidentally, an article appeared in the newspaper about another local child who had butterfly dystrophy, and it said that his parents had decided to take him to Europe for some kind of treatment. My mother commented on the article, and cut it out and showed it to me. All she said was, "This is what Dr. Boyer thinks you might have."

Things grew more strange around the house. Suddenly, my mother volunteered to be the assistant coach on my soccer team. Sports were not her thing; she played the piano, not soccer. But now she was involved—and protective—in everything I did. Just what every 10-year-old wants: her mother on the sideline, but deep down I understood that she was concerned about me and wanted to be close by.

My father, on the other hand, became withdrawn. He was working a lot, as usual. His way of dealing with the trauma was to try to comfort me with sweets: he would come home in the evenings with a six-pack of Pepsi or a Snickers bar, or he'd ask, "Do you want a bowl of ice cream?" Those weren't his favorite foods, or mine, but he thought they would make me happy, so he tried to give them to me. Underneath it, I could sense a constant unease within him. I think he was just very sad.

Finally, it was time to go back to Dr. Boyer for the second appointment. This one would take an entire day; he had scheduled me for a comprehensive exam, a series of procedures. I dreaded the appointment. I hated being trapped in the examining chair, peered at and prodded. By the end of even the most basic exam, my eyes felt violated. The drops to artificially dilate them would leave me blurry and even more vulnerable to bright lights. I invariably left doctors' offices with a splitting pain in my head and my eyeballs feeling scalded.

As much as anything, I dreaded the antiseptic seriousness of eye exams; the lack of anything reassuring or playful for a child in those cold, sterile examining rooms. I remembered Ernie, and to comfort myself I got out a pair of red tube socks that I wore with my soccer uniform, and I made a sock doll. I stuffed a sock full of cotton, and drew a face for her, and gave her blond pigtails with bows, and pinned two little legs and two little arms on her, and put her in an old doll-dress. I named her Sally and took her with me to the appointment.

First, Dr. Boyer dilated my eyes, as usual, and he took a series of photographs of the retinas. Then he put my head into a contraption that held me still, and he put a camera against my face. An attendant reached in and held my eyelids open so that I couldn't blink while the camera shot a series of flash images. I flinched and gritted my teeth, but I couldn't move.

When they finally released me, I pulled my head back, reeling from the flashes. I blinked, and opened my eyes. For a long minute, I saw nothing but purple. Eventually the purple receded.

Next, I had to put my head into a small dome that was dotted by tiny bright lights. It was another way to test my field of vision. I was given a small clicker-control and told to stare straight ahead. If I saw a red light blink on and off, I was to click the control box. If a red light came and went and I didn't see it, the machine would emit a buzz.

A red light flashed somewhere over my head, in the periphery. I clicked. Another flashed somewhere off the side. I clicked again. And again. And again.

And then . . . nothing. I heard a buzz.

Buzz. Buzz. Buzz. I saw no more flashing little red lights. I just heard the buzzes.

After a few minutes, a machine spat out a printout. On the page was a diagram of my responses, a kind of graph, with a distinct oval shape. It was, as it turned out, a map of the blind spots in my eyes. They looked like empty spaces, holes in the universe.

Next, Dr. Boyer took me across the hall and sat me in a chair, and an attendant placed electrodes all over my face. More readings were taken. After that, I hoped they were done, but they had saved the worst for last.

Dr. Boyer showed me two small discs in the shape of contact lenses. But these weren't regular lenses; these had wires protruding from them. A nurse opened my eyelids and put these wired contacts into my eyes. They were so big and protruding that I couldn't close my eyes. They were up under my eyelids, and they were excruciating. I had to hold my eyes open that way for two minutes. I felt like something out of Dr. Frankenstein's laboratory.

By the time they were removed, I was completely limp. Still clutching Sally under my arm, I staggered out of the office. To protect my eyes from the daylight, I was given a pair of dark plastic glasses. They were ugly and uncomfortable, and I hated them. They scratched my nose and my cheekbones. My mother wore the large-framed sunglasses of the day, in that 1970s Elton John style that suited her blond, permed hair. To console me, she let me wear those huge glasses, which sat easier on my face.

We had to wait another two weeks for the results of those tests. As soon as the results came in, my mother and father drove straight to Los Angeles to hear in person what Dr. Boyer had to say.

They sat in that office, where they had received such dreadful news a month earlier. The door swung open, and as soon as Dr. Boyer entered the room, he said, "Well, I am now the second doctor to misdiagnose your daughter."

My parents stared at him, dumbfounded.

"You aren't going to believe this, but I'm wrong, too," Dr. Boyer said. "She doesn't have butterfly dystrophy. She has Stargardt's disease, and it's not progressive."

"What does that mean, it's not progressive?" my mother said.

"It means she won't become totally blind," he answered.

Dr. Boyer explained the specific effects of Stargardt's to my parents. The disease would damage only my central vision and would leave the periphery intact. However, central vision, provided by the hypersensitive macula, is what determines visual acuity. My visual acuity would be forever impaired, not correctable with contacts or glasses. My vision would be something like a camera with "bad film": no matter how much you focus the lens, you won't get a clear image.

I also had a case of myopia, or nearsightedness. My vision was

20/800 in my left eye and 20/1000 in my right. While contacts could correct the myopia to 20/200 in both eyes, the damage caused by Stargardt's was not correctable. There was no cure.

In the years to follow, my corrected acuity would actually slip to 20/300 in my left and 20/400 in my right. "Legally blind" is defined as a best-correctable visual acuity of 20/200 or worse, often identified by "the big E" on the eye chart.

In time, even the Big E would become indistinguishable to me.

Dr. Boyer explained that my only option to function in the sighted world was to use technology, such as a closed-circuit television for reading and a visual aid called a monocular, which looks and works something like a telescope, for distance. Since my eyes could not be fully corrected, I would have to learn to "correct" my environment, by bringing the world closer to me or by making things larger.

Stargardt's typically affects children between the ages of 7 and 12, and although the damage eventually ceases somewhere short of total blindness, the effects are irreversible, he explained. It strikes one out of about every 15,000 people.

But virtually everything else Dr. Boyer said that day was lost on my parents. All they heard was that I wouldn't be totally blind. Stargardt's wasn't bad news to them; it was great news. In fact, it was astonishingly great news: I wouldn't lose all of my vision.

Dr. Boyer tried to impress on them that Stargardt's was serious enough. I was already legally blind, and my vision would probably get worse before it stopped. He wanted them to know what we were in for, so he spelled out all of the limitations he thought we would be faced with.

"She won't be able to drive," he said. "She would need help to go to college. You've probably already noticed that her grades are slipping. High school is going to be very difficult for her. She's going to need a lot of support."

But my parents were just grateful to have a definitive diagnosis of what was wrong with their daughter. The months of mystery and pain and confusion were over; we finally had an answer.

I was partially blind, yes. But I could see a little, and that was enough for them. And in time it would be for me, too.

3. Surrounded by Music

One night, as I lay in my bed, I noticed an odd splotch on the ceiling of my bedroom. The lights were out, and the only illumination in the room came from the doorway, which my parents left open a crack to allow in a sliver of a beam from the hallway. Even in the dimness, I knew that the ceiling above me should be perfectly white—or at least that it always had been before. But now, as I lay there, I saw an oval-shaped gray blot, as if there had been a water leak and moisture had seeped through and ruined the ceiling. The large gray stained area seemed to cover five or six feet of the ceiling above me.

What's that? I thought. I moved my eyes across the ceiling, surveying it. . .

The stain moved.

I shifted my eyes, scanning back again.

Wait a minute—where did it go?

I moved my eyes to the left.

The stain jumped to the left.

I shifted back to the right.

It jumped to the right.

I moved my eyes all over the ceiling, trying to figure out what it would do next. Finally, I stared at the ceiling above my head. The stain hovered there, and I stared at it until I fell asleep.

The next morning, I told my mother about it. "There's this gray blob on my ceiling," I said. "Like a stain."

"That blob isn't on the ceiling," she said. "It's in your retinas. That's the scar tissue in your eyes."

I was 11 years old, and it was the first time that I realized that Stargardt's disease had literally left a mark on my eyes. From then on, I saw the blot whenever I looked at a solid field of color. A white kitchen floor. A grass lawn. Even the blue sky, while lying on my back.

The specific realities of Stargardt's began to set in. Dr. Boyer had tried to prepare us for the frustrations. Initially, my parents were so relieved by his revised diagnosis that they were unbothered by his warnings, but as the long-term consequences became real, we all became less sanguine.

For months, my parents had clung to the idea that once I was properly diagnosed, the problem would be fixable. My father would say, "Let's go fix it." Now came the realization that it couldn't be fixed.

It became apparent that reading would be a constant problem for me. Given a powerful magnifying aid, I could read—sort of. Often, I had to try to recognize the "shape" of a word, because I could only make out the first and last letters. For example, I might mistake the word "partly" for "partially," or read "family" as "finally." I had to guess at the words from the context of a sentence. My ability to read was dependent upon my familiar vocabulary.

If a teacher gave me a list of new words to look up in the dictionary—forget it! The microscopic print was all but impossible for me. But I still tried. Also, cursive script or any other individualized handwriting was becoming impossible for me to read, or to produce. The up-and-down swirls all looked the same to me. This was a huge disappointment to a fifth-grader, because learning cursive was a rite of passage—it meant you were learning to write like an adult. I made a go at it. But I figured out later in life that it wasn't all that important.

On Dr. Boyer's advice, and with the help of a local advocacy group called the Lions Club, my parents got me a closed-circuit television, or CCTV. It served as a giant reading machine with which I could do most of my schoolwork. It was a large, heavy, two-piece arrangement, with a desktop monitor, a camera, and a sliding tray. The idea was to put the book on the tray and slide it underneath the camera, which then magnified the print and showed it on the screen. The tray was moveable, so I could slide it back and forth and up and down while reading. The enlarged image would move correspondingly on the screen.

But it gave me terrible vertigo. Every time I moved my book, the print veered and skipped crazily across the screen, until it made me dizzy and nauseated. That thing could give me a headache after ten minutes. I would place a book on the tray and slide the tray under the magnifying lens—and the print would go flying by, until it made me ill.

Everything seems difficult when you're 11, but now reading

seemed doubly so. I would bring a book home from class or the library and try to read on that thing, and I'd end up on my bed in a fit of weeping.

Don't get me wrong; I was grateful to be able to read anything at all. But the CCTV was so huge that it took up an entire desktop. It seemed gigantic, and mortifyingly conspicuous. I thought it was more than I needed, more than was necessary. Why did I have to rely on so much machinery? It made me doubly self-conscious when we put the machine in my fifth-grade classroom. One morning, my mother drove it to school and set it up in the back corner of the room, where it required an entire table of its own.

Each time I turned it on, it gave off a high-frequency squeal. I would slip to the back of the class with a book and quietly pull a chair in front of it, hoping to be discreet. I'd flip the switch—and it would emit a long "*eeeeeeek!*" It was a peculiar tone that was especially hard on the sensitive ears of children. It wasn't as obvious to adults like my parents or teacher, because adults are less sensitive to the higher frequencies. But to me, and to the other kids in the room, it might as well have been a fire alarm. I'd turn it on, and every child in the room, including me, would clap our hands over our ears and groan. So much for "silent reading."

My mother went on a hunt for more convenient visual aids. I quickly acquired an assortment of them. She ordered a magnifying glass on a stand that I could slide over my books, and she got me a monocular, a little tiny telescope that I could hold up to my eye and with which I could read assignments on the chalkboard. She found my fifth-grade math textbook in large print. This was a blessing and a curse, because the large-print version took up four whole volumes. They were hardbound and green-covered, thick as encyclopedias, and they made me self-conscious. Like the CCTV, they seemed conspicuous.

I still had not completely accepted the fate of Stargardt's. These measures all seemed so unnecessary. Why couldn't the doctor just make me a pair of glasses that would correct my vision? After all, other people got eyeglasses all the time.

One day, my mother and I went into the local pharmacy, Sprouse Retz, where I came across a rotating stand of glasses. They weren't sunglasses, but *real* glasses, with varying degrees of magnification. I took a pair off the rack and put them on. They had brown frames and were clearly made for an adult.

"Hey, Mom, why don't we just get these?" I asked.

Problem solved.

"Do they help?" she asked.

"Yeah . . . uh . . . everything is a little bigger," I said.

"You've got to be kidding me," my mom said.

Looking through the glasses, I stared at the assortment of candy near the checkout counter. Everything was a little bigger, yes, but the glasses also made objects softer and more blurry. The glasses were made for reading, not everyday use, and the magnification was very weak—maybe only a 2 power.

She bought the glasses, to humor me, but perhaps she also wanted to entertain the idea that a five-dollar pair of adult reading glasses could help me. It was the granny glasses all over again—only this time, I really couldn't see.

Now that my mother had a concrete diagnosis, she could attack the problem. She went into her Supermom mode. In those days, my school district was at a loss as to how to accommodate a child with a visual impairment, so my mother had to do everything that the school district should have done.

My mom opened whole new doors for me with monoculars and magnifiers and enlarging machines—and when she couldn't find any more visual aids, she invented her own ways to help me get along in the classroom. My fifth-grade homework assignments came on ditto sheets—these were the pre-Xerox days—and at the start of the week my mother would go to the teacher and ask for the whole week's assignments.

Then she copied them over in large print. By hand.

My mother became utterly focused on me. She was sure that I could make it through a regular school, despite what the doctors told her. Something else was at work too: it's embarrassing to say it now, but it was traumatic for her that her daughter might have to go to a special school. She wanted to avoid it if it was at all possible.

My parents were struggling emotionally. Although they tried not to show it to me, they were distraught day and night. My mother kept a stiff upper lip as she drove me to and from school, but there were times, after I'd gotten out of the car, when she sat in the driver's seat and sobbed.

One afternoon, she went to a Christmas brunch and ran into an old friend, Shirley Smithro, who also had a daughter with a visual impairment. They hadn't seen each other in months.

Shirley Smithro stared at my mother in shock.

"You've lost twenty pounds," she said.

"Well, here's what's happening," my mother said.

She poured out the whole story. She told Shirley about my incorrect diagnoses and the Stargardt's disease. She described how difficult it was for me to see the chalkboard and do my homework, and her fear that I wouldn't be able to keep up and would have to go to a school for the impaired.

"But there's a school right here that has special services for visually impaired children," Shirley said. "Right here in our county. That's where she should be." Shirley told my mother about a place called Williams Elementary School, which happened to be in the next school district over, an hour away in a community called Hueneme (pronounced "Wy-nee-me"). It was a standard elementary school, but it offered a program for VH (Visually Handicapped) students.

My mother was becoming increasingly frustrated with our own local public school. The staff seemed to her either unwilling, or unable, to cope with my vision loss. My mother had to do everything herself: she found visual aids, she implemented them, and she made sure that I had my assignments. Despite her best efforts, I was still floundering. I wasn't failing, but I was barely getting by.

Shirley Smithro told my mother that her 6-year-old daughter, Robin, was enrolled in Williams Elementary. "They have VH teachers, and all of the equipment already set up," she said. "It's great." There was even a school bus that picked up students from neighboring counties and took them home after school.

A couple of days later, my mother drove me over to visit Williams Elementary. We wandered through the hallways until we came to a classroom with a plaque on the door that said "VH." We opened the door. . .

. . . and I wasn't alone anymore.

There were other kids who couldn't see. I didn't realize until that moment how isolated I had been by my vision loss. In fact, I had been desolate. My only company was my mother—not exactly an ideal environment in which to mature socially.

The first thing I saw when we entered the room was that it was designed entirely for people like me. Each desk had a stand with a light and a magnifier. In the back of the room was a bank of CCTVs, at least five of them. A dozen or so children were working quietly at the desks; some of them were totally blind, and some had thick eyeglasses. There were four teachers in the room, ready to cope with every conceivable need: there were two VH specialists, a Braille specialist, and an orientation-mobility instructor.

There were several large-print typewriters. A number of the children were being taught to type, and the letters they rat-tat-tatted onto paper were so large even *I* could see them. I got a chance to type a few words myself.

After just two minutes of observing the classroom, my mother said to me, "Oh, yeah, you're coming to this school."

Then the mobility instructor, Carlos Logan, called me over. "Hey, Marla," he said, "look at this." He pulled back his sleeve and showed me his wristwatch. He said, "Watch this," and flipped open the glass cover.

"It's a Braille watch," he said. "You open it and touch the face and you can feel the hands."

I gently placed my index finger on the open face of the watch, careful not to break the tiny hands. I could feel little raised bumps: the numerals in Braille. I stared at the watch in wonder and kept moving my fingertips over it.

Next, he pointed to something hanging on the wall. I peered at it.

"This is a large-print map," he said.

As we continued to observe the class, it seemed to me that it offered the best of both worlds. The VH room was a convenience; it wasn't meant to separate me from the rest of the students. I would spend most of the school day in a standard classroom with the mainstream student body, but I could use the VH room whenever I wanted to or needed to. I loved the atmosphere of the room; it was casual and unstructured, but it wasn't out of control. The kids had freedom to move around the room—to get up from their chairs and go to another desk—but they also worked quietly.

What I liked best of all was that when I was in *this* room, no one expected me to be able to see fully. It was okay to be partially sighted, or even blind, and in fact, it was no big deal.

The realization hit me that this was where I belonged. I didn't even want to go home. Finally, we got back into the car for the drive back to Camarillo.

"Mom," I said, "we gotta get me into that school."

But we were about to enter a world of red tape—and not for the last time, either. When we got back home, my mother immediately called an administrator in our school district. She told them that I wanted to be transferred to Williams Elementary in Hueneme.

The administrator, with a voice as dry as dead leaves, informed her that before I could be transferred I would have to undergo a series of placement tests to ascertain my academic grade level.

And they wouldn't be able to administer the tests for three or four months.

"You're kidding me," my mother said.

"No exceptions," the administrator said.

"But she has special needs. She should be in the other school district, where they can accommodate her."

"There's nothing I can do."

"That's ridiculous."

From that point on, my mother became my chief advocate. She was on the phone every day, nagging at resistant administrators. She began to think they were dragging their feet intentionally. It seemed that it would take an act of God to get me into that school.

Finally, it occurred to my parents that the school's real interest in keeping me was so that they could meet their head count for public-school funding. My parents believed that it was strictly a matter of bureaucratic stonewalling that prevented them from giving me the placement test.

Finally, my mother became so angry that she pulled me out of school. "Well, I'll tell you what," my mother announced. "If you won't test her, she's not coming to your school." She withdrew me, and for the next several weeks she tutored me at home.

I continued to participate in the after-school activities, however. I still played soccer, and in the middle of my fourth-grade year, I had begun violin lessons with a man named Dr. Krusch.

One afternoon, my mother dropped me by the school for my usual music lesson. As my mother sat idling in our van in front of the school, the principal walked over and said, "Why isn't she coming to school? We can meet Marla's needs. She should be here."

"When can she take the test?" my mother asked. "She's not going to school here, and that's that."

In the meantime, my father researched the legalities of the situation and discovered something called Public Law 94–142. It was an education act for children with disabilities, and it said that if a child had a disability, the school in the child's community was responsible for providing the appropriate assistance and services so that the child could be educated. Which my school had failed to do—from the start. The only assistance I had received had come from my mother.

My father picked up the phone and read the law to the school-district administrators. For one of the few times in his life, he raised his voice. "You're liable," he said.

The following day, our phone rang. It was a school administrator.

"Marla can come in today and we'll test her," they said.

We drove to the school, and they administered the test—in small print.

I remember just one part of the test: it was a cartoon of a guy walking in the sun. "Is anything wrong with this picture?" the administrator asked.

"Yeah," I said. "His shadow is in the wrong place."

But that was the only easy question. When the results came back, I had done poorly. It turned out I had fallen two grade levels behind: I was a fifth-grader but functioning at a third-grade level. My mother was perplexed. She knew that I had been struggling, but she didn't think I was that bad off academically.

A couple of days later, the school psychologist called and said, "We're very concerned because Marla only tested at the third-grade level."

"Well, did you read her the questions? Or give it to her in large print?" my mother wanted to know.

No. Of course they hadn't. It only confirmed to my mother

that she was right in fighting to get me out of there. The transfer finally came through.

By the time it took effect, it was springtime. I went to Williams Elementary for just three months before the school year ended. The bureaucrats were the real winners.

Everything was an ordeal. That was my mother's favorite word, and I was learning to appreciate its meaning. The following year, I entered a junior high school in the same district, EO Green, which had an even better program for the visually impaired. Still, sometimes even the smallest detail could seem like an insurmountable problem to me.

On the first day in my new school, I found my locker. I stared at the combination lock with its tiny little numerals. I told myself that I could deal with it. My brother had taught me how to open a combination lock years earlier when we had locked up our bikes back in Camarillo.

I began to twirl the dial. But to me, the numbers were just white marks on the black circular disc. I had no idea what numbers I was looking at. *Man, these numbers just keep getting smaller,* I thought. I kept twirling the dial and yanking at the handle of the locker. But it would't budge. After the fifth attempt, I got angry.

I went to the VH room and found my teacher, John O'Looney. I cried, "I can't even open my locker to get my dumb old books."

"Calm down," he said. "We'll get you a padlock."

He led me to an area where four lockers had been set aside right next to one another. These lockers were different; their tiny black combination locks had been removed. Instead, each was fitted with a large padlock that could be opened with a key. These lockers were reserved for the special kids, the ones who were "incapable" of using a standard combination lock.

I wasn't incapable. I just couldn't see very well. But more often than not, others viewed those two conditions as one and the same.

I was beginning to grow self-conscious about my vision. I was deeply grateful to have the VH room, but I wanted to seem like any regular student. I went to the VH room for one period each day, and I used the time to catch up on schoolwork—work that other students did as a matter of course, but which took me twice as long to complete. Often, I would have assignments retyped in large print by our trusty Braillist. I was glad to have the assistance, and to have so many new tools to help me get by in school. But it was not the same as being "normal."

My answer was to spend more and more time outdoors. There, I didn't feel blind. I felt like the fastest kid in the world.

Each day after school, I ran for the Cosmos, a kids' track club in Camarillo. I ran in tennis shoes on a dirt track. I ran on blacktop in the playground. I ran up and down our backyard. I was the fastest kid in my school.

From the beginning, I hated the feeling of running as fast as I could and being passed by somebody. It made me feel powerless, as though I couldn't do anything about it. Much the same way Stargardt's made me feel.

One of the first formal races that I ever competed in was a 200-meter sprint on a dusty local track in Camarillo. My running shoes were a pair of worn-out old sneakers. I was racing a group of older girls, and I ran as hard as I could. I was leading off the turn, and then all the other girls began passing me. It made me frantic. I ran harder, and harder, and harder, pushing myself to catch up.

Suddenly, everything in my body locked up.

My muscles seized. I was trying so hard that my 10-year-old body tied up, and I just fell flat, face-first in the dirt. My father was sitting in the bleachers, and I've never seen him move so fast. My sedate banker father vaulted over a chain-link fence and reached me in the space of seconds. He ran over and picked me up.

"Are you okay?" he asked.

"I'm okay," I said, wriggling. "Put me down."

It became a matter of pride with me to prove that I could do anything, to seek out those things that *ought* to be most difficult, and to show that I could master them. Track was one of them. Highjumping was another—even though I couldn't see the bar.

My dad and I made a high-jump pit in our backyard. He took two wooden poles and hammered nails single-file down one side of each of them. Next, he made a base out of scrap lumber. We used a piece of white PVC pipe for the bar, balancing it on the nails. I dragged a couple of old mattresses outside for a landing area. The bar couldn't have been higher than four feet, but I was obsessed with leaping over it.

My father stood in the back patio wordlessly and watched me measure off the distance. I ran toward it and kicked over the bar, just as I had seen Olympians do on television. My dog, Freckles, ran around chasing me. I did it again, and again, and again. I'd race toward the bar with Freckles behind me, and leap over it and flop on the mattress "pit."

My father never stopped me. Instead, he went inside and reported to my mother that I had a natural talent. It was the first of many times when my parents might have felt overprotective but quelled it. Their philosophy was to *let me show them* what I could and couldn't do.

They accommodated me in whatever I wanted to do, no matter how much trouble it was. Although it was a one-hour commute between Camarillo and Hueneme, my mother drove over in the afternoons to pick me up from school so I could make it back to Camarillo in time for track practice at my old school. She never once complained. She drove back and forth just so I could run and jump. It was just another example of what she was willing to do for me. Which was everything.

I signed up for every kind of activity. I ran, I played soccer, and I took violin lessons.

I was a strong soccer player, and I hid how elusive the ball was to me by running the entire distance of the field in every game. It was the only way I could see what was going on—I had to run there. I would beg my coach to let me play center halfback so that I could have the freedom to cover the field. I didn't want to be a ball-hog, I just wanted to see what was going on, so I could be ready to react. I had to divine where the ball was from the way the other girls chased it. Once the ball was away, I had no idea what was going on. Time to run.

The only sport I couldn't master was softball; I ended up hating that game. I only played it when I absolutely *had* to, during P. E. class. I couldn't catch. I used to say, "Put me way, way out in the outfield." I would go to the farthest fence, and just hope that my teammates would get the fly balls. At the plate, I could occasionally hit a ball. But catch one? It was never going to happen. I was afraid of that large white object that would come flying at me out of the sky. Whenever I thought it might be coming my way, I'd throw my arms over my head and duck. I thought it was a dumb sport, and, for me, it was a dangerous one.

On the track I could prove my superiority, because there was nothing to see but the ground in front of me. I loved middle-school P. E. class, because it was structured and organized. Each morning, we did warming-up exercises in unison. After we'd done our jumping jacks in orderly lines, we'd run a lap around the oval dirt track. The top ten finishers each got a point, and at the end of the year, the kid with the most points got the Golden Tenny award. The Golden Tenny was an old size-12 Nike shoe, spray-painted gold, with a plant in it. I won it all three years of middle school, and I was proud of that shoe. I set it on top of my desk, and it stayed there for the whole day.

There was one thing I badly wanted to do that my eyes prevented me from doing: I wanted to read music. The tiny notes on the delicate lined paper defeated me. How could I ever play an instrument without reading music?

One afternoon, when I was still in the fourth grade, Dr. Krusch had come to my Camarillo school to offer introductory lessons in the violin. He explained that he taught via the Suzuki Method, a Japanese means of instruction for young musicians that stressed form and technique. It was based on listening, and on learning to play by sound and by fingering, without learning actual notes at first. The idea was that it would eventually create a more whole musician, one who could play by ear.

Most important to me, I didn't need my eyes to play via the Suzuki Method. I wouldn't be required to read notes for the first year of the course.

I came home and told my mother that I wanted to take up the violin.

"The violin?" she said. She was surprised, but also privately elated. She had never forced her love of music on me or Grady, and except for the *tink, tink, tink* that I produced while sitting next to her at the piano when I was small, I'd never played an instrument. She was very happy to nurture my interest in music, especially since it had come from within me.

The Suzuki Method was a ten-book progression of Baroque music including Bach, Vivaldi, and Seitz. Eventually, my favorite pieces would be the Concerto in A Minor by Vivaldi and the Concerto for Two Violins by Bach, also known as "the Bach double." But that was all a long way off. The first thing I learned was how to bow to the instructor. I always began and ended each lesson with a bow of respect. Next I learned how to hold the violin. In fact, for the first four weeks of instruction I did nothing but make a violin out of a cardboard box with yarn for strings and a ruler for the neck. I learned how to cradle it properly, and how to delicately hold the bow, and so on. It seemed like there were a thousand disciplines to learn before I would actually learn to play a note.

Finally, I was allowed to have a real violin to replace the cardboard one, and I learned the names of the strings, E-A-D-G. I immediately started squeaking away around the house. I learned the first four notes of "Twinkle, Twinkle, Little Star," which was just a matter of sawing at two open strings, A-A-E-E. That was it. For days that's all my parents heard, A-A-E-E. A-A-E-E. A-A-E-E.

At first, it was easy. I could memorize the strings and the fingering, and carry off a song as simple as "Twinkle, Twinkle."

I worked hard, practicing on that violin. I spent at least an hour a day at it. I practiced in the mornings, in the kitchen, while I waited for the school bus. I even went to Suzuki camps in the summers, at UCLA and San Francisco State University.

My new school, EO Green Junior High, offered a strong music program and an immense orchestra for the sixth, seventh, and eighth grades. There must have been twenty violinists and twelve cellists and ten trombonists in it. We even had an oboe and a bassoon. And this orchestra didn't play the classics like Bach and Vivaldi; instead, it played swinging and kid-friendly pieces like "Jingle Bell Rock" and "The William Tell Overture." I was thrilled by the idea of it, and I was dying to join. Thanks to my Suzuki training, I was good enough.

But if I wanted to participate in concerts, I would have to read music. And, of course, to read it, I would have to see it.

Music from this point on would become an intensely visual exercise, and a complicated one. I would have to learn the notes on the staff; half notes, whole notes. But the distinctions between the lines and spaces were just too difficult and delicate for my eyes to discern.

My mother bought me some sheet music and set about thinking up ways to help me. How would we solve my vision problem? With Dr. Krusch, I tried to read music for the first time on a CCTV. I would play the violin, while he'd move the music on the tray.

It didn't work. The CCTV made the notes *too* large, so large that I could only see one or two of them at a time. That was no good. I started to cry.

I went to bed and cried harder. I had dealt with losing much of my vision, but this was a huge sweeping sense of loss—to lose all of music. That seemed too much to bear.

I was 10, and I wanted my mother. But she was out that night, singing with a musical chorus called Sweet Adelines.

I padded into my parents' bedroom. My father was sitting up in bed, watching the news. I stood in front of him, crying.

"I want my eyes to get better," I said. "I want them to get better so I can read my music."

My father stared at me. And then he began to cry, too.

It was one of the few times that my dad had ever cried in front of me. All I was crying about was the violin. His crying was about something larger. He cried because he wanted to give his daughter normal eyesight, and he couldn't.

"Dads are supposed to fix things," he always said.

For some reason, finding a way to read music suddenly became the most important thing in the world to me.

Once again, it was my mother who came up with the solution. Through the VH program, we found some large-print music paper. It came in 11″-by-17″ pads. An oversized four-line musical staff was printed on each page.

I would bring home my sheet music, and my mother would transfer it by hand with a thick black marker, note by note, to those oversized musical staffs. Even then, sometimes I still couldn't see exactly which line a note was on. To help me further, she would write out the fingering above each note with a red marker.

But I felt guilty, as if I weren't playing properly. "I want to read the music just like everyone else does," I said. "I don't want to cheat." My mom finally grew exasperated. "That's ridiculous," she said. "If you can do it, you can do it."

On Sunday afternoons my father would sit in the family room watching football, while my mother spent hours on the tedious job of copying out the music. She would copy each note exactly as it appeared on my sheet music, and then she would add the fingering along the top. It could take the better part of a day.

Each time a new piece was handed to our orchestra, I would rush home and say, "We got a new one today." The process would start all over again. She would spend hours, with sheets of paper arrayed on the floor and magic markers spread around her. Sometimes I'd sit with her and try to help, and we would talk about the music as she wrote. "This is a fun one," she'd say, humming the melody. "You'll like playing this one."

But the longer pieces were a problem. One standard-sized sheet of orchestra music would take up four or five 11″-by-17″ sheets—as much as five feet of paper. We had to find a way for me to see it all. The answer was to use more music stands. I sat alone, instead of sharing a stand with a partner like everyone else, and spread my oversized sheet music across three black stands.

It was a tedious balancing act, but it worked. I sat on the edge of my chair, violin in position, and twisted myself around from stand to stand, never missing a note.

It seemed that my mother's musical handwriting was everywhere. The oversized music staffs, with the giant notes, swirled around me.

I was surrounded by music.

I played the violin through the ninth grade, and I was as proud of my music as I was of my track career. They were my only two successes at a time when I felt hampered at everything else. The violin gave me focus, and a feeling of excellence when I craved it. And it emboldened me.

One morning, I walked into the kitchen and said, "I'm trying out for first violin today."

"What?" my mother said.

"I'm trying out for first violin in the orchestra."

"How many people are trying out?"

"Fourteen," I said. "The whole second-violin section."

"Okay," she said. "Good luck."

I was ambitious: I wanted to become first violin and eventually make it to first chair. First-chair violin meant that you sat closest to the conductor. During a concert, you were the actual leader of your section. Before the concert began, the orchestra would sit down and the first-chair violinist would walk across the stage and tune the orchestra. Finally, the conductor would come out.

"You know, first-chair violin is really important," my mother once told me. "If something happens to the conductor, the first-chair violinist has to conduct."

After orchestra rehearsal that day, all the students were dismissed except for the second-violin section. Our teacher, Mr. Verdades, and two of the cellists acted as judges. They sat with their backs to us as we each played the same selection of music.

I won.

I came home that evening and set my books down and said, "Well, I made it."

There was only one problem: first violin played a different piece of music. As first violin, I would play the melody while the second violins played the harmony, one octave lower. My mom had to rewrite all of my music—again.

By now, the music situation was getting out of hand. Three music stands were no longer enough. There just wasn't room for all my large-print sheet music.

Again, my mother found an answer. She invented a contraption. She found an old silver folding music stand, the kind that has a crease in the middle. She hole-punched my music sheets in the middle and put a large key ring through them. The ring hung right in the crack in the middle of the stand. She bought two large magnets with clips on the top and clipped the last sheet of music to the stand. Now I had all the music piled on to one stand, and I could flip the pages down as I went through them, playing. The music hung on the ring, like flip charts. My mom even figured out how to copy the music so that a rest came at the end of each page; she would break the music into sections so I had a few beats of rest in which to flip the cards. I could do it quickly enough to play in time with the rest of the orchestra. During recitals at other schools, our teacher would assign a student to be my "page turner" so I wouldn't have to worry about flipping the cards.

"You know," my mom said, "even famous pianists have page turners."

To help me even further, my mother took me to the Santa Monica Center for the Partially Sighted to be fitted for a new visual aid. It was called a bioptic, and it looked like something a jeweler would use to examine fine stones. It came in the form of a pair of heavy black eyeglass-frames that held in place a small telescope lens, about three inches long and one inch in diameter, directly over my right eye. If I placed a small additional lens on the end of the telescope, I could see things as close as eighteen inches away from me. Like music. But to do so, my left eye was blacked out with a cover that snapped over the frame.

On the day we ordered the bioptic, my emotions whipsawed. I was alternately thrilled and apprehensive. When I overheard my mother talking with the technician as she paid for it, I was plunged into instant distress. It was so expensive! It cost over a thousand dollars, which seemed like a fortune to me.

I began to worry. *What if it doesn't work? What if they got the wrong prescription in the telescope? Or the wrong power? What if I still can't see the music with it?* I cried all that night, worried about the money, and worried that the bioptic wouldn't be right.

The following week, we went back to pick it up. I was elated—it worked! In fact, by twisting the lens and changing the focus, I could actually enhance the magnification, or pull back, make the power a little weaker, to see more of the notes.

The bioptic, like any visual aid, was tricky. If I moved my head too much, the lens went out of focus. It had to be just right. But I could see the music, and, more important, I no longer stood out as the obvious problem child in the orchestra.

I could use the same sheet music that my classmates did, and a single music stand like everybody else. I had to sit closer to it, but I was almost normal. I was as close to normal as I could be.

With one exception.

I hated the school bus.

The "bus" was a small yellow van that picked up all the handicapped children in my district, all eight or ten of us, and drove us to school.

The other kids called it the Retardo Bus.

It came right to my house each morning, and I dreaded it. I would drag my feet getting on it. All of us were lumped in together: mildly visually impaired, totally blind, hearing impaired, learning impaired, you name it. To me, it was a bus for outcasts— for the nerdy and the dorky. Like all kids, I was trying hard just to fit in and be like everybody else.

The bus set us apart. For one thing, it seemed to be always, always late. We'd never get to school before the first bell had rung;

often, we didn't arrive until after the second bell—the tardy bell. One morning, I walked in and my teacher said, "Well, Marla, you're late."

"My bus was late," I said. "My bus is always late."

"It doesn't matter," he said. "You're late."

The penalty for lateness was to do a lap around the school grounds, circling the tennis courts and back again. Morning recess came, and he ordered me to run the lap. I thrust my jaw out.

"But my bus was late," I insisted. "I can't do anything about my bus."

"Start running," he said.

I knew I was right.

So I walked. I walked out the gate. I walked around the tennis courts. And I walked right back in. This was one occasion in which I had no intention of running.

The bus represented stigma to me. It was everything I hated about my impairment. Too often, others equated being impaired with being dumb. Just because I couldn't see something, people assumed that I couldn't read. It was an automatic equation: if you can't read, you're stupid.

I knew otherwise. Yes, academics were more difficult for me, and for other kids who were visually impaired, but only because every task took longer. To conceptualize and problem-solve with numbers, words, or letters was a never-ending task of "bottom-up" processing; of trying to recognize things by their familiar shapes or a few visible characteristics until the brain could fill in the rest. It took a lot of time. Others immediately associated that slowness with mental slowness, a lack of mental acuity.

On the contrary, it took a great deal of mental creativity to make up for vision loss.

On that bus, there were kids with all kinds of disabilities, all different kinds of problems. But to outsiders, we all had the same big brand on us. It was the "problem" bus, the "special" bus.

My mother should have said, "Marla, get over it. It's just a stupid bus ride." But she was desperate to make life easier for me. The problem was, this time she couldn't.

The bus was just one of many ways in which I was becoming ever more embarrassed by my sight. As much as I loved the VH room, and as much help and relief as I found in there, I never wanted other students to see me go into the room. Its door was labeled "Special Ed." I didn't want to be associated with that room.

I would dodge in there, and dodge out again.

Once I was in there, I loved it. I was crazy about my VH teacher, John O'Looney, who was the first person I met who could treat a disability with humor. He was determined to make us all laugh. One of my classmates, a boy named Sam Bushman, was totally blind. Sam compensated for his disability by making an extra effort to appear totally cool. One afternoon Sam opened what he thought was his lunch bag and reached inside. He pulled out a handful of snails. Mr. O'Looney had struck.

We were a group of kids grown grim from coping with serious problems, and "Mr. O," as we called him, could make us laugh, lighten our moods and our loads. He was also a great motivator: no kid from the VH room had ever made the Honor Roll until he arrived. He told us, "There are four quarters in the school year. If you get on the Honor Roll in any of the four quarters, I'll take you out to lunch." I ended up making the Honor Roll all four quarters for three straight years. He had to take me to lunch twelve times.

But during my eighth-grade year, Mr. O finally said, "Marla, I am not taking you out to lunch four times again this year. We'll go once and call it even." We went to a nearby Mexican restaurant, and over our combo plates, Mr. O asked me to consider something when I moved on to high school the following year.

"I think you should go out for the track team," he said.

I laughed. Mr. O told me he was serious, but to me it was a pipe dream. I was afraid of high school. It was another, bigger place, with older kids, and I was not ready to face it yet. Thank God it was still a summer away.

The more my eyes betrayed me, the more determined I was to become an academic overachiever, and an athletic one, and a musical one, all at the same time. I had to prove that I wasn't dumb, and that I could do all the things that came naturally to others. My mother would say to me, "Marla, there are few things you can't do, but everything just takes longer."

It was important to me to be articulate; to be able to communicate well and express myself without stumbling. I had to be word perfect, because I wanted others to know I was intelligent. I put unnecessary pressure on myself to excel. It didn't come from my parents or my teachers. It came from me, and me alone. *I'm gonna show them* was my motto. And my motivation.

I expected a lot from others, too. I could not understand how some of my fellow students could be so lackadaisical about their work; about assignments that were incredibly time-consuming for me. Why didn't they use their vision to the fullest? It seemed to me that they were wasting perfectly good eyes. At times, the feeling was alienating.

I was in danger of becoming socially impaired. There was a dramatic side effect of vision impairment: I had spent too much time alone. By the end of junior high school, I had not matured the way I should have, because I had neither the knowledge nor the opportunity to interact with my peers and develop basic interpersonal skills. Junior high is an awkward age for anyone, but it can be especially difficult if you don't know how to meet people, how to express interest in their lives. Or even how to simply say "Hello."

Everyplace I went, I was with my mother. And she did all the talking. I stood one step behind her, quiet and shy. I looked at the ground, or off into space. I slouched.

Finally, my mother took notice of it and said, "Marla, look at people when they speak to you." I wasn't even aware of the extent to which I had withdrawn. From that day forward, I tried to make an effort, but effort wasn't any good if opportunity didn't accompany it. Until I found some friends my own age, until I could venture out into the world without my mother at my side, I was never going to grow up.

I had one good friend at EO Green Junior High, Tracey Reagan. We were in the sixth grade together, and I met her at recess in the first week of school. "Hey, do you want to play hopscotch?" she asked.

I had never played hopscotch. But I was eager to learn. Tracey and I became instant friends, and we remained friends through three years of junior high. She was, quite literally, my accompanist; Tracey played the piano, and we performed together for our eighth-grade music-appreciation class. But she was my only friend. I didn't know how to begin to make more. If I had at least tried to associate more with the other kids at school, I would have learned that they were, in their own ways, as insecure as I was. It was a crucial piece of missing information.

There was one tantalizing clue to the kind of social life others had: my brother, Grady. By now, Grady was a tenth-grader at our local high school in Camarillo, and he was becoming an enormously popular guy. He and all his friends would burst into our house, laughing and punching each other and teasing. I didn't complain—I liked it. I liked his friends, and the house seemed more at ease when there were other voices around. Sometimes I tried to hang out with them, the quiet little sister in pigtails who stood in the back of the room and smiled. Grady was too nice to tell me to beat it, and his best friend, Glen Dutro, a big guy with curly blond hair and a riotous sense of humor, was one of the few people who could draw me out and make me laugh. The truth was, Grady knew how much I admired him, and while he teased me like a normal sibling, he watched out for me, too.

I thought Grady was so cool that it never occurred to me that he might have his own problems. We all relied heavily on Grady's good nature. Unlike me, he was dependable emotionally, always easygoing and laid-back. He was a continual help to my parents; if my mother had to make a long commute to pick me up, we would invariably return to find that Grady had emptied the dishwasher and set the table. We took it for granted. Grady never whined. But he had to grow up too early.

Simple tasks made difficult were becoming a way of life for me. Example: I hated clothes-shopping. I still do. An activity that most girls my age loved, I despised. It was always an "ordeal," that favorite word again. I never knew what was cool and what was not, and frankly, I was past caring. My main objectives were to find something that fit and get out of the store as quickly as possible. But the only thing I could do quickly anymore was run.

I couldn't see the sizes or the price tags on anything I took off the rack. Nor could I see the mannequins or other displays, the way everyone else could. If I wanted to know what that reddish thing was on the wall, I had to get my hands on it, feel the fabric, and figure out exactly what sort of article of clothing I was dealing with.

I didn't want my mother's help. What 13-year-old girl wants her mother to pick out her clothes, much less read the tag? But until I came up with another solution, Mom did most of the choosing. The result was a closet full of clothes that my mother thought were "adorable" and that I refused to wear. I wore jeans and a sweatshirt every day of my life. I told myself, *I'm not a girl, anyway. I'm an athlete.*

The violin was growing more difficult by the day, too. I continued my Suzuki lessons with a teacher in Camarillo, Ms. Gasteneau, but the music was complex, and it required hours of work. I remember trying to learn a piece that was seven or eight pages long, and the laborious task of trying to make it out with my bioptic.

With the three-inch-long bioptic in my eye, I would peer at five notes of music, my face pressed to the page, too close to the stand to hold my violin. After I had memorized the five notes, I'd set down the bioptic, pick up my violin, and play the notes. Then I'd set down the violin again, put the bioptic back in my eye, and study five more notes.

It took an hour to learn just two lines of music.

This went on and on. Eventually, it just became too difficult. I decided that I'd rather be outside, running track or chasing a soccer ball. I gave up the violin.

There could be no real escape from my disability. I learned that on the day I graduated from junior high school, at the very moment when I thought I finally *had* escaped it. After three years, I had transformed myself into the top student in the school, and I was invited to give a small valedictory address, something simple about setting goals.

I took my place in line for the walk into the arena for the ceremony. The graduating class was split into two groups alphabetically, so that A to L was on one side of the outdoor amphitheatre and M to Z on the other. We were supposed to file down the central aisle and form a pair with someone from the other line, and take seats together.

I turned down the aisle . . .

. . . and one of my bus-mates fell in beside me.

Imagine the chances, as the lines merged, that a kid from the hated bus would be my partner. I couldn't believe it. It was the ultimate irony. The sad thing is that he was a terrific kid, bright and funny, and we would know each other through high school and into our twenties. I liked him immensely. But on that day, when I was 13 years old, he represented being an outcast and a loner.

I wrote a poem at the end of that year. It was about living life with a sack over my head. My teachers read it and called my mother to suggest that she take me to a counselor. But I refused: I didn't think I needed counseling. I just needed my eyes back.

Life is a bore
Life is a drag
Life is like a hole in a bag
Everyone's inside
Everyone but me
I can't find the hole
I can't see

Even if I didn't need counseling, my parents did. One evening, they went to a center for the partially sighted and joined a discussion group with other parents who had blind or partially blind children. They didn't attend for long. In the end, they felt that the discussions weren't productive. Too many parents would talk *for* their kids about what they could or couldn't do. My parents came home from these sessions determined not to set barriers for me, artificial or otherwise. They decided to let me determine my limitations for myself.

At some point during one of those evenings, my parents made the decision not to treat me as impaired. They didn't ignore my vision—that would have been impossible—but they essentially made no concessions to it.

I was beginning to adopt a similar philosophy—only mine was angrier. To me, my vision wasn't impaired. My environment was.

4. My Secret

In every town there's a rivalry between the two big high schools. Marla was just a sophomore at Camarillo High, but she was already on the varsity, and she was supposed to run the 400 meters in the big meet against Camarillo's arch-rival, Rio Mesa. Well, Marla came home three days before the meet and said, "I'm pulling out. I just found out I have to run against Mary Bittner." Mary was the big deal in southern California high-school track before Marion Jones, a very prominent local athlete. That day, and all through the next morning, it was all Marla would talk about. She was wringing her hands about running against Rio Mesa and Mary Bittner. On the day of the meet, she came home with a splitting headache. She threw herself on the bed and said, "I have to take a nap, and I'm not running the race."

Marla would do this. She would find something to focus on, and obsess on it, but it wasn't the real problem. Finally you'd find out what was really bothering her. Well, it turned out she had never run at night, and she was afraid of losing her way or wandering out of her lane in front of everyone. Finally she admitted it. She was worried about the floodlights, about the glare.

She woke up from the nap and started to cry. She said, "Mom, I'm not going to run the 400, I'm just not." I stood there like John Wayne. I said, "Marla, you can't let your team down, or your coach. It's too late. It doesn't matter whether you want to or not. You're going to run it." It was one of the few times I put my foot down.

We got into the car to go to the meet, and lo and behold, it was foggy. Like pea soup. We got to the track, and this fog kept rolling into the stadium. I sat there watching it get thicker, and by the time those girls lined up for the 400, you could not see the straightaway. You could not even see the bleachers.

The gun went off. Everyone started screaming and yelling, and off she went, into the first turn—and into a bank of fog. She just disappeared. I stood up, and I thought, I pushed my daughter into this. I felt so responsible because I didn't usually push her. Everyone around me was screaming and yelling, and no one could see what was happening.

Finally, out of the fog comes this body, around the far turn. Of course it's Marla. And she's about ten yards in front of the field. I stood there and bawled. Not because she won it, but just because she did it. Not another person in the stands knew what I knew; how she had felt before the race, or for what reason.

It was just a race. But it was so much more than a race. She beat Mary Bittner in the fog, and all. And we didn't even get to see it.

—Valerie Runyan

My vision was my secret. Virtually no one knew about it. Even the few who suspected that something was wrong had only a vague sense of what it was. It was a hushed thing, *there's something wrong with her eyes but we don't know what it is.*

I became so good at hiding it that I tricked everybody, from the very first day of high school. I went to extreme measures to behave as normally as possible. I wanted them to treat my vision problem exactly the way I treated it—as something nonexistent, and certainly nothing to be discussed.

I enrolled in Camarillo High—my home district had finally implemented a visually handicapped program—which meant that I would go to school with Grady. It also meant that I'd have to start all over again academically and socially at a new school, where I didn't know anyone but my own brother. Grady could have balked at being responsible for his impaired kid sister, but he did exactly the opposite. He looked out for me, in his own quiet and subtle way.

Before the fall semester started, Grady took me over to the school, with my class list in hand, and we hunted down each of my classrooms. I memorized where they were. I couldn't see the numbers on the doors, but on the first day of school, I walked straight to my classes as if I could. I never had to ask for help. I faked it. I seemed as competent and self-assured as anyone else.

Every morning I rode shotgun with my brother, who by now was cool beyond description, clean-cut and sleek behind the wheel of his black 1982 Firebird, in which he had installed a high-tech stereo system, with equalizers. He would turn the knob on the stereo each morning and the speakers would crackle and hum, and within seconds Oingo Boingo would blast away. He parked at the back of the school because it was the cool thing, even though it meant trudging up a dirt hill to the rear door. We always walked together up the hill and across the grass, until finally we would go separate ways to our classrooms. For those few brief moments as we walked across the grass, I would feel cool, too. But then Grady would say, "See ya," and I was on my own.

The first great crisis for any freshman is who to eat lunch with. If you had to eat lunch alone, it was like hanging a sign around your neck that said, "I don't have any friends." My brother called up one of his buddies who also had a younger sister, a sophomore, and they arranged that I would eat with her. Each day at lunch we'd meet under a particular tree, and I would have lunch with her circle of friends. This went on for weeks, until I got to know people on my own.

I finally found my niche on the track team. I decided to accept Mr. O'Looney's challenge, and I made the varsity. On the afternoon of tryouts, I went through my warmup strides around the dirt track without mentioning my disability to anyone. It never occurred to me to tell my coaches and teammates about my vision, because I genuinely thought it was irrelevant.

After I had run a couple of 100-meter sprints, the coach wandered over to me. "You have a natural stride," he said.

I was thrilled. I had found something that I was good at, and I would have a presence in the school instead of being just another face in the hallway or the odd girl who always ate lunch by herself. I couldn't wait to get out of the classroom, put on shorts, and go outside to run.

There was one drawback: when they handed me the uniform, it consisted of a skimpy tank top. I was flat as a board. I was so embarrassed to wear it that I wore a T-shirt underneath it and a sweatshirt over it. I would take my sweatshirt off at the last second before a race, run my race as fast as I could, and then throw the sweatshirt back on.

Track and field was my rescue from the constraints and frustrations of the classroom. I was becoming an accomplished high-jumper, good enough to compete at the state level, and I loved the sensation of hurling my body through the air. There was something gratifying about clearing the bar; a sense of an obstacle overcome. I could hardly see the bar—and it didn't matter. I would take off down the runway toward the invisible goal, and only after four or five steps would it come faintly into view. Then I would accelerate, and by the time I got there, just a moment before I jumped, I would see it clearly.

Instead of vision, I relied on counting off the steps. I would walk backward down the Tartan, counting stride by stride. Then I would place a mark in the ground where I needed to begin my approach. My father even made me a personal marker: he hammered a nail into a golf ball, then sawed it in half so there was just a small spike showing. He painted it Day-Glo orange. I couldn't miss it. I'd run my approach in the other direction, stick the golf ball in the ground, and that's where I'd start.

I continued to believe that my sight was only a problem indoors. I genuinely thought that my vision was normal when I was outside. You can call it denial, or you can just call it ignorance. If I couldn't see a group of people across the field, I assumed nobody else could, either. It never occurred to me that other people saw things that I wasn't seeing.

Occasionally, I'd get a small, telltale clue to what others saw. One of my friends and teammates was a girl named Tricia, who was so studious that she would bring her books to meets and study in the grandstand. She'd find a sunny spot in the bleachers and read in the sun while she was waiting to run. I envied her; it seemed like a pleasant way to study. I couldn't read anything without a magnifying glass, and even with that, not in the bright glare of sunlit bleachers. The one time that I tried to read in the sun with my magnifying glass, my book almost caught fire.

Sometimes I would lie on the infield grass and stare up at the blue sky, and I would know for a fact that I was seeing something others weren't: large black specks floated in front of my eyes. They drifted back and forth, as if suspended in water. I learned from my doctors that the specks were pieces of dead retina tissue loose in the interior of my eyes.

But I was determined never to use my vision as an excuse. If I couldn't do something, I never said, "It's because I can't see." If the cause of failure was not my eyesight, then it had to be a deficit in my effort or skill. I told myself to work harder, and I was intensely critical of the final product.

My mother called it the Great Illusion: I was becoming so good at hiding my disability that I almost convinced myself it didn't exist. I practiced hiding it every day, at school and at home, and I got better and better at *seeing* fully sighted.

Early in my freshman year, the school held a "backwards dance," in which the girls invited the boys to be their dates. I mustered the courage to ask a guy on the track team, a senior. He said yes. We arranged to go to a local Italian restaurant, Ottavio's, and then the dance. But I had forgotten one detail.

"Mom, I can't read the menu," I said.

My mother said, "I'll go to the restaurant and get a menu, and we'll read it ahead of time."

It worked. I decided what I would order three full days in advance. When the waitress came to take our order, I held the fine-print menu two feet from my face, pretending to read it, and then glanced back up at her and said, "I'll have the rigatoni with marinara sauce, please."

In a way, I lived in a double world: the sighted and the unsighted. But in doing so, I put myself in a no-win situation. My ferocious independence made me resist all attempts to help me—especially if they were made by my mother.

When my English class was assigned a term paper, I insisted on typing it like everyone else in the class. It was tedious work. I sat hunched over the typewriter, peering at the keys and jabbing at them one at a time. I could barely see the letters, and I had to use my magnifying glass to see which letter I'd actually typed.

I typed in the morning, and I typed into the night. I even came home from school during my lunch hour to type. Sometimes it would take me an hour to type one sentence. Sometimes frustration got the better of me, and I cursed at the typewriter.

"Let me help you," my mother would say.

"NO!" I'd shout.

"Then don't do it," she'd say, throwing up her hands. "Why put yourself through this? Just stop."

"I can't do that," I'd reply.

I'd go in my room and rest for a while, but an hour later I'd be back at it. My mother would hear the typewriter going again and bury her face in her hands at the painstaking pace of it. Click. Click. Click.

My mother later told me that she'd considered sneaking in a couple of sentences while I was at school.

Finally, after hours of anguish and tedium, I finished it. It was a thousand times harder to type it than to write it in longhand, but to accept help was to admit defeat.

I would go out of my way to take on tasks that no one believed I could do. Like photography. I became fascinated with the idea of seeing my world through the pictures I took and developed. I would snap a picture of a person, object, or scene with an old 35-millimeter camera, then rush back to the classroom to find out what I had actually captured. I developed the film and enlarged the images in the darkroom, and there, in the dim red light, a clearer and larger image would appear. *Oh, so that's how it looks,* I would think to myself. I also used photography in reverse—to show others how I saw the world. For a class project, I purposely created softer, blurry photographs of the chalkboard and the print in my textbooks so that my teacher could see how things appeared to me. I loved photography, and I was good at it. I even won First Prize in a county contest. I photographed a friend of mine, Carla Myers, reading Braille. Just her hands are in the photo, with the light positioned so that the raised dots are visible under her fingertips. I titled it "A Touch of Sight."

My parents rigged a darkroom for me in a rarely used bathroom at the back of the house, and they had an exhaust fan put in to dispel the chemical fumes. I used the darkroom so much that the chemicals eventually stripped all the paint off the walls.

My parents and teachers learned not to offer help, and not to sugarcoat the results. Tell me the truth, or say nothing.

Even when my reading load grew increasingly heavy, I refused to take shortcuts. I read *The Sun Also Rises,* and *The Catcher in the Rye,* and a heavy novel that baffled all of us, irrespective of sight, *A Portrait of the Artist as a Young Man.* In my senior year we had to read fourteen novels in a single semester.

I could have gotten those novels on tape, from a service called Recordings for the Blind. But I was determined to do everything the way my classmates did, even when it was nearly impossible for me. I considered books on tape unacceptable shirking. My mother could see another ordeal coming. "It's not worth all this, Marla— don't do it," she'd say.

Instead, I insisted that my VH teacher photocopy the entire novel in large print so I could read it with a magnifying glass. "Otherwise, it's cheating," I said.

In retrospect, how do I explain my stubbornness? I was afraid to use my vision as an excuse, because I suspected that if I gave in to it on the smallest matter, I would be tempted to give in to it on the larger matters, and for the rest of my life. I didn't want to get into the habit of humoring my blindness; I cultivated denial as a protection from the temptation to become a victim.

On the one hand, ignoring my impaired vision served me well, because there was nothing I wouldn't tackle or try to excel at. But it didn't serve me as well in other ways. When you don't accept your impairment, you inevitably make life more difficult than it has to be. There is a difference between accepting limitations, which I never did and still don't, and accepting the basic condition and making peace with it. I had no peace in high school. What I had was a case of envy for the fully sighted.

Denial, at least at that time of my life, was as helpful to me as a visual aid: I couldn't use my vision impairment as an excuse if I didn't really believe it existed. It was a feat of mental acrobatics—and an ironic one, given that my partial blindness had once been diagnosed as psychosomatic.

My mother, on the other hand, did use my vision loss as the scapegoat for many of my shortcomings and mistakes. She seemed to think that this vision thing explained all; whenever I cried out in frustration or simply because I was a teenager, she immediately concluded that it was because of my eyes. The truth was, I tended to lose my temper over things that were easy for others but not for me, like typing or reading, and I didn't know how to control my anger. I simply vented it. I hadn't learned how to transform a negative attitude into a positive one. My parents loved me, and often excused me—when an excuse was the last thing I needed.

I screwed up sometimes, just like any kid or teenager or young adult on this planet. I made plenty of mistakes in judgment, but my parents, who were so proud of their daughter, and who marveled at how much she accomplished despite blindness, couldn't admit that their little overachiever also had faults. I became weary of what I felt were their irrational rationalizations, and I swore never to excuse myself.

An excuse was tantamount to giving up and becoming truly blind.

I didn't have much tolerance for idle chitchat in high school, and I had even less tolerance for people who didn't try hard. Thanks to that attitude, I didn't have much of a social life in high school, either.

I wasn't the most approachable kid. I couldn't see my own demeanor or how forbidding I was to others. Each morning, I arrived in homeroom and dropped a stack of books on the floor next to my seat with a loud bang. I wouldn't speak to anyone. I just fixed a monocular in my eye, stared at the board, and started copying furiously. What my classmates couldn't know was that I felt pressured every single morning to copy down what was on the board. I was unsociable because I was so preoccupied with keeping up.

My classmates thought I was aloof. My secret was also becoming my trap: I refused to accommodate or even acknowledge my vision loss, but I was hurt when no one understood the extent of my tribulations with it. I walled myself up, and then resented it when I was misunderstood.

One afternoon, I was running on the track when some football players jogged by. All of a sudden they burst out laughing. For some reason, I was sure they were laughing at me. I knew that at the least they considered me standoffish. When I got home after school, I dropped my books on the kitchen table and said to my mother, "I'm going to the T-shirt shop and I'm going to get a shirt made that says, 'I'm really not a snob, I just can't see you.'"

I wrote a poem for creative writing called "Behind My Green Eyes," in which I talked about crawling into somebody's head and looking through their eyes to see what they see. I envied my classmates the easiness with which they moved through the day. I was tired of coping with the fact that in every single classroom, the first thing the teacher did was to write something on the board. And I couldn't see it.

I would immediately have to go into problem-solving mode. First, I sat there and tried to assess how important the information was. If it was just the instructor's name, I didn't care.

Was it something I really needed to know? *Am I going to be tested on this?* I wondered. *Is it still going to be there at the end of class, when we're allowed to get out of our seats and I can walk up and copy it down?*

Maybe not. *If it's not going to be there, maybe I better ask the girl on my left to tell me what it is.*

But that would mean asking for help, which would immediately set me apart from the rest of class. Or, I could get my monocular out and try to read it. I chose that option and rustled around in my knapsack, searching for the monocular. I glanced up.

Now the teacher had written down three more sentences. *I've missed everything he said.*

By now I was hopelessly far behind, and we were only ten minutes into the first period of the day. That was my life.

Inevitably, denial led to anger. Every day, I ran face-first into roadblocks that I wasn't prepared to cope with. I could have made my life so much easier if I had just given myself permission to listen to books on tape, or if I had asked my teachers, "Would you copy something down for me ahead of time, if it's really important?" There were a thousand little ways in which I could have helped myself.

Instead, it seemed as though I was always tired and always had headaches.

And it seemed like it was always sunny and god-damned seventy-eight degrees.

And it seemed like everything was always a problem.

My doctor prescribed a pair of contact lenses because I had developed a case of nearsightedness in conjunction with the Stargardt's. They were daily-wear contacts, and they became the bane of my existence. They always had lint or hair on them. They came with a little heating box and a bottle of cleaning solution. I was supposed to heat the lenses in the box to burn away the toxins from the cleaning solution, but sometimes I would just pour cleanser on them and stick them straight into my eyes.

It was forty minutes of hit-or-miss to put the contacts in. One would fall down my cheek. The other one would disappear in the corner of my eye. I would finally get them in—and by my second-period class my eyes would burn so badly that I had to take the contacts out, because I had misused the cleaning solution.

There was just one perk: they were tinted green, to protect my eyes from bright lights. They made me look as though I had cat's eyes, and people would stop me in the hallway to remark on them. "Wow, look at your eyes, they're so green," someone would say. But sometimes one of them would hurt so badly that I'd have to take it out, and I'd have one green-gray eye and one bright-green eye. Which further convinced my classmates that I was kind of weird.

It didn't help matters that I lived in such a shimmering upper-class, all-white, pseudo-perfect community. The weather, warm cloudless skies day after day after day, represented the conformity that I saw around me and the intolerance for any kind of difference. It was beautiful every day of the year, but no one rode a bike or went for a walk. People all stayed in their houses and watched television. Even if a store was only a half-mile away, no one would dare walk to get there—they'd drive. I was beginning to hate Camarillo.

One of my first new friends was a girl named Amber. I met her as a freshman, when we were both new kids in school. She was from a military family and had just moved to Camarillo, and she didn't know anyone either, so we were relieved to find each other.

Amber's mother, in an effort to help her make friends, enrolled her in a Church of the Nazarene youth group. I had no interest, because organized religion had not been a very big part of my life, but Amber became very involved with the group, from a social aspect as much as a religious one. It became obvious that if I wanted to keep Amber in my life, I would have to join the group. So I did.

I began going to the Church of the Nazarene several times a week. I'd go on Sunday mornings, and again on Sunday nights, and on Wednesday afternoons after school. We had Bible-study classes with a severe young pastor who taught us prayers and told us that it was a sin to dance and a worse sin to wear a bikini bathing suit. I was wide-eyed with shock and didn't understand any of it. Gradually, it began to have a disturbing effect on me.

There was one young woman in the group whom I found especially unsettling. To this day I don't like to think about her, and I don't want to include her name in the book, so I'll just call her Maggie. She told us that she was a "gift of God" because her mother had had several miscarriages before she was conceived. She was 17, older than most of us, and we tended to believe what she said, no matter how far-fetched. Even though I decided that she was a fanatic, I was a little bit afraid of her, too. Unfortunately, she and Amber became close, and we fell into a kind of tug-of-war for Amber's friendship.

One afternoon, Maggie informed me that my blindness was a result of my sins.

"Your eyes are bad because you're being punished by the Devil," she said. "You don't believe in God enough. If you accept

Jesus in your life and become a Christian, then you'll be miracu-
lously healed."

"Why are you saying this to me?" I asked.

"You need to do this right away, so your soul will be saved, and
so you won't go to Hell," she said.

I should have ignored her. But I was 14, and what she said tor-
mented me. For days I walked around believing I was going to
Hell, and that I had brought my affliction on myself through lack
of faith. I didn't know what was right or wrong anymore.

From then on, at every turn, Maggie went out of her way to
sow self-doubt in me. She'd invite Amber and me to slumber par-
ties at her house, and then try to convert both of us, talking about
Hell and sin, when all we really wanted to do was practice our
dance steps.

This was in 1984, and the movies *Fame* and *Flashdance* were big
hits. Every Top 40 song on the radio was a dance tune. Amber and
I liked to go into her garage and practice dancing, and throw in
some gymnastics, maybe a back walkover and some splits. But according to Maggie and the Church of the Nazarene, our dancing
was sinful.

One afternoon I came home from our Wednesday Bible study
in tears. That day the entire topic of our youth-group discussion
was our pastor's insistence that girls who wore bathing suits and
lay in the sun were sinners because they were tempting to males,
and temptation was evil. In the back of my mind, I knew it was a
warped view, but I actually felt guilty, too. I had just bought my
first bikini and worn it in the backyard as I lay next to our pool.
Was I a sinner? Was I evil?

Up to that point, my mother had restrained herself when it
came to the church group. She didn't like any of it, from the bits

of information that she'd gathered, but she didn't want to intervene; she was happy that I had friends, and she wanted me to make up my own mind about the group. But that afternoon, I sat on the kitchen counter while my mother mopped the floor, and I told her exactly what the pastor had said, and what Maggie had said.

As I talked, my mother mopped harder and harder.

"You know what, Marla?" she said, swiping at the floor savagely. "I am so *sick* of that church group. You are the best person you can be, and that's all that matters. You just forget every single thing they've told you."

My mother was doubly furious at the end of that year when she saw what Maggie had written in my yearbook. She'd copied passages from the Bible about being blinded by the Devil and about God healing those whose eyes were afflicted.

"She's ruined your yearbook," my mother seethed. "She's absolutely ruined it."

Having no friends at all was better than having this friend, I decided.

The things I would never do began to prey on my mind. One thing in particular haunted me, because it was so important to any teenager: I would never drive.

For the able-bodied teenagers around me, driving had become everything. It represented adulthood, independence from the parental world, your own wheels, your own set of keys, your own sense of direction and self-determination. It was an essential rite of passage, and when my classmates began to do it, I felt more envious than ever before.

Somehow my parents understood this, and perhaps even had expected it. When I was a kid, I used to say, "Mom, if I can't drive when I grow up, then I'll get a horse and ride along the side of the road."

"Okay," she said.

But now I was 16, and we didn't live on *Little House on the Prairie*; we lived in a paved-over, asphalt-and-cement jungle called Camarillo, and if you wanted to go anywhere, you didn't ride a bike or a horse, or even walk, you drove.

One summer afternoon, after a clothes-shopping "ordeal" in a nearby mall, my mother, Grady, and I piled into our blue Ford van. We sat there for a moment, cooling off from the heat outside.

"Let's go," I told my mother.

But she was wiped out, sitting in the back of the van sipping a Pepsi.

"Fine, I'm going to drive," I said.

"Okay," she said.

She began to give me instructions.

"Turn the key, put your foot on the brake, and put the car in gear."

I did. For the next thirty minutes or so, I drove in circles around the empty parking lot, delighted. But it was just a temporary illusion. If I wanted to go anywhere at all, I had to rely on someone else for a ride. I was 16 years old, and my brother still drove me to school, and my mother still picked me up.

One afternoon, I was hanging around the VH room at school when I overheard our teacher, Cynthia Pontinen, talking about how some visually impaired people were actually able to drive. There was this Dr. Gordon in Encino, she said, who could prescribe powerful bioptic telescopes with which you might qualify

for a special license. In fact, Dr. Gordon had helped visually impaired people do all kinds of improbable things with the use of
powerful magnifiers.

My mouth fell open. I ran to a pay phone on campus and
called home.

"Mom," I said urgently, "Mrs. Pontinen says there's a doctor
who can help me see well enough to drive. Will you take me to
him for my birthday?"

My mother was stunned. I could hear an edge in her voice. She
didn't like the idea at all, and she was resentful that Mrs. Pontinen
had put it into my head.

"The doctor could prescribe a thing, and you know, I could
drive," I babbled on. "I could drive, I could get a thing, and I
could drive, I could drive."

On the other end of the phone, my mother simply said, "We'll
talk about it when you get home."

That night at home I declared, "I want to drive."

My father was aghast. Driving is a source of alarm to any parent, much less the parent of a visually impaired teenager. It was a
frightful thing for them to consider, and they were furious that
anyone would even suggest it.

At first, they tried to stonewall me. "That's all well and good,"
my father said, "but no one will give you a driver's license."

But I wouldn't let it go. Every night over supper, I pushed and
pushed. I accused them of being overprotective, a charge that they
were usually sensitive to, but my father remained completely resistant. "This is not going to happen," he said. "I'm not just concerned for your safety. I'm concerned for everyone else's." Still, I
persevered. My parents had adjusted over and over again when I
wanted to try something new, whether it was skiing or photogra-

phy or track. In time, they would adjust to the idea of driving, I thought.

Finally, they agreed at least to let me see Dr. Gordon—but they weren't happy about it. My father still flatly objected to any mention of driving, while my mother was disapproving to the point of aloofness. She grudgingly drove me to Dr. Gordon's Encino office. "Let's just get this over with," she said.

We parked in the underground structure and were about to get out of the car when my mother suddenly twisted toward me from the driver's seat. She said, "Marla, I think you should just tell yourself that the chances of you driving are not very good. It's fine to see him in case there is something else he could help you with, but let's just forget about the driving thing. Promise me you won't bring it up."

I was crushed—and by then I was as tired of the argument as she was. "All right," I said, unhappily.

In Dr. Gordon's office, I climbed into yet another examining chair, while my mother sat across the room, flipping through a magazine. Dr. Gordon was a very thoughtful-seeming, soft-spoken man. He performed the basic initial eye exam that I had sat through hundreds of times.

"Is there anything in your life that you want to do, that you can't do because of your vision?" he asked me.

I bit my tongue. I wanted to yell "I want to drive!" at the top of my voice, but my mother had forbidden me to.

I sat there for a long minute thinking. I couldn't come up with anything. Finally, I said timidly, "Well, I have to sit on the floor when I watch TV because I can't see from the couch." I felt silly even saying it. Sitting on the floor was not a big deal and certainly not worth coming all this way and wasting this doctor's time with.

"Anything else?" he asked.

I considered the question further. So far, I had been able to master what I had put my mind to, from schoolwork to photography to highjumping. Was there anything I couldn't do? No.

"Not really," I said.

"Huh," he said. "You're the first sixteen-year-old I've ever met who didn't want to drive."

I squirmed.

"Yeah, well, I'd like to drive, but my mom told me that I'm not going to be able to."

"Oh, she did, did she?" he asked.

"Yeah," I said.

"Let's see about that," Dr. Gordon said.

I almost leaped out of the chair. Across the room, my mother cringed.

"But I do want to drive," I said. "I *do* want to drive."

Dr. Gordon began to put a series of bioptic lenses onto a frame. For the next half-hour, he appraised my vision using several different magnifications. He slid various telescopes in and out of my view. Finally, he made a temporary bioptic using a magnification to the sixth power and placed the frames on my face. I peered through the three-inch-long eyepiece. My mother was sitting across the room.

I gasped.

"Mom, I can see your face!" I said.

I'll never forget it. My mother didn't say anything; she was too overcome. But after a minute she got up and went into the bathroom, where she lit a cigarette and wept—and decided that if Dr. Gordon said I could drive, she would have to allow it. It was worth it to know that I could see her face.

After more fiddling with lenses, Dr. Gordon determined that he could give me 20/40 vision in my right eye using a bioptic. I had very limited angles, and it was essentially like looking through a tube—the stronger the power he used, the narrower the field of vision—but it was more vision than I'd ever thought I would have again.

Finally, Dr. Gordon finished his examination. He explained that California was one of about twenty-five states in which driving with a bioptic lens was legal. Then he said to my mother, "Well, Marla has good peripheral vision. What I can do is fit her with a six-power bioptic, and if she practices and learns to use it, and she can scan back and forth, she should be able to drive."

I left the office in triumph. My mother put in an order for the bioptic.

It would take a few weeks for the bioptic to be made, but I wanted to enroll in Driver's Ed and apply for a learner's permit right away.

Getting a driver's license, however, would prove to be as hard as anything I've ever done. It took almost a year of effort to cope with all the red tape.

When you apply for a learner's permit, what's the first thing that happens? They test your vision, that's what. But most people at the Department of Motor Vehicles were ignorant of the official policy on "bioptic drivers."

"What's a bioptic?" was the standard response.

I stood in front of the chart and explained that I was legally blind and could only see the Big E.

"What do you mean, you can only see the E? Hey, George! Get this. This girl thinks she's going to get a driver's license!"

My mother became my lawyer once again. I had to have three

interviews at the DMV, and my mother drove me back and forth without complaint. One administrator looked for "macular degeneration" in her DMV casebook, and it wasn't in there. That led to a bureaucratic snarl-up. First, we had to prove that the disease existed. Next, we had to prove that the disease was not progressive. And finally, we had to prove that with a bioptic, I was entitled to take the driver's test.

I pursued my license quietly, without telling anyone at school. I knew my teachers and classmates would cringe at the thought of a "blind girl" behind the wheel of a car. I had no intention of asking my VH teacher to photocopy the Driver's Ed textbook in large print. Instead, my mother went on a search for a private driving tutor, someone who knew what a bioptic was and could train me to use one in a car. Finally, she found an instructor who agreed to take me on. He showed up at our house one morning in his special car with two brake pedals and said, "Sure, I'll teach her how to drive, no problem."

My mother had spent time and energy looking for "just the right person," as she put it. But I realized very soon that this guy just wanted his money and couldn't care less how well I learned to drive. It was also apparent that he had never worked with a bioptic driver.

I put the heavy black bioptic frame on my face. Inside the frame were two clear plastic pieces, and mounted to the plastic over my right eye was the telescope. It was almost identical to the bioptic that I'd used to play my violin, except that this lens was designed for distance. Since I had worn one before, I was pretty good at peering through it and switching from one eye to the other.

The driving instructor just gazed at me and shrugged, like, "Whatever."

I crept out of the driveway and drove at about five miles an hour to the end of our cul de sac, and then to the end of our residential street. Really, all I did was take my foot off the brake. We reached the intersection at the end of the street, and I stopped.

The instructor said, "Okay, now make sure you look, because we're going to make a right-hand turn."

Peering through my bioptic, I glanced to the right. No cars. Now I glanced to the left.

A car was coming.

I sat still behind the wheel.

And sat. And sat.

Cautiously, I glanced to my left again. The car was still coming. We sat for another long minute.

Finally, the instructor asked, "What are you waiting for?"

"Well, there's a car down there," I said.

He said, "That car is going in the other direction."

This was the problem with a bioptic: the magnification was so powerful that it tended to distort my distance perception, so an object that was three car-lengths away would appear to be right in front of me, and a car a half-mile away would seem to be coming right at me. The car that I had seen with the instructor was blocks away—but it seemed closer. Dr. Gordon had said, "Now, you have to understand, you can drive down the street and something will look like an elephant, but you won't be able to see its tail."

Gradually, I became accustomed to the bioptic and learned how to use its strengths and weaknesses. I played it safe by finding a quiet route with few cars, and I would never vary it; looking for alternate routes was too difficult for me because it was such an effort to read street signs.

My distance perception improved, and I was ready to take the Driver's Ed course. But first, as a bioptic driver, I was required to have a special form filled out by my doctor—and then the DMV lost it. We had to drive all the way to Encino, have a new form filled out by Dr. Gordon, and drive all the way back to the DMV. Again my mother made the round trip without complaint.

By this time she was determined to help me surmount any limitation, even one that made her afraid. She didn't expect that I would drive on a freeway, but she did want me to be able to move through the world as ordinarily as possible; to go to McDonald's, to drive myself to and from school, or to go out to a movie.

When it was time to take the written test, I went to the DMV with a hand-held magnifying glass, and I took the test over to a corner of the room. I hunched over with my back to the front desk and checked the tiny boxes. I did well enough to obtain a learner's permit.

With my learner's permit, I began to broaden my horizons. I started by driving cautiously to school one morning, with my mother in the seat next to me. It meant everything to me to arrive at school behind the wheel of a car. My mother and I practiced the two-and-a-half-mile route together, plotting each street and each turn.

It was a process of trial and error. We learned that I should always avoid left-hand turns, for two reasons: first, when turning left I had to look in two directions, and it took me longer to scan with the bioptic. Second, a left-hand turn meant yielding in front of oncoming cars.

My parents decided to get me an appropriate vehicle, and that touched off a long round of discussions: we already had our van, Grady's Firebird, my father's sedan, and my mother's classic 1959 Triumph, a collector's item that remained parked in the garage. By now we had become the total southern California family.

My parents didn't feel that any of those cars was safe enough or suitable for me. They wanted me to have a car with exceptional sight lines, so they mulled over a convertible, but I objected. "People will be able to see my bioptic," I said. "I don't want people to see that." After test-driving a few used cars, we decided on a hardtop Volkswagen Rabbit. It was a box—basically nothing in the way to block the driver's view. But it wasn't exactly the safest car, either. It was the closest thing to a golf cart—basically a Pepsi can on wheels.

Each morning, I slid behind the wheel of my Volkswagen Rabbit, and my mother climbed into the passenger seat in her bathrobe, holding a cup of coffee. I wasn't wild about arriving in front of Camarillo High School with my mother riding shotgun in her bathrobe, her hair messy, but I didn't have a choice, and I was just thankful to drive there. I would hand her the keys and she'd drive home. After school, she'd wait for me in the Rabbit, and I would take over the wheel and drive us both home.

After months of Driver's Ed and special training with the bioptic, I was ready to get my license. By now it was December and I was 17, and I had spent months working toward this moment.

Finally, I was ready for the test. I passed with flying colors: I parallel parked, the whole deal. Afterward, I rejoined my mother in the car, and she said, proudly, "Do you want to drive home?"

I said no, because I wasn't familiar with the streets in Oxnard.

But as soon as we got back to Camarillo, where I was more comfortable, I got behind the wheel of my Rabbit.

That afternoon, I drove to McDonald's and pulled up to the drive-thru. It was the first thing I wanted to do. I rolled down my window and yelled into the drive-thru speaker, "A large Coke, extra ice, and one Chicken McNuggets with barbecue sauce!"

It was official: I was an adult. From then on, I drove myself everywhere. It was just a puny two and a half miles to school, but it represented more than that to me. Sure, I could have walked there, or run, or ridden a bike. But it wasn't a matter of distance, or of transportation. It was a matter of driving. And to me driving meant one thing:

I was out of there.

The natural next question, now that I was of age and had a car, was what to do with the rest of my life. I believed that I had to know beyond a shadow of a doubt what my career plan was before I graduated from high school. Sometimes, I tried to make the decision in a single night. I would lie in the dark and tell myself, *By morning you have to make up your mind.* Most of my classmates were going off to four-year colleges, but I dreaded the idea of floundering.

I told my parents, "There is no way you're going to drop me off at a four-year university somewhere, without a plan."

I was a straight-A student, and I even received a recruiting letter from Harvard, but I was so tired of my classroom struggles that I wasn't sure I wanted to apply to four-year schools. I hated books and everything associated with them at that point. It seemed that all I had ever done was labor through class after class.

Homework took me twice as long as it took everyone else. After six hours in school, I would go to track practice—an all-too-brief respite of two hours. Then I'd come home and spend the next four hours bent over my books, peering through a magnifying glass.

I was fed up. I could barely stand to be in my own home. I was fed up with school, with the town, with the house we lived in. Everything that happened seemed just a clone of the day before. The monotony was driving me crazy.

I felt underestimated. Life had become a tug-of-war with my mother. She had fought long and hard for me, and she'd made everything possible, for which I was grateful. But the role she had undertaken when I was first diagnosed with Stargardt's had not changed, and now I was 18. I wanted freedom. I wanted to have a phone conversation and not feel she was listening, and to make a decision for myself without worrying about her judgments and opinions. I wanted the opportunity to make choices, and even mistakes.

So I had to have a plan. My number-one priority was to get in and out of college as quickly as possible. For that reason, I was thinking about enrolling in a southern California junior college, Mesa. I used to joke with my mother, "Let's see. Should I go to Harvard, or Mesa Junior College?" I took the SAT, and did well—the test was actually administered in large print, and I took it with a special test proctor. My eyes entitled me to take twice as long to complete the test, and between the math and the English portions it consumed about six hours.

I was seriously considering Mesa. It was in San Diego, only three hours away, and it had a veterinary program that I was interested in. I had done volunteer work for a woman veterinarian in

Camarillo for much of my senior year, a significant confidence-builder for me and an escape from the monotony of school. But then I found out that I'd have to take an extra year of general-education coursework to qualify. More coursework? I couldn't face it. I simply didn't have the patience for it. My Mesa plan fell apart.

Again, it was track that saved me. By now I was a fairly renowned local athlete, though not quite top-tier. I held the school record in the high jump at 5'7", and I had won the Marmonte League title in my junior year. I also ran the 400 meters and anchored our high school's 1600-meter relay team. I never made it to the California state finals, although I did reach the level one step below the finals in the high jump for four straight years, and I was getting quite a few recruiting letters.

My mother called around to some of the state colleges, making inquiries about their track programs and services for the visually impaired. More often than not, they didn't have any aid to speak of. She called one prominent track and field school and spoke with a coach. "Are you kidding? Enlarged-print books? What are those?" he asked. She hung up.

May was approaching, and I still had no idea what to do with my life. I was beginning to panic. Then one afternoon, I got a call from the track and field coach at San Diego State University, a gentleman named Jim Cerveney. He asked me if I would come take a look at his program.

"We'd really be interested in having you highjump for our team," he said. "If you come down to San Diego, I'll give you a tour of the campus."

I thought, well, why not? I agreed to come—and never mentioned my vision. But without my knowledge, my mother called Coach Cerveney back and said, "This is a unique girl." She explained my impairment. Coach Cerveney said he would do some homework and get back to her.

When he called back, he described their disabled-services department, and he said, "It's not perfect, but they do the best they can. Please visit, and I'll show you what we've got."

It was good enough for my mother. Coach Cerveney said, "This will be a unique experience for me as well."

My mother and I piled in the car and made the three-hour trip to San Diego. When we arrived, Coach Cerveney met us in a parking lot, and we strolled the white stucco campus. He showed us the track facilities and the dorms, and then he escorted us to an appointment with a disabled-services administrator. The counselor we met with was visually impaired herself, and she was also in a wheelchair.

I sat down and began to fill out an application. I struggled, however, because I hadn't brought my visual aids. Finally, the woman said, "Why don't I do that for you?" Next, she asked me what my grade-point average was. I replied, "It's 3.98." Coach Cerveney's eyes almost bugged out. He knew me as a highjumper, not as a student.

Finally, the woman put down her pen and explained what sorts of services would be offered. If I expected sympathy, I was quickly disabused. She was stern and frank about what I could expect. There would be no large-print books, because textbooks were revised every year and it wasn't practical. Instead, I would have to use books on tape or hire readers.

"No one's going to take care of you here," she said. "You have to be responsible and do everything on your own. This isn't high school. You'll have to be very independent."

"Well, I am," I shot back.

If she was trying to discourage me, she had the opposite effect. I had already made my decision: I would go to school there.

This time, I really was out of there.

5. Learning to Ask for Help

My whole life was "special." I rode a "special" bus, went to a school with a "special" program, and according to my mother, I was a "special" girl with "special" needs and "special" equipment. But I wasn't special, I was angry. I had lost all patience with the world around me. I railed at the absurdity of it, and at the effort required of me to be a part of it.

I left home for San Diego State, like any freshman off to college, with every expectation of a more independent life. But I had simply replaced one sun-stained, cement-covered leisure community for another, and my problems followed me south. If anything, I felt more impaired than ever. The glare in San Diego was even more torturously bright than in Camarillo, the college textbooks were thicker, and the words I stared at were smaller.

On the first day of classes I walked into a lecture hall of 250 seats for Biology 101. The room looked more like a beach than a class: everyone wore tank tops, shorts or skirts, and sandals. Girls clicked their gum and flipped their hair over their shoulders, while the guys strutted around with bulging biceps and gel in their spiked hair, saying things like "Hey, dude, what's up, going to the party this weekend?" SDSU was ranked the No. 3 "party school" in the nation in 1987, and it was hardly a magnet for conscientious scholars. I scanned the students enviously through the monocular fixed to my right eye.

Another fifty or so "crashers" sat in the aisles; these were students hoping to get into the already overcrowded class. The professor stepped to the lectern and surveyed the masses. "No crashers," he declared. The crowd of bodies moaned and left like a herd of sheep.

Next, the professor said, "Look down the aisle, because two of you in every row of ten are going to fail this class."

We all shifted nervously in our seats. He then launched into a lecture on the basics of protein synthesis. Behind him were five white eraser-boards. As he spoke, he began to scribble on the first board. He wrote as quickly as he talked.

I grabbed a pen and a notebook, and I turned my monocular toward the board. The monocular was the same pathetic little device that my mother had bought for me when I was in the fifth grade—and it was of no use. Whatever the professor was writing up there at the lectern nearly fifty meters away was lost in the glare of that white, white, board.

As soon as he'd filled the first board with his indistinct writing, he moved over and began writing on the next one. He crammed the open white space full of notations. When that one was full, he flung it up on a tracking system, and it hung there, high on the wall, while he started writing on another board beneath it.

Then he pulled another one down, and he wrote and wrote and wrote, and then he threw that board up, too.

Now it was gone.

He would write on a board, and throw it up high, and then start writing on the one below that. I just sat there, frozen, with my monocular.

Okay, what's that first word? I thought, and I wrote down, "synthesis."

I watched the people around me. They would glance upward, and casually put pen to paper and write. All around me, beachy-looking girls crossed and uncrossed their legs, and bounced their feet over their knees, all while easily copying down everything the teacher wrote. Most of them looked bored. *If I had your eyes, I would not only know what is on the board, I would get an A in this class,* I thought to myself. All around me, I saw 20/20 eyesight being wasted. *I want to be like that. Why can't I?* I thought. They all looked like geniuses.

In the space of a single hour, my vanity crumbled. My determination to *appear* sighted no matter what, my insistence on doing things the same way everyone else did, vanished. I didn't have that luxury anymore, I realized. I needed help, or I would never make it.

As soon as the lecture was over, I raced to the disabled-services office and explained my problem to the young girl behind the desk. This time, I was not taking my distress to an adult, but to someone my own age. "You'll have to hire a note-taker," she said, pointing to a notebook in which students looking for work had written their names and numbers. In small print. Irony of ironies, I had to read small print in an effort to find a note-taker.

As it happened, a student named Scott was in the office at that very moment looking for part-time work. He agreed to be my note-taker for four dollars an hour. From then on, he sat with me during class and wrote down all the visual notes, while I wrote down the auditory ones.

As far as I was concerned, I got a two-for-one deal. Scott was cute, and he was nice, and I was no longer in danger of falling behind. I didn't have to cringe when the teacher lunged at that white board, marker in hand. Instead, I looked over at Scott, who copied it all down with a large black pen.

"Is this big enough for you?" he asked.

Now I had someone to talk to, and walk into class with. I wasn't a loner.

But my problems were just beginning. In every single class, I had to make some kind of adaptation. I would hire readers to help me—and they would lose my books. Or not show up.

Recording for the Blind only offered a couple of my textbooks on tape; the books were updated so frequently by the professors that it was impractical to record them. I tried to get ahead of the game by hiring a reader to put a couple of textbooks on tape, borrowing a tape recorder from Disabled Services. But one day the phone rang.

"Marla, uh, my backpack was stolen and it had all the tapes, and the books, and the recorder inside."

No matter how I tried to compensate, it seemed that I was always behind.

Yet again, track saved me. Not long after I arrived on campus,

I reported to the training room for my physical. All the track team members were required to pass a basic medical exam, measuring height, weight, and blood pressure. A doctor took down my medical history, and then a trainer asked me to take a vision test.

"Well, I'm not going to do very well on this test," I said. "I'm legally blind."

The trainer stared at me. "Well, we don't know if we can allow you to be on the team," she said.

"What do you mean? I was recruited to be here. You can't tell me I can't be on the track team. That's why I came."

"Wait here." The woman got up from behind her desk and returned a few minutes later. "I guess it will be okay," she said. From then on, nobody paid any attention to my impairment. They never even asked about it. Nobody ever said, "What can you see, and what don't you see?" I suppose it was because I made a good show of appearing sighted.

The track program at SDSU was a struggling one. The coaches couldn't have made more than a few thousand dollars a year, the tartan track was so beat-up that it had holes in it, and the high-jump pits were so old and dusty that there were something like colonies of amoebas living in there. We actually flipped the high-jump pits upside-down and landed on the plastic part, because if you landed on the cushiony part, you'd get totally covered in dust and bugs. Whatever was living inside the foam was producing spores. But I loved it, every bit of it. I loved it so much I hung out there all day, and I never wanted to go back to my dorm.

My "special" dorm room was not so special. It was more like a large apartment complex. I had three roommates, and they were all in sororities. They sang their sorority songs and chants—"We tease all the boys and we treat 'em like toys!" (I rolled my eyes)—and they strutted up and down the hall talking about rush week and guys and going to Tijuana and other things that I filed under "Girl Crap." *More total waste of good eyesight,* I thought, resentfully.

Our dorm suite had a living room, a kitchen, and two bedrooms, and there was a long waiting list to get in. I was there thanks to my mother. She had lobbied long and hard with the disabled-services department to put me in that dorm, which was the most modern and desirable on campus, because she said that I needed "special" accommodations for my visual aids. My mother was always animated, and when my happiness was at stake, she wasn't above exaggerating.

I lasted four weeks with the sorority girls. One night, one of them had a group of UCLA students over to party. They were in the process of drinking themselves into oblivion, with plans to head off to Mexico for more booze and dancing. I sat in my room, listening to a cassette tape, "Fundamentals of Biology," from Recordings for the Blind. A monotonous voice droned on about mitosis, while in the background I could hear yells and chants and laughter coming from the living room, where the drinking games were in progress. "This is ridiculous," I said out loud.

The next afternoon, I lay on the high-jump pit after track practice, brooding. Two hammer throwers, big guys, came over to me and asked me what was going on.

"I hate my roommates and I don't want to go back to the dorm," I said. "They're all sorority girls."

That was all I had to say. The entire track team despised the Greek system; it was a famous campus clash. As a joke, we named ourselves Alpha Zappa Tracka.

As it turned out, a friend of a friend on the track team had a large apartment, and he needed a roommate in a big hurry, because his two current roommates were leaving. "I'll take it," I said. My two hammer-thrower buddies offered to move me that afternoon.

My two huge friends burst into my "special" dorm, and we packed up and stuffed all my belongings into my little Volkswagen Rabbit. I drove three blocks down the street to my new apartment. It was a cockroach-infested, dumpy place next to Interstate 8, and my rent would be $375 a month—and I loved it. I had no bed, but I hung a beach poster on the wall, turned on my stereo, and lay on the floor, happy.

I could afford the apartment because of another "special" consideration: On my 18th birthday, I qualified for Social Supplemental Income, which was essentially money given to you by the federal and state governments simply because you were blind. If you worked, the government reduced the SSI stipend, but if you didn't work, you received the full amount of $618 a month. I saved all of my SSI my senior year of high school and used it to pay my rent. The SSI money gave me independence.

It took me a few days to tell my parents that I'd moved and that I was living with a guy. It was a harmless arrangement, since we had our own bedrooms on opposite ends of the apartment, but I knew that my conservative parents wouldn't see it that way. I figured that since I was paying my own way, they couldn't forbid me to live there.

I finally called home, and my mother answered.

"I moved down the street into an apartment, and I have a roommate named Kevin, and I need to give you my new phone number."

"Okay," my mother said, in a controlled tone. "I have to hang up the phone now." And then she did.

Within a couple of days, my parents were at my door with a van. They had brought me a dresser and a bed from home. My father had also brought a deadbolt lock for my bedroom door. They marched right into my apartment, and the first thing my father did was get that lock out and start up his drill. He started drilling screw holes into my bedroom door for the padlock. The noise of the drill echoed through the apartment. I was mortified for poor, innocent, 17-year-old Kevin.

The track team was my strongest connection, my source of friendships and social life on campus. I lived at the track; it was the only place I really wanted to be. I spent most of my time with a group simply known as "the jumpers," about thirty male and female longjumpers, highjumpers, triple-jumpers, and pole-vaulters.

I had never trained seriously before: we ran hills, we did bounding drills in the grass, and on Fridays we ran a 4-mile hill circuit. We lifted weights together, and I established a personal relationship with the squat-bar rack and Olympic-lift platform, bearing up to 285 pounds on my shoulders. I learned how to clean and jerk, and how to snatch.

I also learned what a keg was. I was tired of everything being so much work—and now here I was at the No. 3 party school in the nation, living on my own, with an ample supply of party favors around me. For the first time, instead of turning away, I joined in.

During that freshman track season, I highjumped 5'9", which ranked among the all-time top five performances at the university and put me second in our conference. I got my picture in the school paper and all that. But I went into the conference championships tired and exhausted from the workouts, and placed last. I was devastated. I thought it had all been a waste, all those hills and weights and jumps for nothing. I felt miserable.

I arrived home from the conference meet at nearly 3 A.M. and told my new roommate how awful I had been. We invited some friends over, put the Rolling Stones on the stereo, and partied into the dawn. The party lasted not just the whole night, but it went on for weeks. I still managed to ace my finals, but immediately afterward, the party resumed and lasted all summer. I was an extremist. *If you're going to do something, you might as well do it all the way,* I thought. That was my motto.

Every afternoon at track practice, I studied the sprinters and hurdlers curiously. They were coached by Rahn Sheffield, an intense man who had been a prominent local sprinter in his own day. He had a big voice, and he was always driving them—screaming at them, or yelling some kind of encouragement—as they pranced around the track. They looked so fast.

I was fascinated—and also intimidated. Whenever the runners came past, I always squinted at them with mixed feelings and wondered how they did it. Meanwhile, Rahn was watching me, too. Every now and then he would notice me in the jumping area; I had a powerful bounce in my step that suggested to him I might be as much a runner as a jumper. Finally, early in 1989, when I rejoined the team for my sophomore season, our curiosities met.

The occasion was an intrasquad competition called the Red and Black Meet, for which the coaches divided the team in half.

They set odd distances for the races: rather than run the usual 400 meters, we might run a 300. Rahn strolled over and asked me if I wanted to fill out the field in the 300-meter race. I said, "Sure."

I didn't have any running spikes, just my high-jump spikes, so I borrowed some from a teammate, tied my shoelaces, and went over to the starting line. The other girls set up their starting blocks, but I didn't even know how to use them—that's how raw I was. Instead, I just faked it. I did a standing start.

I held my own for 200 meters, came off the curve, and with 100 meters to go, I took off. No one went with me. I crossed the line in front.

Afterward, nobody said much—except for some of the sprinters, who explained to Rahn that their legs were tight because there had been no warmup. Rahn just smiled.

When I showed up for practice the next day, Rahn said, "Hey, Runyan, you're working out with me three days a week."

"Okay," I said.

You were guaranteed one thing if you ran for Rahn: it was going to hurt. Rahn put a painful emphasis on interval training, with limited recovery time. He would put me through a series of 200-meter sprints, demanding that I hit a certain time, and give me just two minutes to recover after each one. Or he might tell me to run 500 meters, followed by 400, and then 300, and follow *that* with four straight 200-meter sprints. He would stand in the infield with three or four stopwatches all going at the same time, driving me and my teammates. We chased after the times in a panic. "Hit the times!" Rahn would yell.

His voice triggered an adrenaline release. By spring, the pace in workouts had dropped from 64 seconds to 60 seconds per 400 meters. That torturous 5-4-3-2-2-2-2 medley was now run in 75, 60, 45, and 30 seconds. Finally, the university had built us a brand-new, beautiful Mondo track, and I must have run hundreds and hundreds of laps around it for Rahn.

Any time I got discouraged, Rahn would holler at me. It didn't do any good to tell him if you were tired or in pain, because he wouldn't hear of such a thing. He was unsympathetic, and he had a right to be, given his own history. Rahn was a world-class 400-meter hurdler who was preparing for the 1984 U.S. Olympic Trials. He was working for a local San Diego plant, Chemtronics, driving a forklift to earn extra money, and one afternoon he was moving a big aluminum wheel. It rolled off the forklift and headed toward the street. Rahn was afraid it might hit some pedestrians, so he leaped down from the forklift and threw his body in front of the aluminum wheel. It turned over, and 830 pounds of metal came down on his leg.

In the emergency room, he asked the attending doctor, "What are the chances of me keeping my foot?"

The doctor replied, "Fifty-fifty."

Rahn was in so much pain that he said, "Then cut it off, because it hurts too bad."

A surgeon came in and said, "Rahn, we're going to save your foot."

When Rahn came to after surgery, he was afraid to look under the sheet. He sat there for hours, unwilling to peer beneath the covers. Finally, the surgeon came in, and he said, "We saved it."

It took Rahn three years to build his leg back, and, against all advice, he started running again. In 1986, he actually made it back into the world rankings in the 400 hurdles. But he also knew that it was time to retire. By then he was coaching his younger sister, LaTanya, as well as another great young San Diego sprinter named Renee Ross, and he thought they had better Olympic chances than he did. So he retired and became a volunteer coach at SDSU.

When I first started training part-time with Rahn, my high-jump coach, Gary Stathas, was opposed. He said, "Marla, you're not a sprinter, just a highjumper who can run sort of fast." He was right. My motion was raw and out of control: I ran so far up on my toes that the natural curve in my spine would sway into a reverse "C" position. When I was tired and coming down the homestretch of a 400-meter run, it really got ugly. It looked like my back was simply going to snap in half. It quickly became apparent that I would never be a pure sprinter; I could only manage about 12 seconds for the 100-meter dash, 25 seconds for the 200, and 55 seconds for the 400 meters (almost exactly a quarter-mile).

But Rahn decided to try me on the mile relay. He knew he had a runner on his hands, someone he could work with.

The relay was a significant learning experience, and my most important lesson came in an annual meet against UC Irvine and Fresno State. It started as a disaster. By the time the 4-by-400-meter relay—always the last event—rolled around, we were a distant third in the standings. Irvine and Fresno were dueling for the victory, and whichever of them won the relay would win the meet. Since we were out of it, we really had no business sending four girls out onto the track, but Rahn was not one to back away from a race. We knew never, ever, ever to ask the question, "Rahn, do we *have to* run the relay?" Distant third or not, we were running, and that was that.

I volunteered to run the anchor leg that day. We didn't figure to stand much of a chance in the race, but I thought it would be good experience for me. I would run my typical time of 57 seconds and it would be over. No pressure.

We lined up at the start. The gun went off. My teammate Jennifer Nanista stood with me on the grass infield as my narrator. When I ran the relay, I never knew what position our team was in, so Jennifer had to talk me through the race. I couldn't see who was leading or what was happening on the other side of the track.

"Darla looks good," Jennifer said. "She's in first. She's way out front."

Uh-oh, I thought. *We're not supposed to win this race. Pressure's on.*

Darla came around and made the exchange. As the second leg began, I could tell we had a lead of about fifteen meters.

"Okay, now Erica's hanging in there," said Jennifer, my personal commentator. "She still has the lead, but it's getting smaller. She's hanging tough."

I watched the next baton pass from the infield. Our lead had dwindled, but we were still in front.

We'll probably fall behind now, and I'll get the baton so far back that there won't be any pressure.

But we held the lead. I hung on Jennifer's every word. "What's happening?" I yelled.

"Christine's still in first, but barely."

All three teams were charging down the final straight toward their anchor-leg runners, and we lined up on the track based on our teams' positions. I stood in Lane One.

"Here she comes!" Jennifer screamed. "We're still leading, but only by a little."

I looked over my shoulder. Here I was, a *highjumper,* about to anchor a 1600-meter relay against two girls who specialized in the event. They were going to whip my ass down that track.

Finally, I could see Christine, and she looked awful. In total agony she thrust the baton out at me. The cold silver cylinder slapped into my palm and I was off. But by the time I had turned around and taken three strides, the other two girls were on me. They swallowed up our lead in a fraction of a second. Off the first turn, the three of us ran side by side. I had one advantage: I had the inside lane. And I wasn't going to give it up. *You can't have it. No one is getting into my lane.*

I was holding them off. By now all three squads lined the in-side edge of the track, screaming. Off the final turn, we were still in complete unison: the highjumper in Lane One, Irvine on her shoulder, and Fresno on *her* shoulder. As we powered for home, it seemed to happen in slow motion. I gritted my teeth and pawed at the Tartan, pulling myself closer and closer to the finish line. We all three reached it at almost exactly the same time.

Irvine lunged forward, claiming first place. I was second. I stumbled across the line, and Rahn ran onto the track and picked me up and threw me into the air. He was laughing. I was a rag doll, limp and panting.

"But we didn't win," I gasped.

"Oh, yes we did," he said.

He valued my effort over victory. That was Rahn.

A little later, I strolled by Gary and said, "Not bad for a *high-jumper."*

For the next two weeks, Rahn walked around with a smile fixed to his face. Too bad I couldn't see it.

My progress as a runner began to give me bigger ideas. In

the summer of 1988, I had been glued to the television during the Seoul Olympics, and I watched Jackie Joyner-Kersee break the world record in the heptathlon, the seven-event competition that is the women's equivalent of the decathlon. It is a contest requiring supreme athletic versatility, and the winner of it is generally regarded as the world's greatest athlete. I couldn't have chosen a more difficult event to be fascinated by.

As my times improved with Rahn, it began to occur to me, *I'm a good highjumper and a good runner; maybe I could do the heptathlon.* In the high jump, I was clearing 5'10". One afternoon, I mentioned my idea to Jim Cerveney and Gary Stathas. Neither of them seemed very excited about it at first, and I was disappointed. *Why did they react that way?* I wondered.

I didn't know it, because they never mentioned it to me, but they had reservations because of my vision. To compete in the heptathlon, I would have to run the 100-meter hurdles, put the shot, throw the javelin, highjump, longjump, and run 200 and 800 meters.

My vision wasn't an obvious hindrance, but there were telltale signs of it, nevertheless. I had a tendency to run to the outside to get away from the other bodies I felt jostling me. In the relay, since I never knew where we stood in the field, I worried constantly that I wouldn't be in the right place to receive the baton—or that I would try to hand it off to the wrong runner. But the coaches never knew it. Instead of admitting it to them, I asked my teammates to help me; tell me which lane to stand in, so I would be there with my hand out when the runner with the baton came around.

It worked okay, in most of the races. Only once did things not go as planned. I came down the homestretch, finishing my leg of the race, and became disoriented as to where my teammate was. She was standing in the outside lane, and as I got to the exchange zone, I couldn't find her. I heard her say, "I'm over here," and I had to dodge around before I found her and handed her the baton. We wasted over two seconds.

I learned later that Gary, my jumping coach, was so concerned about the prospect of my learning the hurdles that he called my parents. "She wants to do the heptathlon, and that means the hurdles," Gary said. "What do you think?"

My parents were quiet for a minute, and then my father said, "I guess you have to let her try it."

But when they hung up, my father turned to my mother. "Valerie, those hurdles are going to beat the hell out of her," he said. "She's going to lose her teeth."

The coaches gave in, and Rahn started slowly teaching me the hurdles. He set up a series of them and explained that it was all a matter of cadence, of rhythm. I should take eight full strides, running with my head down, out of the blocks. He didn't want me looking at anything but the ground for those first steps. Then I would raise my head, and take two more strides, and I would be over the first hurdle, *boom*. Three more strides, and *boom*, there was the next hurdle. From then on it was a three-stride rhythm, one-two-three, hurdle. The secret, he said, was to avoid looking at each hurdle individually, and instead to look at the very last hurdle, so that I wasn't so much jumping over the hurdles as running over them. "If you're jumping, you're spending too much time in the air," he said.

At first, I leaped over the hurdles with a jerky stag-like motion. It took me close to 17 seconds to run the 100 meters. I was careful to leave all kinds of air between me and those metal frames.

But Rahn told me that, eventually, I would learn to take the hurdles smooth and low. To demonstrate how efficiently he wanted me to clear them, he taped a three-by-five card to the top of each one. I would know I had it right when I ticked each card with the foot of my leading leg. He called it the tap drill. I learned to tap each card with my foot.

Eventually I got the feel for it, the *tap, tap, tap* rhythm that he was looking for. But it took a while, and in the meantime, I got a lot of black-and-blue marks on my legs. Since I couldn't see a hurdle until it rose up directly in front of me, I relied almost entirely on my rhythm. Sometimes, I just plain face-planted. My trailing leg would catch the top of the hurdle, and I would sprawl face-first on the Tartan. Everyone was telling Rahn, "Don't let her do it, you're going to hurt that girl." But I loved the hurdles, I loved the pace and beat of them and the feeling it gave me to conquer them so improbably.

Shortly before my junior year, Coach Cerveney left his job. Rahn was elevated to head coach, and he started training me even harder. He was so consumed with training me that he completely forgot I was blind.

One day I was adjusting my starting blocks, and in order to see them I had to bend down until my face was right on top of them. "What the hell is she doing?" Rahn said to one of my teammates.

"She can't see it," the other runner answered.

"Oh, right," Rahn said.

Even I forgot about my vision sometimes. Training with me under Rahn in the hurdles was Donna Waller, who was perennially ranked among the top ten nationally. While Donna and I warmed up, Rahn would set up the hurdles. But I was never sure how many; sometimes he'd set up three, sometimes four, and sometimes five. Usually, I had to walk down the track and count them. But that day I simply asked Donna, "Do you know how many hurdles are up today?"

Donna glanced up from setting her starting blocks and said, "Five."

I said, "You can see all the hurdles from here?"

"Well, yeah," Donna said. "Of course."

"Really?" I said. "Wow."

I could barely see the first one—which was eight strides away. Strange as it may sound, it had never occurred to me that my competitors could see the hurdles better than I could.

I went from staggering over the hurdles in nearly 17 seconds to regularly cruising over them in under 14 seconds. I was starting to think I was a pretty hot ticket in the event when I went to the Occidental Invitational, a meet at a university about an hour away. As I lined up in the starting blocks, I noticed, in the lane next to me, a pair of shimmering red Nike spikes. I couldn't see the face of the owner of those shoes, but the shoes said everything I needed to know about her—or so I thought. *Doesn't she think she's special,* I said to myself snidely as I lined up. I decided I was going to blow her away, just for wearing those garish shoes. Then the announcer introduced the runners to the crowd. "And in Lane Four . . . the 1992 Olympic Gold Medalist at 100 meters . . . Gail Devers!"

The gun went off, and she was over the first hurdle before I'd taken three strides. I never saw those red shoes again. That's how fast they moved.

6. The Only One
In the Race

When you don't really accept your impairment, it makes life difficult, whether you are willing to admit it or not. If you embark on something without realizing or accepting that you may not be able to accomplish it, you let yourself in for a lot of wrath and some nasty surprises. Similarly, when you do accept your impairment and recognize the ramifications of it, you can make some peace with it. That's what happened to me in the summer of '89.

After the '89 track season ended, I got a phone call from someone with the California Association of Blind Athletes, CABA, inviting me to attend a national competition in St. Louis. I had never been to an event for impaired athletes, and I was curious, so I agreed to go. In the airport, I met my old friend Casey Cook, a former grade-school classmate of mine who was deaf and blind. I remembered how to sign, so I said to him, signing into his hands, "Do you remember me? My name is Marla, and we went to Williams Elementary together." Casey was thrilled. We sat together on the plane, and we visited the whole way to St. Louis, Casey talking to me, me signing into his hand.

Those Games were a revelation to me. We stayed on a small college campus, and for the first time in my adult life, I was in an environment where everybody else was visually impaired or blind. There was something much more important happening there than running or jumping. In that place, it was okay to be blind. In fact, I probably had more vision than anybody else there. Casey was in the swimming competition, and when I was done with my own races I would hang around the pool with him, talking via sign language. We spent most of the week together, and he was a bright, funny, articulate guy.

At one point, I called my parents from St. Louis. I said, "Mom, this is the most amazing thing, because no one expects me to see."

By the end of the week, I was so excited to have made some friends, and so fascinated by my ability to communicate with Casey, that I decided what my college major would be: Communicative Disorders, with a special emphasis on education of deaf and blind children.

There was just one problem: my choice would mean graduate school. In order to get a specialty teaching credential, I would have to get a master's degree and a teaching credential in elementary education. I had instantly sentenced myself to four more years of classroom torture. Also, I had new requirements to fulfill before I could get even my bachelor's degree. To graduate on time, I would have to take eighteen units in the fall of my senior year, and twenty in the spring—and twelve is considered a full load.

It seemed like every time I saw my college advisor, she handed me another piece of paper with more prerequisites on it. Was it worth the effort? That spring, I finished fourth in the heptathlon at the conference championships, and I got a couple of C's in the classroom to close out my junior year. All that work for fourth place and a C?

But that summer, I attended the 1990 World Disabled Championships in Holland, and, once again, being among other disabled athletes restored my perspective. We stayed at an old military base, and the food was awful and I froze in my bunk bed at night, and I ran my races in the rain. But the effort I saw put forth by amputees in wheelchairs, and others who were far more profoundly impaired than I was, made me reexamine my good fortune—and my goals. Again I was relieved to be in an environment where I wasn't expected to see.

I came back from Holland with a new attitude. I would rather struggle with lofty goals, I decided, than settle for more comfortable ones. I signed up for eighteen credits in the fall of my senior semester and twenty credits for the spring. If all went as planned, I would graduate on time, and maybe even earn a plaque for finishing among the top three in the conference in the heptathlon, a goal that had eluded me for three straight years.

I began to show major improvements in the heptathlon. I had been scoring around 4800 points, but early in my senior season I scored nearly 5200 points. The qualifying score for the U.S. Olympic Trials was 5500. If I could improve another 300 points in 1992, I would be a potential Olympian—a level that I'd never even contemplated.

The Western Athletic Conference Championships were held at our home track in San Diego. We had a brand new Mondo-surface track and new high-jump and pole-vault pits. No more amoebas. We were a small but feisty team, with a squad of only fourteen competing against the league powerhouses like Brigham Young, which brought a team of forty. I was so hyped up for the meet that the coaches worried about me. As I got ready for the hurdles, I warmed up by compulsively leaping over the first hurdle, time after time after time. Rahn wandered over to me, concerned. "How you doing, sweetheart?" he asked.

"I'm doing great," I said.

"You need to calm down," he said.

"*Calm down?* Rahn, this is *conference*," I said, waving my arms at him.

Rahn just grinned and walked away. "She's in the zone," he told his assistants. "Leave it alone."

I took second in the heptathlon. I took second in the 400. I anchored the 4-by-100-meter relay, and we came in second. I placed third in the high jump. And finally, I anchored the 4-by-400 relay, and we won. As a team, we finished second to Brigham Young, and I walked away with five plaques.

That spring, I got straight A's in my course load, and then I walked through the graduation ceremony. I graduated *magna cum laude.*

But if I thought I was finished with the idiocy and torments of the basic educational system, I was wrong. It turned out that I still had to take two more prerequisite classes to qualify for the elementary-education program. I had picked an endless major.

I stared at the requirement printed on the sheet of paper that the Education Department administrator had handed me. I had to take Art Appreciation.

I didn't know whether to feel despair or to laugh hysterically.

I went to nearby Grossmont Junior College and enrolled in its Art Appreciation course. I walked into a darkened lecture hall, where a professor clicked through slides of artwork that I couldn't see.

The class syllabus was full of reading—a long list of art history books. My first move was to go to the Disabled Services office at Grossmont College. There, I asked if they would provide me with a reader. I was told, "We're actually kind of low on the budget. So what we would like you to do first is make an announcement in your class and see if there's anyone who would be willing to read to you."

I was reluctant to announce my disability to the class, but I didn't have a choice. The next day I went back to the lecture hall, and during the break I approached the professor, and I awkwardly explained my problem to him.

"I can't see the textbook very well, and Disabled Services told me to ask you to make an announcement to the class and ask if there's a volunteer to read the assignments to me."

Then I took a seat in the front row, where I could stare up at the screen images of artwork.

After the break, the class filed back in, and the professor went to the lectern and made the following announcement, booming into his microphone:

"We have a young lady in the front row here who can't read."

That's what he said. It was my worst nightmare. I slouched down in the chair, my face flushing.

Then he said, "Will you please stand, so they know who you are?"

I slumped instead—as far down in my chair as I could—and frantically shook my head at him, "No!"

"I can read," I said. "I just can't *see*."

He said, "So, we need to know if there's any volunteers who would like to read the class assignments to her."

Everyone laughed. They laughed and giggled and tittered. And nobody volunteered.

After the professor finished his charming little speech, he went back to teaching. I sat there, furious and embarrassed. But then I noticed a girl sitting farther down the front row who was trying to catch my eye. She said, "Pssst—I'll read to you if you want." I nodded gratefully and turned back to the indistinct images on the screen.

The one thing a reader couldn't do for me was see the pictures. I had to figure that out on my own. I could see colors. I could tell that an image on the screen was a statue and not a painting, but I couldn't see particular details, or much in the way of shape. For the most part, statues all looked very much the same to me. They were all gray, nude women with no arms.

I was supposed to be able to recognize which work was by which artist. How was I going to do that? I decided to make notes on each image and describe how it looked to *me*. I would write down, "Reddish-orange color overall, left corner blue, right corner green, looks like a meadow." Then I would add the name of the painting and who had painted it.

I remember *The Scream*.

I studied the image by Edvard Munch, and at first I couldn't find the face. I peered at it through my monocular. Gradually, I discerned the face and the open mouth. *I know how you feel,* I thought.

I was so angry that I didn't care about my grade. I just wanted to be done with the class. I got an A on the first test, quit studying, and got a D on the second one. It had nothing to do with anything except the fact that I despised the class.

I was trying to do way too much. The workload of graduate school finally forced me to take a leave of absence from the track.

In addition to my basic course load, I was in a program to obtain a special credential for teaching the deaf, I was student-teaching in a regular ed program, and I was working in a communications clinic. My ambition of making the 1992 U.S. Olympic Trials in the heptathlon was unrealistic; I simply couldn't train properly.

The year before, remember, I had reached a new personal record by 500 points in the heptathlon. But in '92, I only raised my best score by another 30 points. It was disheartening after all that time and effort. The only good thing that happened on the track was that I showed sudden dramatic improvement as a runner, in the 800 meters. I went from running it in 2 minutes and 17 seconds to 2:08. By the time I graduated, I'd knocked nearly ten seconds off my time.

As a consolation prize, I decided to go to the '92 Paralympics in Barcelona—and gave myself one of the most meaningful gifts I've ever had. Everything was a perfect replica of the mainstream Olympics; we stayed in the athlete's village with all of the same accommodations and volunteers, and the Paralympic flag waved over us. It was like an imaginary world for two weeks.

Everywhere I looked, an athlete was doing something that made my own impairment seem relatively minor. There were athletes in wheelchairs, athletes with prosthetics. I saw a Chinese athlete with no arms swimming the breaststroke.

In Paralympic competition there are five disability groups: blind and visually impaired, amputee, wheelchair, cerebral palsy, and dwarf. You compete within your own disability group, which is broken down into further classifications so that the athletes are equally matched. For the blind, there are three classes, from B-1 to B-3. Someone who is totally blind, with no light perception, is classified as B-1, whereas a B-2 can see the shadow of a hand up to a visual acuity of 20/600, and a B-3 has visual acuity between 20/600 and 20/200. I was classified as a B-3, which is the most sighted category. Compared to everyone else's struggles, a B-3 had it made.

We were there for seventeen days, and I won gold medals in the 100, 200, 400, and long jump.

It was one of the rare occasions on which I gave myself permission to accept special accommodation for my vision. For those couple of weeks, I let go. It was such a relief not to be expected to see like everybody else. Let's take something as fundamental as registration: the pack of papers I had to fill out was in large print. Even something that simple made a real difference.

I saw that in every culture, in every country, there was somebody just like me. We couldn't speak the same language, but we all understood one another. I had spent most of my life insisting on not playing by any rules except those of mainstream society. And yet now that I actually let my guard down, I felt such relief.

But I was torn, too. Personally, I didn't believe in segregation. While the Paralympics were wonderful, I knew that I didn't really belong there. I was determined to compete in the mainstream Olympics, and I felt that settling for anything less would have been using my disability as an excuse to be less of an athlete. I would be a better athlete if I made the commitment; if I maintained the highest level of expectation. To compete in any other kind of race felt hypocritical.

I didn't view the Paralympics as "beneath" the Olympic Games, but literally parallel to them. The athletes were some of the best in the world in their disciplines, and in classifications such as wheelchair, there was no able-bodied equivalent. The "wheelies" battled it out for medals with truly Olympic spirit. My roommate at the Atlanta Paralympics, for example, was Jean Driscoll, at that time the seven-time Boston Marathon champion in the wheelchair division (and still counting). Weighing 110 pounds, she could bench-press twice that.

One afternoon, the elevator in our dorm broke down.

I said, "Jean, how did you get to the fourth floor?"

She said, "I just tricep-dipped my way up the stairwell."

She had hauled herself up three floors of stairs using only her arms.

All of us—blind runners, wheelchair racers, dwarf power lifters—were there to show the world that we were *athletes first, disabled second*. But no matter how fast we ran or swam or cycled, the media confused us with the Special Olympics, which is a competition for athletes with mental retardation, and that was disheartening. I came to hate that word, "special." We were guaranteed to find it in every newspaper article or news short, along with "courageous" and "inspirational." Our accomplishments were always overshadowed by the presence of a wheelchair, a prosthetic limb, or a guide runner. Proving the point was an exhausting task. We always told the press the same thing. "I am an athlete with a disability, not a 'disabled athlete,'" I said, time after time. But they were just words, and I decided that words were not enough to make a difference. I had to do something about it.

But I couldn't do anything about it just yet. When I got home from the Paralympics, I took a year off from training. I knew once and for all that juggling school and track was too much: I had to do them one at a time. I decided to finish school first.

Of all my responsibilities, working in the communications clinic was by far the most grueling, but it was also gratifying. This was hands-on work, not just sitting in class discussing theories on how children should be educated. In the fall of 1992, I began to work with my first child at the clinic. His name was Stuart, he was two years old, and he had been dealt a tough hand: his disabilities fell under the broad description of "deaf-blind," but it was more complicated than that. He was partially sighted, and he had some ability to hear, but he had multiple challenges, physical and sensory. With Stuart, my passion for running shifted to teaching.

At the beginning of each session, I would greet him in the waiting area with a great big cardboard happy face. From a distance, my work with him resembled child's play, but each activity had a purpose. Communication was the name of the game. Stuart couldn't speak yet, although he could make noises to let me know what he was thinking. We worked on sign language as a possible avenue for him, and it was slow, tedious work, but he was a very driven little guy. When nearly half the semester had gone by and I was on the verge of getting discouraged, Stuart suddenly looked right at me and signed "music."

"Music!" I signed back. "You want music? Okay!"

I gave him all the music he wanted.

Breakthroughs like that one helped me cope with the everyday hassles. My biggest problem was not the workload or what to do with the children; the problem was *how* to physically get there. I was trying to drive everywhere I went.

I didn't do it entirely alone. I had a good friend, Sisi, who was enduring the graduate program with me. We took most of our course work together, and she even became my reader. She would drive all the way out to my apartment to read *Piaget's Theory of Cognition and Affective Development* and *Language and Literacy Development in Children Who Are Deaf* to me. Now, that's a friend. She earned a few dollars from the Disabled Services Department, but getting me through all the assignments became almost a full-time job. Sisi never complained; instead we laughed a lot and got each other through a graduate program that truly seemed to have no finish line. But eventually all the work became too much for her, and I learned a valuable lesson: I had to separate "assistance" from a "favor." A favor is something a friend does for a friend, but "assistance" is a job. It was easy to confuse the two, especially when Sisi was acting as my assistant, my reader, and sometimes even my driver. It was too much to ask of her as my friend. The lines and roles were crossed, and I have always regretted it. I didn't need an assistant; I needed a friend. I decided to ask less of her.

Ordinarily, I never drove on the freeway with my bioptic, but with all my classes and clinic work, I had no choice: there was no other way to get to certain places. I would roll down all of the windows in the car, to get as much visibility as I could and to be able to hear traffic.

In an effort to make my life easier, my father had bought a condominium in San Diego County. He did it partly as an investment but also to free me from rent and to be sure that I lived someplace safe and secure. The problem was, it was too far from campus. It was a beautiful condo in an area called Rancho San

Diego, which was in the southeast part of town. But it was a full twenty-five minutes by car from campus, and it made my life both hectic and dangerous.

I couldn't drive at night—but one evening, I was forced to. I stayed too late at the clinic, and when I walked outside, it was already dusk. Nervously, I got into my car and started to drive home. I tried to take all the frontage roads, but there was one stretch when I couldn't avoid the freeway. Whenever oncoming headlights rolled across my windshield, they completely blinded me. I couldn't even see my lane. That's how dangerous it was. Worse, as it grew darker, my bioptic became next-to-useless. There wasn't enough light to make the telescope effective. Imagine trying to look through binoculars at night—that's what it was like.

I almost ended up driving off the road that night. I finally made it safely home, but by then I was in tears. As it happened, my father called that evening. "I can't do this," I said. "I know you had good intentions, but this is ridiculous. I'm going to be dead."

The next day, I put a note on a Help Wanted bulletin board at the university, and I hired a driver to take me home on those evenings when I had to work late. I paid him forty dollars a week, and I hated doing it. I didn't want to rely on anyone else; I prized my independence too much.

Many nights, I agonized about whether I would get home before dark. I was trying to race the sun home.

I used to think that if you slept, you were lazy. I would stay up until midnight or 1 A.M. doing my graduate work, because I figured sleep was the one thing I could sacrifice. What was sleep but a waste of time, anyway? No one ever told me that sleep is when you heal. When I finished my degree in the spring of 1994, I weighed a chunky 142 pounds and I was totally sleep-deprived.

My graduate program had been paid for by a Hilton-Perkins Grant, due to the shortage of teachers in my specialty, and one thing was certain: once I graduated, I was guaranteed a job almost anywhere in the country.

Instead, I immediately leaped back into training full-time with Rahn. But it seemed that I was always exhausted and broken down, and I very often became emotional. I didn't know why. No one had taught me about recovery, or about nutrition.

My goal was to make it to the U.S. Olympic Trials in '96, and perhaps on to the Olympic Games in Atlanta. I trained relentlessly, and I couldn't understand it when I grew fatigued and my performances suffered. I didn't realize that rest was as essential to building a strong, efficient body as the work itself. If all you do is train, you don't build; you break.

I had never allowed myself to explore my full capacities as an athlete; my commitment had always been divided between school and track. But with school out of the way, I became a full-time athlete for the first time in my life. I gave the seven events of the heptathlon the same laser focus and fanatical work ethic that I had given to graduate school.

I worked with Rahn on my running, and with Gary Stathas on my jumping, and soon I had two new coaches to work on my weakness, the throwing events. Rahn said, "Your throwing events are what's holding you back. I think you should try working out with the Pagels."

Ramona and Kent Pagel were a husband-and-wife team who worked and competed out of Mesa Junior College. Ramona had been on three Olympic teams at that point, and she was about to make her fourth. She was also the American record holder in the shot put. She was 5'10" and weighed 215 pounds, and she could throw 300 pounds over her head during a clean and jerk. But she had a sweet, kind voice and personality; so sweet that her nickname was Minnie, after Minnie Mouse. She coached me in the javelin, and Kent coached me in the shot, and they had a lot of patience with me.

I had a color-coded schedule of all the days of the week, with blocks of time for each event. TP was track practice, SP was shot put, HR was hurdles, and so on. I went to Mesa Junior College at noon for throwing with the Pagels, to San Diego State from 2 to 4 P.M. for running and jumping with Rahn and Gary, and to a gym near my house for weight training. If I colored a box red, that meant I was at SDSU; green meant I was at the gym; yellow, I was at Mesa. I spent as much time in the car as I had in grad school—and I was frequently as tired.

Often, because those throwing events gave me the greatest grief, I would break down crying at the end of practice. I would start the work by saying, "I'm going to throw 140 feet today." Then I'd go out and throw 70 feet—and I'd cry.

One day when I was in tears, Ramona came up to me and gently scolded me.

"Of all people," she said. "If anybody should have patience, it should be you. You have your *master's degree,* and you can't see."

I stopped crying. Ramona put up with me, because she understood me. She understood that my tantrums were based on ambition, and she taught me that ambition has to come with the composure and patience to do things right. Ramona and Kent coached me through '95, until Kent was hired at Kent State that autumn and they moved to Ohio.

In 1995, thanks in large part to the Pagels, I took the Olympic Festival bronze medal in the heptathlon. I scored 5,741 points, which qualified me for the Olympic Trials, and I highjumped 5'11½". The medal was only a cheap metal disc, but it was my first medal, and it meant that I now had credibility as an elite heptathlete. The Olympic Festival was a meet designed in part to identify future Olympians, and so it meant the world to me.

By the end of the season, I was ranked ninth nationally in the heptathlon by *Track & Field News,* and I was nominated for the Sullivan Award, which is given to the amateur athlete voted most outstanding in the nation each year. But for all of that, I was still fairly anonymous, even in track circles. I had no endorsements, except a verbal agreement with a Nike representative who secretly slipped me a pair of shoes once in a while. But one day I placed an order, and the shoes never came. I was living on next-to-nothing, leaning heavily on the SSI, and shoes were expensive. I called Nike, and it turned out that my supplier had been fired. The new rep said to me over the phone, "We don't have anything on file, we don't know who you are, and we don't just give out stuff."

I said, "Well, I'm a hepathlete, and the U.S. Trials are coming up. What am I supposed to do?"

"I'll honor one more order," he said.

My chances of making the Olympic team were slim, I knew. But something interesting was happening in my work with Rahn: I was becoming extremely fast in the 800 meters, arguably the hardest part of the heptathlon. Because the 800 always came at the end of the competition, everyone was already exhausted. It was two painfully long laps on dead-tired legs, but it had become my strongest event—so strong that I set a new goal: I wanted to break the American record for the heptathlon 800. It was 2:06.97, and was held by my friend and competitor Kym Carter. I was regularly running 2:08, and I thought the record was doable.

Although I had goals of setting an American record and perhaps making the '96 Olympic team, I felt obligated to compete at the Paralympics one more time. My ambivalence about the Paralympics was bubbling to the surface, however, and now an incident convinced me once and for all that it wasn't the right place for me. It started over a bureaucratic snarl-up, my favorite kind of thing.

I had been told by a coach from the U.S. Association of Blind Athletes that I wouldn't have to go to the Paralympic Trials, because I'd qualified for the mainstream Olympic Trials and that was good enough. It certainly made sense.

But one morning, I got a letter in the mail from the Paralympic organizers warning me that in order to be selected for the 1996 Paralympic team, I had to "participate" at the U.S. Paralympic Trials in Atlanta. No exceptions. The catch was, the Trials fell right in the middle of my training season, and just five weeks before the actual U.S. Olympic Trials, also in Atlanta. And the day before the Paralympic Trials, I was due to be in Santa Barbara, California, for an important heptathlon.

I panicked and made about eight frantic phone calls. "Are you kidding me?" I asked. "I've got to go all the way to Atlanta?" No exceptions, they told me.

"Participate" was one of my least favorite words, right up there with "special." I never participated; I competed. However, I devised a plan: the rules didn't state that I had to "participate" in the same event that I would compete in at the Paralympics. I noticed on the schedule that the 100 meters was to be run on a Thursday, which would allow me enough time to fly back to Santa Barbara for the heptathlon. The Paralympics were still meaningful to me, no matter how torn I felt, so I paid my couple of thousand dollars in airfare and hotel costs and went to Atlanta to "participate" in the 100 meters.

When I arrived, I discovered that there was nobody else entered in the 100 meters. I would have to run alone on an empty track. It was the ultimate administrative Catch-22: there is no race to be raced, because I'm the only competitor in my classification and event. But the rules say that I have to be present and run, or I can't compete at the Paralympics.

That night in the hotel, I alternately fumed and laughed at my predicament. The next day, I took the shuttle from the hotel to the track. My race was scheduled for 11:55 A.M. I got a sore ankle taped, warmed up, and waited for them to call my race. And I waited, and waited. Finally, at 11:45, I went over to the starting line and said to an official, "My schedule says the B-3 100 meters is supposed to be in about ten minutes."

This guy in a blazer looked at me, and he said, "Oh, no, we decided to move that event to Sunday. We're going to lunch."

I froze.

"No, you're not," I said. "No way. No way. I'm the only one in the race. And I'm scheduled to fly out tonight for a meet in California."

The blazer just shrugged. There was nothing he could do, he said. And he wandered off to join his fellow blazers at lunch.

I lost it. I went to the organizers, and I yelled and I cussed, and I told them it was a joke. "I have a plane to catch," I insisted. "You have to run my event—it's on the schedule. It takes eleven or twelve seconds!"

Finally, the organizers capitulated. They rounded up a couple of officials to put on the race, and told me to go to the starting line. As I stood there loosening up, a voice came over the loudspeaker. "We have a change in our schedule because an athlete has to go to California for another competition. So in order to accommodate her we are now going to hold the B-Three 100 meters for women."

Then an official handed me a big number for my chest, and then another one for my back. Then he handed me hip numbers.

I just looked at this guy, and I said, "You're joking, right? I'm the only one in the race."

He said, "No, this is good practice for when you get to elite competition."

I said, "My practice for elite competition is in Santa Barbara, not here."

I put the numbers and stickers all over me, and I stood there looking at the track. "Okay," I said. "I guess I'll run in Lane Four."

It's a good lane.

Nobody else seemed to find the situation ridiculous. In fact, a USABA staff member, Mark Lucas, stood ten feet away and said, "Come on, Marla. You can do it."

I said, *"I'm the only one in the race!"*

It summed up my frustration with the Paralympics. It can be a wonderful event—but on that day I belonged in Santa Barbara.

As I got into the starting blocks, I was still angry—at the absurdity of it, and because I had compromised my training schedule. The gun went off, and I ran to the finish line.

And I just kept on running.

I ran straight to my bag. I whipped off my spikes, threw them in the bag, and pulled on sneakers. I ran to a bus and went straight to the airport. I was out of there. When I landed in California, I had one day to recover before the heptathlon started.

I arrived to find that Kym Carter was entered in some events there, although she wasn't competing in the full heptathlon. A year earlier at the U.S. Nationals, I had told Kym that I wanted to break her American record in the heptathlon 800, and she'd said, "Oh, you go, girl."

At the end of the heptathlon, as I lined up for the 800 with the other runners, Kym came over to the start area. She was dragging a chair behind her, and she had a stopwatch in her hand.

Kym set her chair up in Lane Nine, and sat down. She reclined, and held up the watch. "Okay, Runyan, I'm timing you," she said. I thought it was hilarious.

I didn't break her 800 record. But my 2:10 was good enough to give me a personal best in the heptathlon—even while jet-lagged and numbed by the fiasco in Atlanta.

I flew back to San Diego on the Monday morning after the meet, and the very next day I went straight to meet Rahn at the San Diego State track, because I didn't want to miss a day of practice. Also, I was scheduled to do an ESPN interview, and their crew wanted to film my workout. Ever since I had won the Olympic Festival bronze medal, word had gotten out that a legally blind athlete was a factor in the heptathlon.

But I still hadn't learned the principles of recovery. I continued to operate on my graduate-school philosophy that sleep and rest meant laziness. I hadn't had a day off from training and competing in a couple of weeks, and now I hit bottom. I was unbelievably tired. I tried to throw the shot, and I could barely lift my arm. We moved to the hurdles. The ESPN crew wanted to film me doing all the events, and they had rented a golf cart to follow me down the track as I took each hurdle.

But I literally could not get over the first hurdle. I stood on the track, with my head down, trying to get my breath and figure out what was wrong with me. What I really needed was for someone, anyone, to say, "Marla, you're exhausted. You just flew back and forth across the country and then did a heptathlon. Go home and rest."

Instead, Rahn came over and said, "Get it together."

I walked away and sat down by myself and cried. I couldn't handle it anymore. I was just whipped—by everything. By the mental exhaustion of so many years of school, by the constant enervating struggle to see things that others took for granted, by the needless obstacles, by bureaucrats, by the hundreds and hundreds of sprints I'd run and hurdles I'd leaped over without a decent rest.

From that day on, I was toast—and the Olympic Trials were just five weeks away. My performance in practice steadily deteriorated. Ordinarily I was able to run a workout of three times 200 meters in 24 seconds apiece. Now I ran them in 25 seconds. Everything was falling apart. I was getting slower and slower. Rahn didn't know how to handle it. He felt my frustration and my sadness and my depression, but he interpreted my emotions as a criticism of him as a coach.

One afternoon, after I'd dissolved in tears, Rahn finally lost his patience with me. He screamed, "Get your ass off the track and come back when you're a real athlete." Rahn had a temper, and he knew how to use it, and this was his way of trying to make me snap out of it. But I was too upset; I had tried once again to run a decent 200, and I couldn't do it fast enough. I stalked off the track and went through a black gate toward the locker room, thinking I would get some water and try to calm down. But as I went through the gate, I grabbed it and slammed it.

"What the hell do you think you're doing?" Rahn wanted to know.

"I learned it from you," I said.

That was the end of that. Rahn was furious with me. He started screaming again, and I kept crying, and finally I walked away. In all those years from 1987 to 1996, we had never had such a conflict. But now even our great rapport was falling apart. We never quite recovered it.

For the next five weeks, Rahn and I lived in a state of quiet tension. My mother came down to San Diego to support me; she did some grocery shopping for me, and made meals and put them in the freezer, but as the Trials approached, I only grew more anxious. All of the work of the last several years seemed to be amounting to nothing.

Finally, it was time to go to Atlanta. A contingent from our San Diego State training group was going to the Trials together: Rahn's sister, LaTanya Sheffield, would compete in the 400 hurdles, and the great Renee Ross was making a major comeback in the 800 meters after having two children; she'd run 2:03 to qualify for the Trials. Also with us was Jennifer Nanista, Rahn's top assistant and my good friend.

Jennifer would act as my eyes at a meet: she'd fill out paperwork for me, point out the registration area, and make sure I was well situated. Sometimes she would help me get a feel for the track—did it have wide curves, long straights? The more oriented I felt, the better I could perform.

But at the Trials, the athletes weren't permitted into the

Olympic Stadium until the very start of the event. I wouldn't see the track until I stepped onto it.

The Trials were not at all what I had expected. It was my first time in an event of such prestige and importance, and I was overwhelmed by the sheer size of it. It was big and bustling, and you couldn't go anywhere without moving through a throng of people.

The heptathlon began on the very first morning. It seemed so abrupt. This was the big day, which I had been planning for years, and it was all happening too fast. First, they bussed the athletes from the hotel to the warmup track. I warmed up tensely. There, I saw, was Jackie Joyner-Kersee, the World and Olympic champion.

We weren't ushered in to the Olympic Stadium until just before our hurdles event. I couldn't get my bearings. I was accustomed to doing a few drills to get a feel for the hurdles before the gun went off. Since I couldn't see them, I needed to get a feel for where they were, so I could find a comfortable rhythm. But I only had about thirty seconds to study them once they led us to the track.

We walked out, took off our sweats, set our blocks. There was time to go over exactly one hurdle as a warmup before we were called to the starting line for the race.

Jackie Joyner-Kersee was in my heat—and in the lane next to me. It was a humid day, and raining lightly. The stadium was weirdly empty. It was early in the morning, and the more glamorous events wouldn't begin until later, so the general feeling was one of desolation. The gun went, I started hesitantly—and then it was over. It was a comparatively slow heat, and I finished third.

Next was the high jump. As I walked by the outside rail of the stadium, down the steps came Rahn, Gary, and Jennifer. They were hustling, trying to reach me before I passed by. Rahn wanted to tell me that the heat had been slow and that I had lost about sixty points on the event. He wanted me to know where I stood. But for some reason, their high energy disturbed me. They all seemed to be talking at once.

Rahn leaned over the railing and grabbed my arm—and I reflexively jerked it back. He stared at me, insulted. I hadn't meant to offend him; I was just in my competitive mode, but he couldn't know that, especially after the scene between us five weeks earlier. Rahn backed away, wordlessly.

By now I was rattled. In my warmup, I missed all three of my practice jumps. I still couldn't get oriented in the stadium. I didn't realize it at the time, but my approach was too short, and I needed to move back on the runway. But I just didn't have time to figure that out.

I only jumped 5′6″. My approach was so short and slow that on one attempt to clear 5′8″, which should have been very doable, I took off way too early and actually came down on the bar. That took care of that.

Now I'd lost another 150 points. And the throwing events, my weakest, were still to come. The weather changed; the skies cleared up, and now it was hot—close to 110 degrees down on the track. A couple of us huddled under an umbrella, trying to stay out of the sun. My shot put was awful. I threw 34 feet, while everyone around me was throwing over 45 feet.

Mercifully, there was just one more event and the day would be over. It was the 200, and again, Jackie Joyner-Kersee was in my heat. I didn't do any better in that 200 than I had in practice. I ran

24.6, and by the time it was over I was close to last place in the overall standings. There was no way I would be an Olympian. I was already out of it, and the competition was only half over.

Back at the hotel, I was numb—in shock at how poorly I had performed. I thought of my parents, of what a total disappointment it must have been to them. I called their hotel and left them a message. "I'm sorry you came all this way and wasted your money to see this," I said.

I sat in my room alone for a while, distraught. Then I picked up the phone and called my friend Renee Ross. Renee came over to my room and comforted me, and then she told me to get myself together.

"Oh, Marla," she said. "You've just got to think about tomorrow. What events do you have left?"

"Long jump, javelin, and the 800," I said.

"All right," she said. "You get out there, and you do your javelin, and you do your long jump. And then you go out there and you run that 800, and you break the American record. Just think about that. *Just think about that.*"

That woke me up. And it also got me to think about someone other than myself for a moment. Renee had run in the first-round heats of the 800 that day. I didn't even know what had happened.

"Renee—how'd you do?" I said.

"Well, I didn't do very well," she said. "On the second lap, there was some jostling in the pack, and I bumped a girl by accident, and she ended up falling down. I felt so bad that I slowed down."

Renee had finished in 2:13, after having run 2:03 to get to the Trials. It was a terrible disappointment for her, but she was such a wonderful, sympathetic woman that she was more concerned with my feelings than with her own.

The next morning, I picked up the javelin for my first warmup throw. I could never see the javelin when I threw it. After it left my hand, it would disappear. I could throw 90 feet, or 190 feet, and I wouldn't know the difference.

I hurled that javelin, and I had no idea where it landed. One of the competitors next to me said, "Man, Marla, you just threw 135 feet."

"Really?" I said.

For luck, I decided not to take any more warmup throws. Then the competition started, and I threw 117 feet—a terrible throw by anyone's standards, but it was still one of the best throws of my career. Next came the long jump, and I did so-so. The only thing on my mind was that 800.

At last, it was time for the final event. I went into a bathroom underneath the stadium, and I doused myself with water. I dried off, and I said to myself, *Okay, let's just pretend you haven't done any other events at all.*

I put my headphones over my ears and listened to music and ignored the other athletes milling in the belly of the stadium. They left me alone; everyone knew I was going for the record. I was in 17th place and out of contention for the team, so I had absolutely nothing to protect or to lose in that stadium. I would run all-out; my competitors knew it and so did I.

Finally, we were ushered into the Olympic Stadium once again. This time it was a totally different atmosphere, because it was full. The 100-meter finals also were being held that night, and the crowd was electric with anticipation, primed to see a duel between Gail Devers and Gwen Torrence. We lined up for the 800 while most of the spectators were eating hot dogs or drinking beer. No one was especially watching us. We were just a diversion between the glamour events. Only a few track aficionados actually paid attention as we gathered at the start. One of those watching closely was a man named Dick Brown, a legendary coach who had trained Mary Decker Slaney, among others.

Standing there in my lane in the warm, night air in a magnificently lit stadium, I had only one thought: *No regrets. Run your heart out.*

The gun went off.

We approached the first turn. I cut in—and I was immediately in the lead, running alone in Lane One. I kept up the pace through the 200 mark. I thought, *Marla, this isn't a 400. Take it easy.* My first 200 meters had been 26 seconds.

Way too fast.

Hold on, you've got to chill, you've got 600 more to go.

Dick Brown was thinking the exact same thing. From his seat in the grandstands, he watched as I raced around the Tartan and thought, *That girl's not smart. She's gone out too fast.*

I was still running alone as I passed the 400 mark. A huge digital clock was mounted in the infield just a couple of feet from Lane One, and as I went by, I could read only the last two digits: "9.8." But that was all I needed to know. I knew very well what the first digit had been—a 5.

I'd never run the first 400 meters in 59 seconds before. For a moment, I wasn't sure if I could hold the pace. *This is going to hurt.* But then I realized that I felt strangely good. I was moving smoothly, fluidly, nothing was tensing up. I didn't understand it, but I wasn't suffering—yet.

Even as a baby, I didn't like limits. I probably didn't like this pink dress, either.

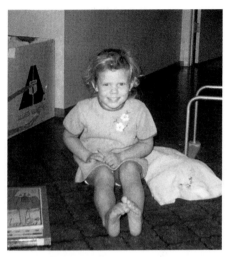

Shoes? What are those? I preferred to feel the floor beneath my feet.

My brother, Grady, and me in Salinas, California.

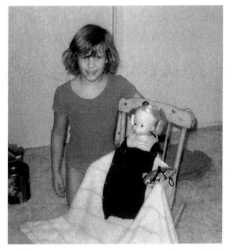

Still wearing my gymnastics leotard. I couldn't wait to get home and play.

"Jump into the air and arch your back," I was told in gymnastics class—so I did.

Fully sighted and totally self-confident, from the looks of this second-grade portrait.

With Grady and his best friend, Glen, showing off our fish after a day on Lake Meade, one year after I was diagnosed with Stargardt's.

Me and my mom, Valerie Runyan, my ally and greatest advocate, who never stopped looking for answers.

With my favorite VH teacher, John O'Looney, who could make me laugh at anything.

In the backyard patio with my dad, Gary Runyan, holding the "Golden Tenny" award from sixth-grade P. E. class—the first of three that I would win.

Playing Bach's Minuet
#3 on a fishing boat
in Hawaii.

When I was in the sixth
grade, my mom thought
I should get a perm. I
wasn't so sure about it.

When I was running,
I felt fully sighted. My
vision didn't seem to
matter when I was
outdoors and on the
move.

With my high school high-jump
buddy, Kelly Maloney

I called it *A Touch of Sight* and won First Prize in the county photography contest.

I started off as a highjumper, and went from a homemade pit in my backyard to jumping 5' 10" for San Diego State University.

I anchored the mile relay for SDSU at the WAC Conference Championships—after finishing second in the heptathlon.

The key to the 100-meter hurdles is rhythm. I couldn't
see the hurdles, but I knew how to get over them.

Winning the 400 meters at the 1992 Paralympics. I wore my first USA uniform . . .
(William Sallaz)

. . . and carried the American flag on a victory lap.
(William Sallaz)

With my former coach Dick Brown and my friend Jennifer at the Amazon Trail. I still had much to learn about running.

Me and Summer on a hike in Bend, Oregon *(Bruce Jackson)*

With Matt and my former coach Mike Manley, who helped get me to the 2000 Olympic Trials *(Michael Kevin Daley)*

Leah Pells and I raced
to a photo-finish in the
Pan-American Games.
"Who won?" I asked her.
"You did," she said.
(AP/Kevin Djansezian)

Matt and me after his
half-marathon in
Coburg, Oregon. He
was "The Rock"and
gave my life stability.

"Thank you," I said to the blue sky above me. I crossed the finish line and became an Olympian—but I was still just Marla. *(Brian J. Meyers@PhotoRun)*

2000 U.S. Olympic Trials - 1500 Meter Run Women (25-2-1)

Finish - Outside

Start: 7/16/00 14:05:36.33

4:06.50   4:06.40 4:02.02   4:01.90   4:01.80   4:01.20   4:01.10   4:01.00
                    4:02.00

Place	Id	Lane	First Name	Last Name	Affiliation	Time	ReacTime
1	456	6	Regina	Jacobs	NIKE - Nike	4:01.01	
2	292	11	Suzy	Favor-Hamilton	NIKE - Nike	4:01.81	
3	796	12	Marla	Runyan	ASIC - Asics	4:06.44	

The order of finish of my race at the 2000 U.S. Olympic Trials
(photo by FinishLynx)

"Bat Girl"

Matt and me after a training
session in Sydney. The
grandstands of the Olympic
Stadium in the distance
were a magnificent sight,
even to my eyes.

The pace began to slow, and I took the lead in the Olympic final. It was a giant risk, but one I felt I had to take. *(Victah@PhotoRun)*

The aftermath of the Olympic 1500 was one of confusion. I tried to comfort my USA teammate Suzy Favor Hamilton. *(AP/Michael Probst)*

The clock at the New York Armory displays my time of 15:07:33—a new American Record in the indoor 5000 meters. *(Stacy Creamer)*

Even Olympians can't escape paperwork. This is how I read with my CCTV. I'm not very fast, but I get the job done.

Summer and I display pride of ownership in front of our new home in Eugene.

Now I came around on the third 200, and I could hear Rahn. He yelled out, "One thirty-one!" It was my 600 time. He screamed, "You got it!" In that crowd of 33,000, I could hear Rahn's voice distinctly. After so many years, I was conditioned to hear it. To me, it was the sound of speed.

I ran the last 200 absolutely as hard as I could. *Don't lock up, don't lock up, don't lock up.* Coming around the turn, I knew that I had the record if my body didn't seize on me. *Try not to lock up, try not to lock up.*

Over the last 100 meters, the noise from the spectators, who had been so distracted, began to build. Gradually, they had noticed that this heptathlete was going to run a pretty good 800. It was the first time I'd ever heard a crowd in a race, and as I crossed the line, they erupted. It was a sound of pure exhilaration.

I stared at the clock: 2:04:70. I'd broken the record by almost two seconds. I couldn't believe it. I just put my hand in the air, and then bent over, hands on my knees, and tried not to stagger.

For a long minute, I wandered around the track, trying to get my breath. I wondered if they would announce the record over the loudspeaker, but it was silent. Finally, an official approached me.

"You need to get off the track now," he said. "The next race is about to start." That would be the women's 100 meters.

"But it's the record," I said.

He had no idea what I was talking about. He just kept pointing me in the direction he wanted me to go.

It was my introduction to the minute significance of this kind of record. A world record, well, that is incomparable. But it's difficult to explain that you just ran the fastest 800 meters by an American *in a heptathlon* when most people don't even know what the heptathlon is. The phrase "a heptathlon 800-meter American record" didn't mean much to anyone but me. In those few minutes, I understood that you have to run a race for yourself and your own satisfaction, because it is not the most recognizable or popular of endeavors. It is, for the most part, a contest of the self against the self, and if you're looking for a lot of external congratulations, you'll be disappointed. I knew it was a record, and that was what mattered.

There was one other person in the stands who knew I had set a record, and who was impressed: Dick Brown. I had shown him some potential. As I crossed the finish line he said to himself, *She's in the wrong sport.* In his opinion, I wasn't a heptathlete at all. I looked like a runner.

I moved into an area called the media chute, where the press could interview me from behind a set of ropes. I was so excited by the record that I jumped up and down like a kid, but the press seemed no more aware of the record than anyone else. The only people who understood were the other heptathletes, some of whom began to congratulate me.

At that point, I heard someone say, "Marla!" I turned around. It was Renee, and she was crying. She reached over the ropes and gave me a big hug, and she said, "You did it, you did it!" Whatever disappointment I felt at the lack of recognition by the press evaporated. I hugged Renee back and thanked her for what she had done for me.

Next, Jennifer Nanista made her way through and congratulated me. I looked over her shoulder. "Where's Rahn?" I asked.

She said, "Uh, he's up in the stands." Rahn was still angry with me for pulling away from him, I guessed.

I put my sweats back on and got ready to catch the bus back to the hotel. Gwen Torrence had edged Gail Devers in the 100 meters, and everyone else had come and gone. I was walking through the tunnel when, finally, here came Rahn and Gary walking toward me.

Rahn patted me on the shoulder and said, "Good race."

And that was it. Gary had nothing to say. I was completely undone by their lack of response. We sat in an uncomfortable silence on the bus all the way to the hotel, and when we arrived I went to my room without a word. I thought I had reason to be congratulated: that 800 had taken me from seventeenth place to a tenth-place finish among twenty-six competitors, and instead no one had much to say.

I called Ramona Pagel. "This is Marla," I said. "Guess what? I broke the record in the 800. I'm an American record holder—sort of. Not the same as you, though."

"YEAH!" Ramona screamed. "That's awesome!"

I clung to the record as the one and only reward for those years of effort. After the other six miserable events, it was all I had. And it would be the one thing that prevented me from quitting the sport altogether.

I went to bed and slept until noon. When I woke up, I realized that my relationship with Rahn and Gary had run its course. As much as I'd learned from them, it was probably time for me to move on. I hadn't significantly improved in the hepathlon in a year of training. Perhaps I was competing in the wrong discipline.

Jennifer was my roommate, and as she stirred in the bed next to me, I said, "You know, I think maybe next year I should run the 1500."

Jennifer looked skeptical. "No, you're not a 1500 runner. You're a 400-800 runner," she said. But I wasn't so sure.

I was invited to run in a 400-meter exhibition relay for blind runners at the end of the U.S. Trials, so I stayed in Atlanta for the duration of the meet, and so did Rahn. We managed to get through it.

I dreaded the exhibition race because it meant another week in Atlanta, but I felt obliged to do it, because I wanted to be more involved with the USABA. I decided to use the exhibition as a test, to help me decide whether or not to concentrate on the 800. I was deeply curious to see what I could run. Why not give up the heptathlon, with its arduous multi-event training, and concentrate on running?

I ran that 400-meter leg of the relay all-out, as hard as I had run my 800 meters in the Trials. I was fresh after a week of rest, and it was an opportunity to see what I could do on new legs. As I crossed the line, I felt I had turned in a good performance. But then my time came over the loudspeaker: 58.6 seconds. *Huh?* That was slow, much slower than I had hoped.

I sat in a tunnel under the stadium, crushed. I couldn't believe that I'd only managed a 58.6. There was no way, with that kind of time, that I would ever be a good 800-meter runner. It was a good thing that I'd gotten my teaching credential.

I got on the bus and went back to the hotel. In the lobby, Jennifer came running up to me, with Rahn's stopwatch in her hand. She shoved it in my face. "Look, look," she said, excitedly.

"Jennifer, I can't see it," I said.

"It says 52.6," she said. "You ran 52.6 on your relay leg."

I said, "Well, why the hell did they say '58'?"

"I don't know, but we had three watches on you, and you ran 52.6."

It was the fastest 400 meters of my life, and the confirmation I had been looking for. With that one relay leg, I decided to commit to four more years of training, this time as a runner. I knew it would mean more years of living hand-to-mouth and working part-time, but my sudden speed was just too intriguing. I had to pursue it.

I went to the Nike hospitality room on the Olympic grounds, hoping to drum up some kind of financial or shoe support, but all I had on my résumé was my top-ten heptathlon finish. I sat down with the rep whom I'd spoken to on the phone. He immediately launched into a discouraging speech. "Nike really doesn't need to sponsor top-ten athletes," he said. "We just look to sponsor the top three in the world. We're condensing the number of athletes wearing the swoosh [their logo] next year, and we're not looking to put it on any new athletes."

Finally, he finished talking.

I only had one card to play, and I played it.

"Well, I just got a call from ABC-TV and, um, they want to do an interview next weekend," I said.

I don't think I'd even finished the sentence before he said, "You know what? We probably should go ahead and put you on the list for some equipment next year. Let's just do that. And, hey, let me give you some stuff right now so you'll have it for the interview. And when I get back from Europe, I'll send you a formal contract."

He handed me a Nike backpack, and started whipping T-shirts and hats at me.

I was relieved: I had Nike for another year. But I still had a larger question to answer: who to train with? I needed a new coach, someone to teach me how to run longer distances. And I needed a change.

I started doing some investigative work, checking out coaches at other tracks and universities, but I didn't get anywhere until, one afternoon, my mother called me up and said, "Did you watch the women's 1500 at the Olympic Trials?"

I hadn't. I had been sitting in the tunnel, brooding over what I thought was a lousy time in the 400. My mother said, "Well, there was a girl in that race named Vicki Huber, and she finished third, and when they interviewed her afterward, she thanked her training partner, Suzy Hamilton, and her coach, Dick Brown, and said they live in Eugene, Oregon, and they're just like a family. Maybe you could go there and train."

"Mom, Dick Brown wouldn't coach me," I said. "He coaches Olympians. Those girls both made the Olympic team." I also informed her that he had coached Mary Decker Slaney to her World Championship medal performances.

"Well, I just thought they sounded like nice people," she said. "It might be something, you know, worth looking into."

At first, I ignored the suggestion. But as the days went by and I couldn't find anyone to work with, I decided it was at least worth a try. I got Dick Brown's number from a coach at the University of Oregon, and I called him. I got an answering machine, and I left a stammering, hesitant message.

"Uh, hi. You don't know me, but my name is Marla Runyan, and I, uh, I ran at the Trials. And, um, I, I did the heptathlon, and uh—I ran the 800 in 2:04, and I was thinking about maybe just running the 800 next year and, uh, I'm kind of looking for a . . . a new coach, and, um, I wanted to kind of look at what my options might be, and I'd like to talk to you. And if you could call me back I'd appreciate it."

I left my phone number and hung up, and immediately thought, *Aaah, God, that was so geeky.*

That afternoon, the phone rang and I unthinkingly picked it up. The voice on the other end said, "Hello, Marla, this is Dick Brown."

"Oh, hi," I said, and gripped the phone hard.

"So, I saw you run that 800 down there in Atlanta," he said. "And there are only two new athletes that I saw at the Trials that I would take next year to coach . . . and you're one of them."

My knees almost buckled. I sank into a chair. Dick Brown, the legendary Dick Brown, was willing to coach me. We chatted for just a few more minutes, and by the end of the brief conversation I was ready to move to Eugene the very next day. Done deal. I didn't even ask about his training methods or his philosophies. All I knew was that he coached people who made the Olympic team.

A few days later, Dick had to be in San Diego on other business, and we met. He was a rangy, extremely thoughtful man who was easy to talk to. Dick told me that what had impressed him was my combination of strength and speed, and my ability to focus at the end of the race, even when he knew I was tired. He asked what I had been doing in terms of training. I gave him a brief description. Dick listened and nodded, and then he began to talk about his philosophy.

"I'm a very patient person," he said. "This is key: you won't build up anything overnight. If you work with me, you'll have to build an endurance base, slowly. You still haven't made the full transition from collegiate athlete to world-class yet. But you could be a great runner."

After that lunch, I knew I was right about moving to Eugene.

But first, I had to tell Rahn. I dreaded the meeting, but I knew I had to get it over with. I went over to his office, and hesitantly stuck my head in his door, and told him we needed to talk. I told him the story of how Dick Brown had watched the 800. I had made a final decision to abandon the heptathlon, and to train for the 800. Then I braced for his reaction.

He got up out of his chair, came around the desk, and gave me a big hug. "I'm really happy for you," he said. "I'm here if you need anything."

I hugged him back. Then I went home and started packing.

7. Eugene

I arrived in Eugene, Oregon, on a fresh September morning, and as I stepped out of the van and took a deep breath, it was as though I had never inhaled before. The air was cool and easy and settled into my lungs, and as I looked around, the view of the town had the same easy effect on my eyes. There was something soft and forgiving about the light, which wasn't half as blinding as the California sun that had ricocheted off the freeways and buildings and cement malls. Here, the sunlight was filtered and absorbed by an arc of surrounding piney green hills, and by deep, rolling fields of turf. It was quiet, too. Instead of sidewalks, there seemed to be woodchip footpaths everywhere, and the general impression was of a muffled softness. Even the traffic sounds were assuaged by the soothing hush of the Willamette River.

I moved there with no preconceived notions, not really caring where I lived. Eugene was a means to an end, a place to train and learn from a first-rate coach, Dick Brown. But I knew instantly that it suited me. It was as though the entire town had been designed for people in running shoes. Everywhere I looked was a health-food store, or a bike path, or a wood-chip trail. It's the world capital for runners, and now I understood why, because its pure air seemed to invite your feet to move, and that concentrated greenness seemed to foster singleminded purpose, the kind that makes people run hard.

Eugene had long been the home and training venue for distance legends such as Steve Prefontaine, Mary Decker Slaney, Alberto Salazar, and Bill McChesney. It was also the home of a less renowned but no less influential figure, Bill Bowerman, the father of the modern running shoe, and the man who may have singlehandedly provoked the running boom in the United States. Legend has it that Bowerman, who was the head coach at the University of Oregon, met with Arthur Lydiard of New Zealand, who is considered the architect of modern distance-running theory. Bowerman brought Lydiard's methods and views on physiology back to the United States, thereby launching Americans into a jogging craze. Bowerman also invented a new type of sneaker, one he began developing with a waffle iron in his garage, and named it *Nike.*

As a result, Eugene was nicknamed "Track Town USA," and on the corner of Franklin Boulevard and Agate Street, you could even find Track Town Pizza. Groomed running trails wind through the town paralleling the Willamette River, and running connoisseurs have serious arguments about which of these trails they treasure the most. Most of the residents are die-hard track fans and would stand on their feet in the rain to watch a 5000-meter race, and they have a deep sense of history. A conversation with a Eugene resident will likely include the words, "I remember when . . ."

I had been sprinting, jumping, and throwing for nearly ten years before I ever set foot in Oregon. But it was not until I pulled into Eugene at age 28 that I finally learned *how* to run.

On the day I arrived, I didn't yet know what it meant to be an elite runner. I only knew that I had big plans: in four years, I intended to be an Olympian in the 800 meters. But in order to make the U.S. team, I would have to do something I never had come close to doing: run the event in less than two minutes. My personal best, still the 2:04 that I'd run at the '96 Trials, was mediocre by the standards of the women who specialized in the event. I would have to completely remake myself as an athlete. I'd have to reshape my bulky heptathlete's physique, and I'd have to retrain my mind as well.

I was searching for a new mind-set—and still grappling with a case of lingering exhaustion from my years in San Diego. Sitting with my parents one night on the front patio of their home, shortly before leaving for Eugene, I said, "I just want to go there and enjoy the process. I want to enjoy running again. I don't want to say that I *will* run 2:01 or 2:02 next year." This was a new attitude for me, and a less-stressful one. But if 1996 had taught me anything, it was that basing my self-worth and happiness upon the outcome of a single competition left me empty.

My parents decided to help me make the trip to Eugene, and I sat in the backseat of my father's minivan with my golden retriever, Summer. A good friend of mine from grad school, Lisa, and her husband also accompanied us, driving a U-Haul packed to the ceiling.

For the next two weeks, we stayed together in a Eugene motel and looked for a rental apartment. My father drove frantically through the neighborhoods around the Oregon campus, looking for a place that would accept dogs. I felt completely capable of finding my own place to live, but this was my father's way of being helpful and of showing his support of the move. He searched through countless newspapers and classified ads, but not even the executive vice president of a southern California savings and loan could persuade the rental agencies to bend their "no pets" policy and accept Summer.

At each apartment complex, he tried to explain to my potential landlord that Summer was a "special" kind of dog.

"He's practically human," my dad would say.

We stopped at a promising duplex, an old brown house that had been built in the 1940s and was being renovated and converted to apartments. The landlords, a couple, came out to the porch, and my father said, "How do you feel about dogs?"

"He's not exactly just a dog," I interrupted. "He's an aide dog."

But the man didn't hear me and quickly answered, "No pets."

The next afternoon we drove past the same old house. The door was standing open.

"Pull over," I said to my dad. Reluctantly, he did.

My parents sat, quietly exhausted. It was time to take matters into my own hands. I hopped out of the car, clicked Summer's harness around his middle, and we walked across the street to the house. As I slowly climbed the porch steps, I heard a voice from inside say, "Hello?"

"Hello," I answered, not sure exactly where to look. A woman appeared.

"You came by yesterday, didn't you?" she asked.

I said that I had.

"I want to apologize," she said. "We didn't know . . ." She paused. I knew what she meant: they hadn't realized I was blind.

"That's okay," I said. "This is Summer. He's a guide dog."

The truth was, Summer would have walked in front of a bus if I'd let him. And he was even afraid of the toaster. But I was determined to get an apartment and ship my parents back to Camarillo.

The landlady welcomed me inside, and she warned me about all the obstacles in the room, such as the paint cans and equipment that they were using to fix the place up. I walked through the old house with Summer, and he led the way like a pro, as though he had been a guide dog his whole life.

"You're welcome to fill out an application," she said, sweetly.

"Okay," I said, and thanked her. When I was done, I crossed the street to the van and hopped in.

"I got it," I said.

I moved in two days later. I was relieved to be settled—and that my well-meaning parents were on their way home. As my mother would say, "What an ordeal!"

I called Dick Brown to set up our first workout.

"What should I wear?" I asked.

"Jeans," he said.

"Jeans?"

"Just jeans," he said. "I'll pick you up."

As it turned out, this was no ordinary "workout." It took place in the study of his home in Coburg, Oregon. In fact, it wasn't really a training session at all—but it would have a significant influence on my running in the years to follow.

Dick was a tall, ambling man with a soft voice and a philosophical turn of mind. To him, coaching was like putting together a never-ending puzzle. "No matter how long you've been doing it, you always come across another piece that was missing," he liked to say. He was always looking for newer information, the most modern theories on optimum physical performance. The basis for what he did, however, came from the philosophy of Arthur Lydiard, the New Zealander who believed that one's aerobic capacity could be greatly increased by running high mileage. Really high mileage. In fact, in his prime, Lydiard had sometimes run the marathon distance of 26.2 miles *twice* in one day—once before work and again after. But Dick merely used the Lydiard methods as a foundation, and his own ideas for training elite runners were constantly evolving. Dick had a Ph.D. in exercise physiology and taught classes at the university.

We sat in the loft of Dick's home, a large, open room with new wood floors, large windows, and a perimeter of built-in bookcases jammed with volumes. Looking out of those large windows, I could only see a haze of colors, the smeared grays and greens of Eugene, green-carpeted hills, and the misty white threads of clouds around them that showered like a continuous sprinkler. You didn't often get a full day of sun in Eugene, but I didn't miss that.

Sitting on a bookcase was a framed photo of a runner. I picked it up.

"Who's this?" I asked, squinting at it.

"That's Mary Decker Slaney," he answered.

I felt like an idiot—I hadn't been able to make out the face in the picture because of my vision. There were other photos: Suzy Favor Hamilton and Shelly Steely, who were also Olympians trained by Dick. Suddenly, I was intimidated by all those photographs. They were greats. What was I doing here? I wondered if I truly belonged in the room. Was I talented enough?

Dick grabbed a textbook off a shelf and asked me to sit down. I took a seat next to him on a sofa, and he opened the book in front of me and turned over some pages, pointing at some charts and graphs.

I listened intently to what he said, but I couldn't make out the graphs.

"Can you see this?" he asked, suddenly concerned.

Dick knew of my impairment; he'd read about it, and I'd explained the basics to him. But I hadn't made a very big deal out of it, and consequently he paid little attention to it and was far more interested in my running. Which is exactly the way I liked it.

"It's okay," I answered, not wanting to hold up the lesson.

In fact, to see the words and the graphs printed in that complex physiology book—to read even a few pages—I would need my CCTV and about three hours. It was impractical for me. Instead, I just nodded at Dick and tried to form a mental picture of what he was talking about; to fill in what I could not see.

Dick balanced a pad of paper on top of the book and began drawing something.

"You essentially run with two bodies. Body Number One functions aerobically. That means you use oxygen for energy. But when the oxygen you breathe can no longer be converted into energy, you switch over to Body Number Two, which functions anaerobically."

He continued to draw on his pad of paper while I waited to hear something that made immediate sense. Something that I could conceptualize—and visualize.

"Using the anaerobic system is expensive. The pyruvate, which is created during glycolysis, backs up. And when that happens, you can't enter into the Krebs cycle."

"Okay," I said.

"Pyruvate is converted into lactate."

"Lactate, like lactic acid?" I asked. Finally, something I understood.

"Yes," he said.

Lactic acid, I knew, was the stuff that killed your legs at the end of a race. It flowed into your muscles with a burn like white-hot alcohol and paralyzed you, making that final straightaway a fight to the finish. Anyone who has ever raced 400 or 800 meters knows exactly what I'm talking about.

"So," Dick continued, "the goal is to stay in Body Number One for as long as possible. Delay dipping into that costly anaerobic energy system for as long as you can."

"How do I do that?" I asked.

"By increasing your VO_2 max," he said firmly.

"Uh-huh," I said.

Once again, I didn't have the faintest idea of what he was talking about.

"Look," he explained. "Your VO_2 max is the maximum volume of oxygen your body can consume per kilogram of body weight per minute."

By now, Dick could tell that I still didn't completely understand. He decided to put the concepts into examples that I could grasp.

"In a world-class 1500-meter race, almost everyone will arrive at the 1200-meter mark at about the same time," he said. "The question is: What do their bodies look like on the inside? Who is the most anaerobic? Who is the least?"

The race scenario got my attention.

"It's not just about speed," he said, and now his voice gained urgency. "With 200 meters to go, it's not about who's the *fastest*. Everybody out there is fast. It's about who is the least anaerobic—it's about who's able to *access* their speed."

Now I was getting it. Dick jabbed at his pad of paper.

"If you are here"—he pointed at a graph—"and the other runner is here, then she will win. All things being equal, the runner with the higher VO$_2$ max will win."

But this concept, *all things being equal,* was foreign to me. I'd always thought running was about effort, will, guts, and tolerance of pain. I thought that slowing down was due to weakness. When I got beat in the 800 meters (usually on the final straightaway), I thought it was because the other runners were simply tougher than I was. I was trained to believe that losing was due to a flaw in my character, not in my physiology.

"What if the runner who has a lower VO$_2$ max just wants it more and pushes herself harder?" I asked.

"She will slow down, no matter how hard she pushes," Dick answered. "She will tie up. Trust me. When you run anaerobically—when lactate builds up and fills your muscles—you will fall behind, no matter how mentally tough you are, because you don't have the body to support that mental strength."

This was fascinating, and a relief. It was as though a huge

weight had been lifted off my shoulders, and my conscience. Dick was telling me that my failures up to this point were explicable. There was a science to running, and what I thought was a battle of will against body was really about training different energy systems and allowing the body to support the mental strength that had brought me this far.

Just when I was catching on, Dick said something that plunged me back into confusion.

"If you can learn how to train, you can finish a race faster than you started it."

"What?"

I was completely thrown off by this concept.

"The best runners finish strong, because they can access their speed even at the end of a 1500- or 5000-meter race," he explained.

Now, this really made no sense at all. My experience with the last 200 of any race was one of pure pain. The last straightaway appeared a mile long and it took every ounce of strength to scratch and claw to the end. Running that straightaway had always been a matter of "holding on." But to Dick, the last 200 meters was when a runner should be "picking it up."

To run faster at the end of a race, instead of slower? It was a eureka concept. I would do anything to experience that. More than anything, I wanted to believe in it.

Dick handed me a packet an inch thick. Inside were charts and graphs, and a four-year training plan in which he outlined a steady increase in the total mileage I would run. It was a program that would require patience and trust.

Trust I had, but patience would be a struggle. I was anxious to get started, but, as it turned out, my left knee was not. I'd had a nagging case of patellar tendinitis, and in fact I'd been injected twice with cortisone to get me through the '96 Olympic Trials and the Paralympic Games.

I listed for Dick the treatments that I'd received over the last two years and explained that none of them had really remedied the problem. "That's ancient stuff," he said. I suddenly felt like I'd been in the wrong place doing the wrong thing for a very long time.

Dick took me to Sacred Heart Hospital to be examined by Dr. Stanley James and Dr. Ken Singer, who were two of the most prominent orthopedic surgeons in the country.

An MRI (magnetic resonance imaging) showed some scar tissue within the tendon, and Dr. Singer advised me to have surgery. But he also informed me that patellar-tendon surgery was not always successful. Surgery was a "Catch-22," since the procedure itself causes scar tissue.

"If it works, you should be able to run again in three to six months," Dr. Singer said.

Dick and I looked at each other, and shrugged. That would still leave enough time for me to train for the outdoor track season. But my hopes of running the 800 in under two minutes were probably shot for the year.

I said to Dick, "Well, maybe I'll have to settle for 2:03 next year."

"I don't see why not," Dick said.

On October 10, 1996, I had surgery on my left knee. I spent the night in the hospital and woke up the next afternoon to find that Dick, as well as his runners Vicki Huber and Jennifer Bravard, had brought me a Dairy Queen Blizzard upon my request. After they left, I threw it up, but their visit made me feel that in moving to Eugene, I had come to the right place.

I also woke up to find a brace on my leg from my hip to my ankle. I wasn't in any pain and I wanted to go home, but Dick thought it would be a better idea for me to stay with him and his longtime live-in companion, Marlene. He brought Summer to the hospital when he picked me up, and he drove both of us to Coburg, where he installed us in his guest room. While I recuperated, I spent my time staring through a magnifying glass, trying to read the physiology notes and articles that Dick had given me.

One article was entitled "Hans Selye's General Adaptation Syndrome." I peered through the magnifying glass at a graph with the vertical axis labeled "Resources" and the horizontal axis labeled "Time in months." Dick had tried to explain the graph to me, but I hadn't really understood the point of it—until now.

"Training is stress to your body," Dick explained. "It's *challenge* to your system. Your body will use up its resources to cope with the stress." He gestured at a lower point on the graph. "But if you rest and recover, your body will adapt to the challenges that you give it. *You adapt stronger than you were before.* It's all a delicate balance of challenge and recovery."

If one did not allow oneself adequate recovery from training, one's fitness—"resources"—would drop. Performance would suffer. Dick handed me a list of symptoms indicating that this had occurred. They read something like this:

1. Challenges seem harder
2. "Psyching up" seems harder
3. Irritated easily
4. Disinterested in surroundings
5. Abnormal weight loss

6. Increased exercise heart rate

7. Increased morning heart rate

"This is me," I said.

I'd experienced every one of the symptoms on the list leading up to the 1996 Olympic Trials. I'd thought I was weak, when actually, I had simply overtrained and not allowed myself any recovery. I'd been beating myself up for months, and now this wise man handed me a piece of paper with an explanation for it.

"You were exhausted," he said.

In all the years I had been an athlete, I had not learned this simple theory: that training must be balanced with rest. I'd considered sleep a needless waste, and I'd thought a "good" workout was one that was hard, fast, and painful.

"No pain, no gain," the cliché went.

But not only was it a cliché, it was an ignorant philosophy to train by. It had taken me nearly ten years—and a trip to Eugene—to figure that out. Here I was, bedridden, with my leg in a brace, but I suddenly wondered if it was the best thing that could have happened to me. Perhaps this surgery had happened for a reason: to force me to rest and to teach me patience.

Eventually, I went home. By now I was well enough to look for a job, and I found one at the YMCA. Each day, I hobbled on crutches down the street to the Y, where I made $5.18 an hour working at the front desk.

I could have gone back to teaching, but that would have meant applying for a temporary teaching license in Oregon, and I dreaded the prospect of all the paperwork and bureaucracy. I wanted something that was simple and less stressful, and that would be compatible with my running career. At the Y, I could cross-train before and after my shift. As soon as I was able, I got onto a stationary bike and pedaled with one leg.

Obviously, I was slow to learn patience.

The decision to move to Eugene, and to work at the Y, meant an economic change for me. The SSI stipend that I'd been living off in California was $200 less in Oregon. Also, Oregon did not have a clear policy on bioptic drivers. I mostly used the bus system or rode a bike. I lived on my minimum wages from the Y, as well as my SSI and food stamps. The total came to about $800 a month. I decided that I was going to make it work—no matter what.

But if I thought the Y would be low-stress, I was wrong. My first task was to collect membership cards as members came in to use the Y, and then to hand them back when they left. The cards were laminated, and the names were typed on them with a regular typewriter. I was supposed to place them in a blue file box as the members entered.

I could not see the names on the cards. Even with my 8-power magnifier, I had to go through the whole stack of cards, holding each one up against the lens over my right eye, until I found the right one.

At first I was self-conscious about displaying my disability so publicly, but pretty soon I just didn't care. I sat there and endured the comments.

"Those glasses don't work too well."

"You might want to get your eyes checked."

"You need a new eye doctor."

In Eugene, I was quickly becoming a nobody. I was just that woman at the Y who took an hour to find a membership card, the one who hobbled around with a brace on her left leg. I thought I would pick up where I had left off after settling that American Record at the U.S. Trials. But instead I felt I had lost my whole identity. I was starting all over again.

Six weeks after surgery, Dick took me to the swimming pool at the Y and allowed me to aqua-jog with a smaller brace on my leg. When I saw my quadriceps after taking off the large brace, I couldn't believe my eyes. They had shrunk to half their size, and all that remained was a small soft lump of tissue, mostly fat, that jiggled.

As Dick and I bobbed around in the pool for thirty minutes or so, I could feel how weak I had become. I had lost most of the muscle in my leg, and the rest of me was starting to jiggle, too. My metabolism had slowed, and I was gaining weight fast. The scale was an enemy. In fact, my body was becoming my enemy.

For the next several weeks, all I could do was cross-train on an Aerodyne bike, a stationary apparatus with arm handles and a firm resistance on the pedals. I could only get my heart rate up into a respectable range on that particular bike. I did my best to cross-train, riding the bike in the morning, swimming in the afternoon, and doing some lifting, although I couldn't lift with my left knee, in the evenings. But still, I ballooned to nearly 150 pounds. I was miserable.

Finally, after three months, the doctors decided I could begin to run. Dick picked me up in his car and took me to the Amazon Trail, a soft wood-chip path in south Eugene. We walked to the lower end of the trail, where there was a 600-meter loop, bordered by some light poles. Dick could sit on a bench at one end and see the entire loop.

"Okay," he said. "I want you to walk to the first light pole. Can you see it?"

"No," I said, but that didn't matter. It would come into view eventually.

"Walk to it, then start to jog to the next pole," he said. "Then, stop and walk again to the next pole. Do this all the way around the loop," he said.

"Okay," I answered impatiently.

I had been waiting for this day, and I was dying to run. But I followed Dick's directions and I walked, reluctantly, to the pole. Next, I moved into an easy gait that felt more like a shuffle than a jog. Everything on my body shook like Jell-O, and my pace was so slow that a woman walking her dog passed me.

Finally, I made it around the loop, in what had to be the world record for slowness.

"Now what?" I asked.

"You're done," he said.

"That's it?" I said, stunned.

"That's it. Right now the challenge is to your knee, not your body. That has to come first."

This was too much. This required faith, not just patience. How in the world would I ever make it back at this pace? All the expectations I'd had when I hurried to Eugene to work with Dick, to be an Olympian in four years, now seemed further away than ever.

Everything was changing, and nothing was what I had hoped it would be. Within a week of my arrival in Eugene, Suzy Favor Hamilton announced that she was moving back to Wisconsin to her hometown. Next, Michelle Ave, another elite 800-meter runner of Dick's who had broken the two-minute barrier at the U.S. Trials, dropped out of the training group, because she lived in Portland and the two-hour commute to Eugene was too long. That left four of us under Dick's tutelage: Vicki Huber, the two-time Olympian; Claire Taylor, an NCAA champion; my good friend Jennifer Bravard, an Olympic Trials qualifier at 1500 meters—and me.

I'd had images of running side by side with the best runners in the country. I'd daydreamed of working out at Hayward Field, the atmospheric track stadium at the University of Oregon where Bill Bowerman had coached and Prefontaine had ruled, and where Decker Slaney had set records. It was an ambient old stadium, with old wooden benches under elegant clapboard eaves, and if you climbed to the back of the bleachers you could find a bronze plaque in honor of Bowerman that had been mysteriously bolted to the wall one night. I'd had an image of myself trotting around that track, training and socializing on a spring day, but now it appeared that that was never going to happen.

The first time I showed up at Hayward Field, I felt like an intruder. Looking for Dick, I strolled through the gate with Summer trotting next to me, and I gazed around at the bleachers. I stopped a runner who was leaving.

"Is Dick Brown here?" I asked.

"He's not here and you have to leave," he said curtly. "No dogs allowed."

Instead of joining the Hayward Field legends, I spent all my time on a stationary bike at the YMCA, or in the pool running in one place, or at the front desk being asked, "Why don't you get glasses?"

Or, worst of all, I jog-walked up and down those wood–chip trails. I hated those trails at first, because they represented a world of uncertainty. They meandered around, twisting and turning and borderless, and their texture beneath my feet was new and strange.

After years of running safely around on the simple oval of a fenced-in Tartan track, I found the trails of Eugene to be an exercise in anxiety. I ran them uncertainly, as if there were eggshells beneath my feet, unsure of the footing and of where the next turn was. In time, I would come to love the trails and know them as intimately as I knew the carpet in my own home, but that was months, even years, away. It was January, and I was a stranger to trails, and I wasn't even sure that the surgery had been successful. My knee still hurt, and I could only jog continuously for twenty minutes or so.

The progress was too slow. I could hardly bear it. I hauled my overweight and unfit body down the trails, stomping over the wood chips like an elephant. I told Dick that I felt like a sea cow in the pool.

"You mean a manatee?" he asked.

"Yep, that's me."

Even when Dick increased the miles and the volume of my training, I was uncomfortable. My heptathlete's body groaned and complained at the new distances and demands. I couldn't find the right shoes. My feet always hurt. I put in an order with Nike for some new training shoes. When they never arrived, I called the number that the man in Atlanta had given me.

A woman answered. "What's your name again?"

"Runyan," I said. "R-U-N-Y-A-N."

"We don't have you on the list. We don't know who you are."

That about summed it up.

So, I went to the sporting goods store and bought a pair of ASICS shoes—on sale.

Typically, I wore training shoes that were a little bit too small for me, because I tried to simulate the snug fit of a spiked track shoe. But I didn't realize that small shoes aren't suitable for distance running. Not too long after I started jogging again, I noticed a sharp pain in my left foot.

Once again, Dick and I sat together in the waiting room of the orthopedic surgeon's office.

"It's a neuroma," the doctor said after examining my foot. "An inflamed sensory nerve between the third and fourth metatarsals. Worst-case scenario is, we have to perform surgery to remove the nerve."

Surgery it was. In March of 1997, I had an operation on my left foot, and that put any idea of a competitive season out of the question. Once again I was on the bike and in the pool. By then I could have aqua-jogged my way to China.

Even after surgery, the injury continued to nag at me. I felt shocks of electricity each time my foot struck the ground. I tried my own invention: using a kitchen sponge as a shoe-insert.

Nothing was going right. My health had become a constant topic, and I was sick of it. Finally, I couldn't contain my impatience and frustration any more. I sat in the small café at the Y with Dick, and told him how I felt.

"This just isn't working," I said. "All I do is the jog-walk thing, and then come here and go in the pool, or ride the bike."

"I wish you could just let go of everything and allow your body to rest, and give it the chance to heal."

Rest from what? I wondered.

I was overweight and out of shape. How could I possibly need rest?

"Do you want to go to the movies?" he asked.

I tried to laugh. But I felt Dick's calmness was a refusal to acknowledge my crisis. I was of the verge of giving up the idea of ever becoming an Olympian. Dick still believed that I was capable of it, and he sympathized with my sadness and frustration, but he had no easy answers for me. He knew what I didn't: that the surgeries and nagging injuries were the price of overtraining, and now of retraining my body; and that there was no shortcut.

Dick suggested that I give up everything except the running. No more pool or bike—we would focus instead on trying to adapt my body to running.

Thanks to Dick's lessons in patience and his constant encouragement, I got through the next several months of forced inactivity. Finally, after ten months and two surgeries, the pains diminished. Dick was right: I was able to run again, and I felt stronger. By summer I could put in nearly fifty minutes, and soon I was running along the Willamette River bike path for over an hour. I was losing weight and feeling better.

But I was still slow. The kind of running I was doing now bore no resemblance to a fast 800. I tried not to complain—and gradually I began to look forward to those long, long runs. I couldn't see a standard stopwatch, so I bought a basic hand-held watch with very large numbers and tied a string to it. Each morning, I wrapped the string of the watch around my left hand and held the watch in my palm. It seemed almost permanently attached there. I ran alone, along concrete bike paths where the footing was surer, rather than on the wood-chip trails that made me uneasy. Every time I'd cross a small footbridge over the rushing waters of the Willamette, I was deeply thankful to be in Eugene, and to be running—even if I was slow.

Finally, one afternoon in the late summer, Dick summoned me to Hayward Field to run a workout with Vicki and Claire.

"It won't be anything too hard," he said.

I was thrilled. I rode my bike over to the track and listened raptly as Dick outlined the workout.

"You will each run 100 meters, like a relay, and then rest while the other two run the distance. Next, we'll do the same thing with 200s, and then with 400s."

All summer, I had run Dick's high-mileage program to elevate my anaerobic threshold. The theory, so carefully outlined in those textbook graphs, was to eventually make it easier to maintain a faster pace. Now I was ready to see some concrete results. *This should feel different,* I thought.

It felt different, all right. It felt awful. The switch to track work was too dramatic after months of slow mileage. By the time we got to the 400s, I had so much acid in my muscles that I could barely take the first couple of strides. My body felt heavy, the running laborious—so much effort for such slow times. Actually, Dick was pleased; I had done exactly as he expected. This wasn't a race, and he didn't want me running anything remotely resembling race-pace. But I didn't know any of that. Running an eighty-second 400 was not my idea of a track workout. I still had a lot to learn.

I wandered slowly to the end of the straightaway, swallowing hard and fighting back tears of frustration.

Dick came over to talk to me.

I said, "You took away everything that I once had that was good and replaced it with nothing."

It was a harsh statement, but it was exactly how I felt at the time. I was slow. I was weak. My endurance had always been my weakness, but at least I'd had speed. Now, the way I figured it, I had neither.

Dick stayed calm. This tall, quiet giant, who had tolerated my impatience for more than a year, continued to talk to me with that same positive, philosophical voice. We leaned against the chain-link gate on the perimeter of the track, and he said, "My goal for you is not this year or even next year. I don't care about the U.S. Nationals or any other meet. What I care about is watching you come down the final straightaway at the 2000 Olympic Games chasing an American record. And I believe that will happen."

I tried to envision it, but it seemed so far off. At that moment, I hated my own body. But Dick's calm was contagious. For at least a little while longer, I believed.

By that fall, I was putting in seventy to eighty miles a week. Every morning, I rose and went out the door into the cold, wet air and headed down High Street to a familiar paved bike path. I still chose to run on asphalt, because I just couldn't get used to the trails. The soft surface seemed to absorb my energy and make the run more laborious. But the hard surface came with a price.

In November, I noticed a pain in my left heel. I thought nothing of it, assuming it would disappear as I warmed up. But soon it was difficult to use the arch of my foot, and by the last few miles I was running on the edge of my left foot. I decided not to tell Dick about it, because I knew it would mean time off—and then back in the pool aqua-jogging or, worse, back on that 600-meter loop of walking and jogging. No way. I couldn't bear it.

So I kept it to myself. Big mistake. By January, I was in trouble again; any attempt to rise up on my toes was nearly impossible. Still, I kept the injury a secret; my first race in two years was coming up in March, a simple all-comers meet in which I would run the 800 against a field of mostly collegiate runners. I wanted desperately to compete again.

I ran the 800 in the rain against the college girls, and that finished the job. As I came down the final straightaway, my arch tore. I felt a burn that was almost like relief. I crossed the line in third place, but as soon as I'd stopped running, I could barely walk. This surely meant the end of another season.

By morning, I really *couldn't* walk. This time I had to tell Dick, and once again we sat in the surgeon's waiting room. By now, Dick and I had gone to more doctors' appointments together than track meets.

The diagnosis was "plantar fasciitis," a shortening and tearing of the muscle sheaths in the arch. The injury had its own vicious cycle. The torn tissues would lay down scar tissue, and each morning when I put my foot on the floor, the tissues would re-tear, and scar more, and the cycle would continue. Running was impossible. Dick ordered me to take a week off, but rest was no real remedy. It was one of those chronic things that had no real cure.

I was back on the bike, this time in tears. It seemed hopeless. First the 1997 season had been lost, and now it looked like 1998 was lost as well. I tried everything. I tried massage three times a week, and that exhausted my minimal finances. I tried acupuncture, a cortisone injection, and ultrasound. Nothing had any effect.

A week turned into a month, and I had nothing but time on my hands. Fortunately, I met a woman who would become my closest friend; one afternoon on the trails with Dick I met Susannah Beck, a 10,000-meter specialist who was considering moving up to the marathon. Susannah was different from anyone I'd known. She didn't wear makeup or store-bought clothes, and her passions were gardening and animals. She was a strong-minded and opinionated woman in a petite distance-runner's body.

Susannah began to come to the Y in the off-season to work out in the weight room. She wasn't a big fan of lifting, but she felt it might help her running. I created a light program for her. In return, she did something for me.

One day, she came into the Y and handed me a piece of paper. It was a letter she had written to the Moving Comfort apparel company. "Hopefully they will send you some training gear—you need it," she said. Susannah could see how thinly stretched my finances were. She wrote Moving Comfort that I was an elite athlete living and training in Eugene and desperately needed appropriate training gear. She described how I would go for two-hour runs in cotton T-shirts in the rain. She didn't bother to mention that I had not competed in over two years. Within a few days, a box arrived at my apartment, full of long-sleeved, all-weather Lycra shirts and running tights. I was so thankful.

Susannah and her boyfriend, Erich, rented a trailer on fifteen acres of land adjacent to the Willamette River. They had a garden in which they grew all their food, and Susannah also made her own clothes. On Sundays, Summer and I would show up at the trailer, and Susannah and her dog Gigi would take us on long hikes up in the mountain, where we would soak our various aches and injuries in the cold river.

"I don't know if I'll ever run again," I told Susannah one day as I sat waist-deep in the freezing river.

"Yes, you will. We both will."

Susannah was a realist. She dealt with injuries with common sense, not panic. She didn't have the resources or the motivation to seek out a quick fix, and, she figured, time would resolve most wounds and you just had to wait it out. She had what I didn't: true patience.

After our hike, we sat in her kitchen and drank coffee and ate fresh muffins that Erich had baked that morning. The trailer always smelled like a bakery, or herbs, and dinner at their house meant taking a walk through the garden and throwing some kind of baked good in the oven. I loved it.

Sipping my coffee and picking at my apple-cinnamon muffin, I said, "I don't know what to do about my foot. I've been paying this massage therapist forty-five dollars a week to work on it, but I can't afford it anymore."

"You should call Matt," she said.

"Who's Matt?"

"He's from Boston, he's a runner. He's in massage school, and he has to do a certain number of hours of massages for his class. He does it for free."

"Really?" I said.

"I'll call him for you," she said.

I went back to my one-bedroom apartment. I had moved out of the old house and found a place that was cheaper, but with a lot less charm. Okay, it was a dump—but it was across the street from a running trail.

The phone rang.

"Hello?"

"Hi, is this Marla?" a male voice asked. "This is Matt. I'm a friend of Susannah's."

"Yes, she told me about you."

"She says you need some help with your foot."

His name was Matt Lonergan, and he worked at the Oregon

Medical Lab during the week as a technician and took massage classes at night, so his schedule was tight, he said—but he could see me that very evening. As it happened, he lived just a few blocks away. At dusk, I rode my bike over to see him.

I couldn't see the address numbers on the houses. I got off my bike and was squinting at a white house that I thought might be the one when a voice said, "Hello." I turned toward the garage, where the voice seemed to come from.

"You can put your bike in here," he said.

I walked up the driveway toward the voice. Someone took the handlebars of my bike. I turned my head slightly, and he came into view. *Too young,* I thought.

I would never have admitted aloud that I was looking for a relationship. But I must have been hoping, because I immediately sized him up as a prospect. He had thick dark hair and a small frame, and he seemed to weigh even less than I did. He looked right at me and smiled and said, "I'm Matt."

Inside, I sat down on a lumpy futon, and he handed me a piece of paper to fill out.

"I need you to fill this out for my class, if that's okay."

I cringed. Paperwork.

I looked at the paper and managed to make out a line where I assumed I was supposed to sign my name. But the rest was a blur. I pushed the "play" button on the broken record in my brain and explained my situation.

"Actually, I can't see very well, and I'm not able to fill this out."

"Okay, I can read it to you."

He seemed to accept my explanation without comment.

"Have you ever had surgery?" he read from the paper.

I laughed out loud. I told him the history of my two surgeries in two years, and all the other treatments I'd endured. Matt listened knowledgeably. He had a bachelor's degree in Athletic Training and Sports Medicine, and he was a marathoner himself. He understood exactly what I was talking about.

"Now, I'm still just a student," he said.

"That's okay," I said.

Actually, I decided, it was better than okay. The fact that anyone would rub my foot for free was quite a deal.

After the paperwork was completed, we talked feet.

"So, it's your left plantar, right?"

"Yes," I leaned back on the futon and straightened my leg out and showed him my foot. Matt ran his hands over my arch. He could feel lumps of scar tissue about the size of quarters. When he pressed hard against them, it was like running his fingers over broken glass.

When people ask how Matt and I met, I hesitate. I don't like to say, "He was my massage therapist." That paints a picture of some guy rubbing naked bodies in a dimly lit room. It was nothing like that. The only article of clothing I took off was my sock. I just sat there, with one sock on and one sock off, on a very lumpy blue futon that Matt had bought for seventy-five dollars. There was no dim lighting or soft music, just dusk through the blinds flapping in the breeze coming through the open living-room window, and Matchbox 20 on the stereo.

Matt's deep-tissue work broke down the scar tissue in my arch. It helped—but his kind voice and calm nature may have been just as therapeutic. We became friends. I had no money to pay him, so

I offered him food. I thought he needed it, because he was so thin from running high mileage. One day I brought him a loaf of apple-crisp bread from Great Harvest. And one night, after he had hammered my foot, we sat and talked for at least an hour, and I asked him if I could treat him to dinner. He accepted.

There was only one problem: he didn't have a car. I would have to ride my bike back to my apartment, change clothes, then drive back to his house before dark. He would then take the wheel and take us to dinner. And it was already dusk.

I sped away, jumped on the bike path, and pedaled toward home. The blurry world streaked by me, and I could only hope no one was walking up ahead.

I wanted to shout, "Blind girl on a bike . . . *look out!*"

I burst open the door of my apartment, threw on jeans, and slammed back out again. I climbed behind the wheel of my Chevy pickup, and I sat there for a moment. I rarely drove anymore. In Oregon, no one seemed quite sure of the policy regarding a bioptic driver with an out-of-state license. The local DMV administrator had responded as most people did: "What's a bioptic?" he asked. I'd had my truck registered in Oregon, but I had no in-state license. I sat there and debated whether or not it was legal for me to drive. *It's only a few blocks. You can do it. Just go real slow.*

I started up the engine, but by now, other cars had turned on their headlights, and for me, that meant trouble. I sputtered out of the parking lot at two miles an hour, peering through my bioptic into a gray and barely lit road. On Hilyard Street, a main thoroughfare, the artificial lights of the oncoming cars glared at me. *Don't look at them, just keep going.*

Finally, I made it. I arrived safely on Matt's block, Alder Street.

Relieved, I made the right-hand turn into Matt's driveway. But the driveway was much shorter and narrower than I realized.

My right wheel hit the curb. With a loud thump I launched the Chevy truck right up onto his front lawn.

Matt strolled out of the house. I didn't need to honk. He knew I had arrived. In fact, the front grille of the truck was only a few feet from his living room, and the lights were glaring right through his front window.

Matt opened the driver's-side door and said, "I think I'd better drive."

I agreed.

We went to Track Town Pizza. We sat in a booth and ordered chicken artichoke pizza, and he pointed out all the famous runners in framed photos on the wall and told me their names, personal bests, and career highlights.

I told him my story; about San Diego, the Paralympics, and the Olympic Trials. He knew of the Paralympics, I was pleasantly surprised to learn. A friend of his from high school had competed in Barcelona. "Really?" I responded. He seemed to know so much—about running, about people. About everything. I'd seen a movie a few years earlier, a so-called "chick flick," *How to Make an American Quilt.* In the movie, the main character compares a relationship to making a quilt: if you put two patterns together that work, their colors and brightnesses will complement each other, but if you put the wrong squares side by side, their brilliance will fade and become dull.

Until I'd met Matt, this had been the story of my life. Every relationship I'd been in had seemed to drain me and make me feel that I had to apologize for who I was. I doubted myself rather than trusted my instincts. Matt and I complemented each other.

One night, he came over to watch television and hang out, and as we sat on the sofa he said, "Do you think this could turn into something?"

"I'm not sure," I said. But I knew as soon as I said it that I was sure. We started dating, and pretty soon we were living together.

Matt worked his heart out on my foot, but with little success. Despite three sessions a week, the scar tissue wouldn't break up. It was now almost May, and I tried to accept the idea that I would have to watch another track season from the stands.

But I tried one last-gasp measure. I called my old chiropractor in San Diego, Dr. Gary Wood, who was now practicing in Colorado Springs with his mentor, a Dr. Mike Leahy. Dr. Leahy was the creator of a soft-tissue technique called Active Release Therapy, or ART.

I bought a ticket to Colorado Springs, where I sat on Dr. Leahy's table with a high-altitude headache and went through my history. He barely seemed to listen. He took my left foot in his hands and pulled my toes down toward the floor. Then he flexed my toes back. It was like massage, sort of. After about fifteen minutes, he said, "I'm done for today. Come back the day after tomorrow."

That was it? I've come all this way for fifteen minutes? And now I have two days to kill until I see him again?

I left his office and started walking back to the Olympic Training Center, where I was staying. My head hurt so badly that I was nauseated and had to stop and sit down. A blue sports car pulled up alongside me and a voice said, "Do you want a ride?" I couldn't see the face behind the wheel, but the voice was Dr. Leahy's.

My impression was of a materialistic doctor who worked three days a week, spent only minutes with each patient, and played with his adult toys on the weekend. The sports car was so low to the ground that it was like stepping into a Go-Kart. I got in, and he drove me the short few blocks to the center. I got out of his car and said to myself, "I came here for *him*?"

But I didn't know Dr. Leahy yet. Nor did I know that he would become essential to me.

I arrived for my next treatment with a bit of attitude. I looked him in the eye and I said, "I really don't know why I've come here."

He was quiet, and then he said, "Sit down."

I sat on the examining table, and he took hold of my foot again. This time, I could feel a change. His tension was stronger, and I could actually feel the lumps of scar tissue breaking apart. It didn't hurt. By this point, my foot had grown accustomed to abuse. He slid his fingers along the arch, and the lumps that had stopped him before were disappearing. He smoothed them away. He told me to hop off the table and stand up.

Just standing felt different.

"Go up on your toes," he said.

I rose up on my toes. And I regretted every negative thing I had ever thought about Dr. Leahy. "When can I try to run?" I asked him.

"Today," he said.

That afternoon, I jogged slowly on a dirt trail down the street from the training center. Afterward, I called Dick, babbling in my excitement.

"Dick, I want to come back and qualify for the Nationals."

"I think you can do it," he said.

"And next year, the Nationals are in Eugene, right?"

"Yes."

"I want to win."

Dick knew I was talking crazy. But he never said I couldn't do it. He understood that I needed to have a plan, a purpose—a goal.

The truth was, my foot still needed a lot of work; months, in fact. By the time I left Dr. Leahy's office, he told me my foot was about 75 percent. I could run, but the plantar fascia was still not completely normal. I flew home to Eugene and to Matt, and we ran together along the river path. After two weeks, my foot pain returned. I had to accept that my season was over.

With that acceptance came a larger one. I finally accepted that if I didn't learn to heal properly, and to train properly, my career might never materialize. Dick had once told me to "let go" and allow my body a chance to heal. I never understood what he meant.

After two surgeries, innumerable cortisone injections, acupuncture, chiropractic adjustments, four pairs of orthotics, and eight months of plantar fasciitis, I finally realized I had to let go.

When I did, I learned how to run a distance race.

8. One One-Hundredth
of a Second

Perhaps only runners and watchmakers truly understand the power and delicacy of time. A subtle regulation of movement makes and marks each second. Running fast is a far more complicated business than most people realize: open the back of a clock and you will see that, in the dozens of tiny dials and cogs and coils that comprise a timepiece. Running is about the body as clock: arms as pendulums, legs as escapement. A runner organizes a million tiny motions, separate and precise, from toe flexes to arm positions, into a natural rhythm. Yet the end result should not be technical. When a runner runs, it doesn't necessarily look fast. It simply looks like a weightless, out-of-body, absence of slowness.

Running is about training the body to imitate physical laws in order to move through space as efficiently as possible. It is the most primary building block of athleticism—there isn't much be-sides golf that you can do without it—and it has a scientific lan-guage all its own. We runners discuss our sport in terms of pace: we spout streams of numbers that are unintelligible and insignifi-cant to anyone but us, we mull over records and time differen-tials—separated not by minutes, but by seconds, and tenths and even hundredths of seconds—as if they were the Dead Sea Scrolls. You might hear me say, "My workout today was three times one-K cut-downs in 2:56 and four times 200 accelerations in 28 to 30." Or you might hear me talk about negative splits, positive splits, pickups, surges, and tempos.

Every runner knows that the clock is not the only opponent. There are actually three races taking place: against the clock, against the other competitors, and against your biggest opponent, the self. There comes a point in almost every contest when you come face-to-face with yourself. The lactic acid fills your body, and the pain consumes you, and you ask the inevitable question, "What kind of person am I?"

The best runners answer the question not with thought, but with instinct. They react. There is no pondering, or questioning, or doubt. They keep moving forward, despite the excruciating pain, and against all common sense. This response is not some-thing that can be coached; an athlete must inherently possess it.

The race against self is the most important, and the most deci-sive, of the three races being run. The race for medals, money, or status is only the most externally important one. At the finish, the medalists will take the podium and be interviewed on television, and the order of finish will be printed in the newspapers. Every-one but the winner is considered a loser. But runners understand that there is a whole set of different criteria by which to judge a race. Even if I don't win the race against my opponents, I might win the internal race against myself by not giving in to pain or self-doubt, or win the race against the clock by setting a personal record. Despite what the spectators see, or what place I finish, I might very well walk away feeling victorious.

But by the spring of 1998, I barely remembered what any of these things felt like, because I had not been in a major race in over two years.

One Saturday afternoon in April, Dick Brown asked me if I'd like to go to a collegiate meet at the University of Oregon. I accepted the invitation, even though it was difficult for me to see from the grandstand. I knew Dick wanted me to study races even if I couldn't run them. I took along my monocular, and we sat in the bleachers above the back straightaway. It was raining, as usual, but the bleachers were almost full, typically. Rain never kept the die-hard Eugene track audience away from a meet.

The last race was the men's 5000 meters. "There's supposed to be a pretty good kid in this one," Dick told me.

I'm ashamed to admit this now, but I didn't even know how many laps a 5000-meter race was, or what was a respectable time. All I knew was that the conversion was 3.1 miles. The gun sounded, and I raised my monocular to my right eye and moved the telescope back and forth until the runners came into view. The runner who Dick wanted me to see was named Adam Goucher, and he was easy to spot, even for me. He went straight to the front of the pack, and he never looked back. He ran like a madman: he completed the first lap in 64 seconds, and each lap after that fell somewhere between 66 and 67 seconds. He ran alone and in the rain, and he seemed to move effortlessly.

I couldn't make out the details of his face, but I could see his movement, which was dramatically different from the pack of runners who trailed him. He was linear, and slightly forward-leaning, with no wasted energy, while the others seemed to bob up and down as if they were hopping in place. When he was leading by nearly half the track, the knowledgeable Eugene crowd rose to its feet and began clapping in sync to his cadence. He continued to knock off each lap at exactly the same pace.

For the first time, I understood the principles Dick Brown had been preaching, because I could actually see them at work. The runner's pace and rhythm were contagious, and I found myself rising and clapping with the crowd. I put my monocular over my right eye and studied him more closely each time he came down the straightaway beneath us. On the final two laps of the race, he actually *picked up* his pace. He charged home with a final 64-second lap.

"How'd he do that?" I wondered.

He had increased his pace at the finish—the very concept that Dick had stressed most, and that I had struggled most to grasp. Now, I had a perfect picture of what he meant.

Goucher's time turned out to be the fastest collegiate performance of the year.

A couple of days later, I told Matt all about the race. But it wasn't news to Matt, who had an encyclopedia of running in his head and who followed every happening in the sport. He could recite every Boston Marathon champion over the last twenty years. He knew who won which medal at which Olympic Games, and by how much, and he knew the personal-best times of international elite runners today, and what they ran when they were in college. Matt didn't just watch the sport; he studied it. And he was becoming as much of a running teacher to me as Dick Brown was.

He read deeply and avidly on the subject: he spent his Saturday mornings in my kitchen sipping coffee and buried in *Track & Field News,* or buried in a book, whether *A Cold Clear Day* or *Once A Runner* or *The Purple Runner.*

What he didn't know from reading, he knew from experience. He had competed in distances from 1500 to 10,000 meters as a collegiate runner at the University of New Hampshire, where he had captained the team and led them to a conference title in his senior year, and he still ran 85 miles a week and competed at distances up to the marathon, in between working at the medical lab and as a massage therapist. Although he stood 5'11", he weighed just 140 pounds in a black T-shirt and a pair of baggy shorts, which he had to pin at the waist so they wouldn't fall down. In comparison, I stood 5'8", and weighed 136 pounds, because I had been working out my frustrations in the weight room, doing pyramid sets of squats and dumbbell bench-presses.

"I want to learn to run like that. I have to get my foot better. I just have to," I told Matt.

"I know," Matt said. "So let's get started."

But by the summer of 1998, I was still trying to find a cure for my foot. Dr. Leahy called it "the worst case I've ever seen." It continued to nag at me, preventing me from working with Dick Brown on anything close to a full-time basis. Instead, I was working full-time at the Y as an aerobics coordinator, teaching senior fitness classes in the mornings and preschool movement classes in the afternoons.

In the mornings, Matt would read aloud from the sports pages for me, narrating the results of the Grand Prix meets in Europe. I needed to know what was going on at the world-class level, but at the same time, it hurt.

"Suzy broke four minutes in the 1500 in Monaco," he said.

"No way," I said.

"Masterkova won, barely, outkicking Szabo. The top eight times were all under four minutes."

Matt was always impressed with other runners, and it began to gnaw at me. I wanted more than anything for him to be impressed with me, too. Instead, I might as well have quit the sport, for all the running I'd done in the last two years. Maybe someday, just maybe, Matt would pick up a newspaper or open *Track & Field News* and it would be *me* he was reading about.

What if I did quit? I wondered. I brooded on that. Could I sit in the stands as a spectator, as I had with Dick at the collegiate meet, trying to squint at the track through a monocular? Could I sit there and wonder, *What if I hadn't given up?* No, I decided; I couldn't quit. Not and be a happy person. And especially not now that I had met Matt, whose passion for the sport I lived with, too.

But something had to change. I wasn't getting anywhere. I would walk with Summer along the Amazon Trail, the meandering wood-chip path that passed near my apartment, and brood as joggers passed me. To me, walking was a grueling and boring activity. *I could have run five miles by now,* I'd say to myself.

One day, while I was working at the Y, Matt called to report that he'd met a chiropractor who had some experience with Active Release, the same technique that Dr. Leahy had used successfully on my foot in Colorado Springs. I couldn't afford to travel to see Dr. Leahy regularly, so the idea that someone in Eugene might be able to treat me meant that I might finally have some prospect of recovery. I made an appointment to see Dr. John LeGat.

He turned out to be a young man in khaki Dockers and a white polo shirt. As he took my foot in his hands, he explained that he would try to duplicate the treatment that I'd had. He could feel the lumps of scar tissue along my arch and heel. From then on, Dr. LeGat treated me every other day for three weeks. The condition got worse before it got better; at work, I had to put my foot in a tub of ice water under my desk while I signed time sheets and did other paperwork. I even bought a rolling pin that I used to roll under my arch. Before long, I was running between seven and ten miles a day, although slowly.

It was too late, however, for my relationship with Dick Brown. He spent most of the late spring and summer traveling with his other athletes, and I didn't mind his absence. Actually, I was relieved not to have to report to him each day the status of my foot—he usually asked me to give him a number between one and ten. I felt a responsibility to paint a pretty picture of what was going on, because I didn't want to disappoint him. But it was a welcome respite when I could just deal with the injury, instead of trying to convince Dick that I was getting better.

The American record in the 800 fell that year—and not to a practiced distance runner, but to a sprinter. Jearl Miles-Clark, an Olympian at 400 meters, had moved up to the 800 and stunned everyone with her performance of 1:56.78. (In the next two years she would lower it twice more, to 1:56.40.) I was more frustrated than ever, and I began to question some of Dick's theories on endurance and what I felt was a lack of intensity in his regimen. I wanted some faster stuff, form-drills, and "strides"—quick bursts of speed at a relaxed effort-level.

Finally, I confronted him. Sitting in the café at the Y, we got into an uncomfortable discussion that left me in tears. I challenged his program. "It's monotonous," I said. And then I accused him of making me vulnerable to injury; the six to seven months of steady mileage had been a significant factor in my foot pain. This was unfair of me: my string of injuries was not Dick's fault. It was no one's fault but my own. But I'd simply had enough. The lack of variety was driving me crazy.

"What about drills, and strides?" I asked. "Maybe even a time-trial once in a while?" Dick said he was agreeable to that. But then I said, "What about breaking apart some of the long runs into two runs in a day?"

"They need to be continuous," Dick insisted.

I couldn't face it. I needed a change. Dick was an intelligent coach and a kind man, and he had taught me everything about how to run. But his program required patience and trust, and by this point, I had neither. We weren't working well together. By the end of the discussion, we agreed to part ways.

After our meeting, I sat in an office and cried. *What the hell was I doing with my life?* I wondered. I was almost 30, and to leave Dick was difficult. I had moved to Eugene for him. I had all but convinced myself that if it didn't work out with him, my career was over.

Running at an elite level now seemed totally out of the question.

But I still had Matt. He became an even more integral part of my life, and gradually, as my spirits improved and my foot felt a little better, we began some light trail running together. "Just a few easy miles, to see how your foot is," Matt coaxed. It felt so good to just run again. I told myself that I was running strictly to enjoy Matt's company and Eugene's beautiful summer mornings. I didn't ask for much more.

Then one day, Matt said, "There's a 5K road race at Alton Baker Park in September. Do you want to run it?"

It was a low-key, 3.1-mile race along the bike path that I was quite familiar with.

"Okay," I said hesitantly.

I won the 5K race with a pedestrian time of 17:57, but, frankly, I was just elated to break 18 minutes. More important, my foot held up throughout.

Soon, I was back running mileage again. I still felt aches and pains—bursitis in my hip socket was injury number four in two years—but gradually they ebbed away, and I wondered if I might resume my career. My mood improved, too, when I left my unchallenging job at the Y and began teaching children again. Initially, I was hired by the local school district to help part-time with an Easter Seals swim program for multiply disabled students, but soon I branched out into home-schooling kids who were too ill to go to class. The income was more than my full-time job at the Y paid, so I quit. Teaching brought back my confidence; I was good at it. And it gave me more free time—which meant more time to run.

I needed a coach, I decided. There were other first-rate coaches in Eugene, I'd learned. One of them was Mike Manley, a 1972 U.S. Olympian in the 3000-meter steeplechase, who had known and trained with the late Steve Prefontaine, possibly the greatest male American distance runner in history. I knew Mike by reputation only—he coached a large group of runners of widely varying abilities—while he didn't know me at all. I called him up cold, one night in December.

"Hi, my name is Marla Runyan, and uh, I run the 800 meters . . . uh . . . I ran 2:04 at the Trials in '96."

"Uh-huh," he said, unimpressed.

"Well, I wondered if maybe you might work with me."

"I've got several runners right now, and I've got my hands full," he said. "I don't think I can take anyone new right now. Call me back at the end of January."

"Okay," I said, disappointed.

I continued to train on my own. One rainy Saturday morning, I suited up and stretched on the living room floor.

"My hip is tight," I told Matt.

"You know, there will always be something," he said. "Sometimes you just have to run through it, a little each day, and it actually gets better."

"Should I go out there?" I asked, pointing to the living room window, which was dripping with condensation. The temperature was about 35 degrees.

"I can't tell you what to do. It's your hip. You can always try, and if it hurts, stop."

It sounded simple enough. Either you can run, or you can't. No more walk-jogging. No more babying my body. Just get out there and get on with it.

I headed out. I'd heard through word of mouth what kind of tough workouts Mike Manley gave his runners, among them a horrendous hill run up in Hendrix Park, over a series of rarely traveled paved roads, rough and full of potholes. The trail wound through a beautiful series of pine- and fern-covered undulations, where some of the wealthier homes in town were. It made for a perfect continuous hill circuit.

I decided to try it. I came to a climb of a quarter mile or so to the top of Hendrix Park. I changed gears and charged upward. Near the top, I did a U-turn and headed back down. I decided to repeat it six times before moving on. Up again, this time faster, trying to maintain my pace from beginning to end. And again, and again.

On the sixth hill, I didn't stop. I kept going, up toward Skyline Drive, where I passed a memorial to Prefontaine. To the right of the narrow road was a wall of rock—the place where Prefontaine had crashed his car and died in 1975. I knew the memorial consisted of a picture and an engraving, from what Matt had told me, although I wasn't able to make it out clearly. Scattered about were old ribbons and medals that local runners had placed there in his honor. As I ran past the plaque, breathing hard from the hill, I managed to say out loud, "Hey, Pre, how's it going?"

I reached the top of Mount Hendrix, and paused for a moment to decide what to do next. A steeper and longer hill to the west looked good, so I headed upward again, and tried to keep my pace steady. I repeated this hill four times. Each time, I talked myself to the top. *This is how it's going to feel, just like this, it's going to hurt. This is the race right here, this is where you have to pick it up.* In my mind I wasn't on a desolate hill in the rain, my breath a cloud of fog. Instead, I was on a track, nearing the final turn, as the burn entered my legs.

I headed back down the mountain, on a winding road through tall trees and ferns, and even though the rain still fell, I wasn't cold. It had been a good day. I arrived back at the apartment and threw open the door, exultant.

"I did it," I said to Matt, "and my hip was okay."

In January, I was dying to call Mike Manley. I knew his group met every Tuesday evening at a certain trail, and I wondered if he would let me join in. I called him one evening and asked if I could just tag along.

"As long as you know I'm not officially coaching you."

"I know," I said.

I suited up in my old Moving Comfort gear and a few Nike remnants: long tights, a long-sleeved Lycra shirt, a second layer on top, a jacket, a pair of Matt's running gloves, and a hat. I laced up a pair of trainers I'd bought on sale. Then I stood in the middle of our tiny apartment waiting for 4 P.M. to arrive.

It was cold and raining hard, and very dark, but I didn't care. I didn't worry about the weather, or if I would be able to see the trail in the dark. I would run no matter what, because this could be my future coach. I grabbed the doorknob and turned to Matt and said, "If this doesn't work, I don't know what I'm going to do." I went out into the dark.

The workouts I'd done on my own paid off: I handled Mike's regimen and stayed with the group easily on that first day. From then on, I continued to run with his group every Tuesday and Saturday, on an informal basis. Each week, I watched enviously as Mike gave his athletes sheets of paper with their week's workouts written out.

One Tuesday evening, after we had finished a trail run, Mike handed me a piece of paper, too.

"I guess I'm coaching you now," he said.

I rushed home and burst through the door. "Matt, come look at this!" I yelled. "I got a piece of paper, too!" I threw it under my CCTV and began to study Mike's writing. I got so much happiness and relief from that single sheet of paper. It meant I had a coach. I had no idea where I would go from here, but I was an athlete again.

Mike and I sat down and discussed my training and my goals for the upcoming season. "I would really like to qualify for the Nationals in the 800," I said. The U.S. Nationals that year would be held right at home in Eugene, and I longed to run in front of that crowd.

I had another, more far-fetched goal. In national and international competition, there are three rounds, or heats. Only the top eight qualify for the final. "Maybe . . . maybe I could even make it to the final," I added.

"That seems reasonable," Mike said.

We got down to work. Mike's emphasis was on strength and stamina, similar to Dick Brown's, but he also introduced me to the "tempo run"—a three-to-five-mile run at an even pace, maximizing breathing, but just shy of oxygen debt. At first, I couldn't maintain the 5:20-per-mile pace like his other runners. But, gradually, I improved. I was getting stronger, and I didn't even know it.

My first test would be an early-season race called the Mount SAC Relays, a popular annual meet in southern California in August, a four-day affair during which high school, college, open, and elite athletes would all compete. The 800 was an invitational event, and in order to get an invite, I needed a fast time. I didn't have a fast time—I had no time at all. My last race had been three years earlier.

I lied on the application. I wrote down a personal record (track people call it a "PR") of 2:03.8, and stated that I had run it in Canada the year before. The truth was, I'd spent the entire season sitting on a stationary bike at the YMCA. I wasn't anywhere near Canada. But I tossed it in the mail and hoped for the best.

I got in. I would be competing in a field of eight elite international athletes, among them Michelle Ave, Dick Brown's former 800 runner. Matt and I packed our bags and headed for California.

There was a lot riding on this race: it would tell all. It would tell me if I was training in the right way, or if my move to Eugene had been one big mistake. What's more, it was my first trip back to California since I had left in 1996, and my parents would be in the grandstand. There was an added element of pressure: I would be running in front of my former college coach, Rahn Sheffield.

The day of the meet was hot and smoggy, with temperatures approaching 105 degrees on the track. I warmed up with a twenty-minute jog in a field behind the stadium, where it was quiet and less crowded and where there was some shade. I checked in at the last minute to avoid that relentless sunshine. The runners crowded together under a small patch of shade provided by an official's umbrella.

Finally, they called our race. I stepped onto the synthetic surface, and my spikes dug in, and I ran down the straightaway. To those in the stands who knew me, I was scarcely recognizable, at 124 pounds and with a completely different build. I wore a red-and-orange Moving Comfort running top and a pair of old black briefs, not exactly cut to modern-day standards. They looked like control-top underwear. I also wore an old pair of Killer Loop sunglasses from 1995, with no idea that they were completely out of style.

I heard a voice say, "All right, Marla!"

It was Rahn. After three years, that voice still meant speed to me. "You got this, girl, you can do it," he said. I could hear a laugh in his voice, and it relieved me. In the back of my mind, I'd wondered if he would hope for me to fail. Instead, he was *cheering for me.* But it made me nervous, too. I wanted to show him what I'd learned.

To calm myself down, I reminded myself to be grateful that I was not on a stationary bike at the YMCA, nor was I aqua-jogging in the pool or running up a lonely hill in the rain. I was about to run a race. Just a race.

The gun sounded. Tina Paulina from Mozambique took off next to me. I immediately fell to the back, holding on at the end of the string of runners. Coming around on the first lap, I was still in last. I thought, *Maybe I'm not ready for this.*

The leaders came across the 400-meter mark in 56 seconds. I crossed the mark in 60-flat—still in last place.

"Catch 'em on the backstretch!" It was Rahn again.

Off the third turn, I started passing people. They began to tire, and I moved up. Now I could see the shapes of the leaders—which meant they weren't too far off. I gritted my teeth. It was starting to hurt.

Everyone began screaming, typical of the audience at Mount SAC, coaches screaming at the top of their lungs at young kids and Olympians alike. As we headed into the final turn, the screams intensified, and so did the pain. But I was still gaining ground, still moving up. I kept my pace even, and finally I passed one more runner. Then I locked up. I held on, somehow—and crossed the line in fourth.

That had better be a PR, was the first thought that entered my mind. For that much pain, there had better be some kind of reward. And there was.

In the infield, I asked an official my time, in between pants and moans with my hands clasped over my knees.

"Runyan? Let's see here . . . Runyan . . . 2:03.81," he said.

"2:03!" I screeched.

It wasn't a lie anymore. The time qualified me for the U.S. Nationals.

Life was good: I was able to train and race again, and I had renewed faith in what I was learning about running. I was able to feel and experience it without pain.

One day at the track as we practiced technique and form, Mike said to me, "You see that line right there . . . the white one?" He pointed to the white lanes painted on the red surface.

"Yeah," I said. I was standing right on it.

"You only need to pick your feet up high enough to step over that line."

His point was that I didn't need to waste time and energy lifting my knees and feet up high. That motion had no bearing on forward motion.

"Run from the inside," Mike would say. He would lean his body up and forward on the track, and insist, "Feel like a rope is pulling you up and out." My form was changing: I could feel my legs underneath me, not breaking my momentum but propelling me forward.

When we ran long intervals or tempos on the track, Mike would stand on the infield and yell, "Rhythm, rhythm, rhythm!" He wanted us to feel the pace, to memorize it and ingrain it into our systems, so that we could find it again in a race without ever thinking about it.

I was good at pace, I discovered. I could find a 66-second pace per 400, on every lap, almost to within a tenth of a second. And I could maintain that pace, 33 seconds flat for every 200 meters, for a full 800. I was experiencing something new, and I liked it. I was beginning to wonder if I was meant for longer distances.

At the end of May, the best runners in the nation flocked to Eugene for the Prefontaine Classic. The "Pre" meet, as it's fondly known, is a Grand Prix event broadcast on CBS and is perhaps the most prestigious annual track event in the country.

For the last two years, I'd watched it from the stands, but this year would be different. Mike went to the race organizer, Tom Jordan, and told him about my 2:03, and asked him to enter me in the 800 meters. Jordan refused; only runners who were sub-2:00 would be in the field, he said. But Jordan did offer me $500 to rabbit the 1500, meaning to run the race as a pacesetter for the real contenders. Or, he said, I could just run the 1500 as a competitor.

Mike reported all this one afternoon about ten days before the meet, after a long trail workout. I looked down at my mud-caked legs—it had been a hard day. I glanced back up at Mike and said, "I'm running."

He smiled. "I was hoping you would say that."

Ten days later I stood on the starting line for the first 1500-meter race of my career. I had no idea whether or not I was ready for this distance, especially not in this company. Some of the best runners in the world were there, including Regina Jacobs, the three-time Olympian, and Leah Pells, the Canadian national champion. I stood way out, in position No. 17. There were seventeen runners in the field, and I was the least of them, just a local girl with no qualifying time.

The gun sounded, and we were off. The early pace was tolerable, I decided, and I found myself near the front of the pack. I didn't know how to feel. This distance was a total unknown to me. *When will I start to hurt?* I wondered.

I remained steady as we approached the end of the third lap. The bell clanged. Now everyone started to move. Time to run. Around me, I sensed the shifting of gears. I started to pick it up, too. With 300 meters to go, I moved into fourth place. I was running just outside the leaders.

Regina Jacobs showed why she was among the best in the world: she moved to the front and took off for home, unchallenged. Still in fourth, I headed off the final turn for home, too, with every bit of remaining energy I could muster. But just before the line I tied up, barely able to lift my legs off the ground. I was passed—and finished fifth.

But for me, this was a victory. I bent over, gasping.

My time of 4:11.81 qualified me for the National Championships. It was a total surprise, and caused a stir in the knowledgeable Eugene crowd.

It also caused a quandary for Mike and me. Not long afterward, we stood on the track at Hayward Field and discussed our options. We had to choose which event I would run at the Nationals, the 800 or the 1500. My performance in the Pre had baffled everyone, including us.

"I still think you can run a good eight," Mike said, shrugging.

But I was tempted to run the 1500—perhaps because it was new, and I felt untapped in my potential at the distance; or perhaps because I suddenly felt there was little room to improve in the 800, while the 1500 had brand-new possibilities.

"Let's flip a coin," Mike said.

He pulled a quarter out of his pocket.

"Heads, you run the 1500; tails, you run the 800, okay?"

"Okay," I agreed.

Mike flipped the coin, caught it, and slapped it on his forearm.

"What do you *want* it to be?" he asked, teasing me.

"Heads," I replied.

Heads it was.

That's how I became a 1500-meter runner.

The 1999 Nationals came to Eugene. I was about to race against some of the biggest names in track and field; people I had only heard about, or read about, or seen on television. I was a total novice, and, to compound my inexperience, the semifinal heats were cancelled. That meant there would be just one heat, the final, and this made me extremely nervous. The race would be my second attempt ever at the 1500.

I stood on that line, in my marmalade-colored uniform, old granny briefs, and store-bought spikes, and as I waited for the gun, I knew that I had no business being in the race.

Regina Jacobs bolted off the starting line. As usual, Regina was the class of the field, a smooth and distinctive runner, all legs, with a pixie haircut. There was talk that she was chasing the stadium record of 4:00, or maybe even going after Mary Decker Slaney's American record of 3:57. Regina was always chasing some kind of record; for some years now she had been America's strongest distance runner, the lone U.S. medalist in the company of Romania's Gabriela Szabo and Russia's Svetlana Masterkova.

When she bolted, the entire field went with her—and I went straight to the back. I was wary of running at such a pace so early. It seemed ridiculous to go out so hard when there were still two and three-quarters laps to go.

At 400 meters I was still in last place, with a lap time of 64 seconds. I began to doubt myself. *Maybe I can't do this. Maybe this isn't my event.* The leaders were not within my view. Instead, I relied on the commentator calling the meet over the loudspeaker to tell me what was going on. *There's nothing like being a spectator at your own race.*

Gradually, I passed a couple of people . . . and then a couple more. I couldn't count how many, but it seemed as though on every turn and every straightaway, I moved up in position. I still doubted myself, however. I ran hesitantly; the leaders were still somewhere beyond my vision. They might as well have been a mile away, as far as I was concerned.

Finally, the bell sounded. The field was thinning in front of me. Things grew clearer. I heard the announcer call off the order of position by last name, like roll call. To my surprise, I was in sixth. And I hadn't yet extended myself.

What the hell are you doing? Go! I went into an all-out kick. It was as if I had finally started running the race. I moved up, and up. Off the final turn, I could see the second- and third-place runners, Stephanie Best and Shayne Culpepper, and I knew I was gaining ground on them.

But the finish line was too close by this time, and I ran out of room to catch them. I crossed the line in fourth.

I just stood there in disbelief. I wasn't even tired. Two competitors were half-carried off the track, completely exhausted. Others were down on their knees. And I just stood there. *I wasn't even tired.*

And that's when it began to hurt.

There is a pain worse than what you feel in a race: the pain of knowing you didn't run your best. That pain, I suddenly understood, I would have to live with for days, months, and perhaps even the rest of my life. It was worse than losing. *There's something worse than losing,* I realized.

Had I finished fourth with an honest effort, after giving it my all, I could have lived with it. Had I been half-dragged off the track in utter exhaustion, I could have lived with that, too. But to walk off the track feeling that there was more inside me that I could have given—that was the greatest pain I've ever experienced. I felt something close to sickness; it was as though my heart had turned black inside my body.

I didn't sleep. It was such a missed opportunity: here were the U.S. National Championships in Eugene—my home—and here I was in a new physique, with a new coach, running well, *and I'd blown it.* Had I run harder, I could have finished in the medals and qualified for the World Championship team. Instead, I had doubted myself.

I lay there in the dark. Matt was fast asleep. I stared at the ceiling, the blot in my eyes flitting across it as usual. Then I noticed something. On the north wall of my bedroom hung the Olympic flag, with the five colored rings intertwined and the giant red letters "USA" just above it. The flag had been there for months. The only light that entered our room came from the parking lot outside, where a floodlight stayed on all night.

A beam of light streamed through the curtains and hit the flag, illuminating it against the wall. It glowed. It was the only thing in the room that was visible to me—everything else was black. I hesitate to tell you this story, because it sounds too stagey, like a cinematic cliché. But the Olympic rings were aglow. I tried to make sense out of what I was seeing. Was it a sign or a message, telling me I was capable of more?

I never did sleep. I stared at the flag, and re-lived that terrible race over and over in my head until the sun came up. I got out of bed, put on my shoes, and went for a run.

Sometimes a mistake is the best thing that can happen to you. It depends on what you choose to do about it: whether you ignore it, and thus repeat it, or whether you decide to learn from it, so as not to repeat it ever again. I decided that I had to right my wrong.

There was a race in Maine on the Saturday following the Nationals, part of a string of meets in the Northeast and Canada known as the Can-Am series. I had every intention of being there. There was still an outside chance that I could qualify for the World Championships, if I could run a fast enough time in Maine.

I whipped out my Visa card, bought airline tickets to Boston for myself and Matt, and laid down the plastic again for an SUV rental.

Here was the deal: the runners who had beaten me at the Nationals, with the exception of Regina Jacobs, had not run fast enough to qualify for the World Championships. To be named to the national team that would travel to Seville, Spain, for the Worlds, you had to log a time under 4:08 in the 1500. There were five of us who still had a shot at it, and we all headed to Maine, where we had hopes of meeting the qualifying standard and thus making the team.

As we lined up at the start in Maine, each of us had one and the same thing in mind: to nail that time.

The gun sounded, and we took off. No doubts this time, and no regrets; I intended to walk away proud, no matter what happened. For the first lap and a half, I was in third place, running stride for stride next to Stephanie Best, who had finished second at the Nationals. Then I picked it up. I passed Stephanie, and then a girl in red I didn't recognize. As it turned out, she was the rabbit—the designated pacesetter for the field.

Matt stood on the infield and gave me my split-time as I passed the 800-meter mark. "2:12!" he yelled. I was on pace, but barely.

I was also in the lead now—and I wasn't looking back. When I had less than a lap to go, Matt tried to shout my 1200 time at me, but it was inaudible because a roar had started to build in the crowd. Bells were clanging, the announcer was screaming over the loudspeaker, and the track was encircled with howling, distance-loving fans.

I bore down, as acid began filling my legs. Just 200 meters to go. 100. I gripped at the track with my spikes as hard as I could— and a white paper banner broke across my chest at the finish line. I stumbled onto the grass. There was a large digital clock just in front of me but I couldn't see the time that it displayed.

"What was my time?" I demanded, gasping for air.

Matt came bounding over. "4:06!!" he screamed, and vaulted over me as I crumpled to the grass.

When I finally got my breath back, I borrowed a cell phone from an official, and I called Mike Manley.

"Mike, we're going to Spain!"

Initially, I cared very little about the Pan-American Games. I was anxious to get to Seville and the World Championships, but first I had to run in the Pan-Am Games. They seemed in the way, an inconvenience.

The Pan-Ams take place every three years and are like a smaller version of the Olympic Games, for countries from North, South, and Central America. On this occasion they would be held in Winnipeg, and the U.S. national team would send two athletes. Regina Jacobs, the national champion, turned down the invitation, and Shayne Culpepper, the third-place finisher, was injured. That left Stephanie Best and me, and I felt obliged to go.

To help me get ready for world-class competition, Matt and I studied tapes of classic races. We watched footage of famous Olympic runners, and studied their strategies, learning from them. Matt got a copy of Steve Prefontaine's famed Munich Olympic 5000-meter race, and I crouched in front of the television and watched him run lap after lap, his hair flying behind him. That race has haunted runners for years, and it began to haunt me.

The race was painfully slow. Early on, the field ran so sluggishly that they seemed to be at a 10,000-meter pace. It was the kind of race that grated the nerves and tested your patience as much as your stamina. Often, races in the Olympic Games or World Championships are slow, tactical ones, because there is no pre-established pacesetter. In races for medals, no one wants to lead. To lead means to jeopardize your stamina. The other runners will "sit" on the leader, who is doing all the work. Physiologically, it takes 10 percent less energy to follow in a race than to lead—much like drafting in cycling. When winners are decided by mere fractions of seconds, this extra expenditure is significant.

Steve Prefontaine found himself in that very situation in 1972. He knew that if he sprinted to the front and took the race out fast, his opponents would use him, only to pass him on the final lap. So, he sat. He ran within the pack, waiting . . . waiting. He was waiting for the *real* race to begin. The result? With a mile to go, fearing that he lacked the sprint-finish speed of his opponents, he began a long drive, hoping to wear the kick out of their legs. With a lap to go, he was in third place. He could have stayed there, and sat, and perhaps taken the bronze medal. But he wanted the gold, because that was Pre, and he went after it on the backstretch of the final lap. He surged to the front, but he didn't have enough left. He had made that last mile the fastest of any 5000 that had ever been run—close to four minutes—but he faltered just five meters from the finish and placed fourth. Even so, Pre's brave tactic became both legendary and widely debated, because every runner eventually confronts the basic dilemma of a tactical race, and fears that sickening sensation of finishing a race with something still left.

The Pan-Ams would be another crucial piece of my runner's education. I arrived in Winnipeg to find that Leah Pells, the Canadian national champion, was entered. Leah had finished fourth at the 1996 Olympics, and she had just run 4:04 for 1500 in Europe that summer. And she would be running in front of a home crowd.

The night before the race, I called Mike Manley from the hallway of the dorm where I was staying.

"Mike, Leah Pells is in the race," I said.

"Well, she's tough," Mike said.

He didn't always say the right thing.

"How do I beat her?" I asked.

"It will be a tactical race," he said. "If you ever take the lead, you had better be prepared to finish with it."

It sounded more like a threat than a piece of advice. I took it to bed with me that night, and I thought about it all through the next day as I prepared for the race.

The following evening, we gathered in the starting area as the sun was setting. The stadium was full, and the air was warm, and as I shook out my nerves, I reminded myself once again to see the race as a blessing and an opportunity.

As Mike had predicted, the race started slowly—so slowly, in fact, that I had never experienced anything like it. We practically walked around the track. We clocked 76 seconds on the first lap. I sat, and I sat, lurking somewhere in fifth or sixth place. *Let someone else lead . . . the race hasn't even started yet.* But always, I kept the red of Leah's uniform within view.

I tried to stay as smooth and efficient as possible. The pace picked up slightly, to a 65-second third lap, but I barely noticed. It felt comfortable. Finally, the bell clanged.

Leah bolted.

She passed Stephanie Best.

I hesitated for a moment. But with 300 meters to go, I told myself, *Now. Go now.* I hoped that I had an edge; that I had conserved that anaerobic fuel tank Dick Brown had taught me so much about. I moved quickly into second place, watching the red of Leah's uniform from the corner of my eye.

She was in front of me by four strides. But gradually, I could feel her coming closer to me. I was gaining.

We flew into the final turn. I didn't dare try to change gears, I just maintained my stride, and I ran wide, out in Lane Two. I came up on her shoulder. The crowd was deafening, pulling for their own runner. But I turned it around. *They're cheering for me.* I knew it was a lie, but I needed their energy.

We ran in unison down the straightaway, arms and legs moving side by side, as if we were attached at the hip. I couldn't move any faster—and neither, it appeared, could she. If I bore down any harder, I knew I would tie up and falter. *Just get to the finish, and get your torso across that line first.* I could feel we were almost there, even though the finish line was invisible to me. I could see shapes of the timers on the infield just to the left of the line.

Moments before we hit the finish, I lunged. I planted my right foot into the ground and thrust myself, like a takeoff for the long jump. We crossed the line.

It was too close to call. A photo finish.

My first thought was *That was awesome!* I didn't care whether or not I had won. I had run the best race I could ask of myself, and the reward was in knowing that.

Leah took my hand and we jogged a victory lap together, still not sure of the order of finish. As we came past the final turn, Leah looked up at the large Magnavision screen, which was displaying a continuous slow-motion instant replay of our race.

Suddenly the crowd moaned. A black-and-white Acutrack photograph of the finish had appeared on the screen, but I couldn't see it.

"Who won?" I asked.

"You did," she said.

I had won—by one one-hundredth of a second.

I threw my arms in the air. As much as I had told myself to run for the sake of running, and not for medals, I did want the gold medal, after all. Leah remained standing as I continued the victory lap down the straightaway.

After the lap, the medalists were escorted to a fenced-in holding area where the media waited. The press came at me like a large, anxious creature. Tape recorders were thrust in my face, and voices yelled questions at me simultaneously. Then one voice separated itself from the others.

"Marla, tell us about your eyes!"

You have got to be kidding me. After I've won a gold medal in only my fourth 1500—you want to know about my eyes?

I wanted to say, "Did you watch the race?" At that moment the subject of my eyesight seemed the most inappropriate and irrelevant topic I could think of. *Weren't they paying attention?* They had overlooked the excitement and the drama of the race itself. Why couldn't they let my accomplishment stand on its own?

I paused. I didn't want to answer the question, especially with my opponents nearby. But I knew if I refused, my answer could be misconstrued, and they would think I was angry or bitter about my disability. I decided to answer the question as quickly as possible, and maybe they'd be satisfied and we could talk about the race.

I took a deep breath and I rattled off, "I have Stargardt's disease, spelled S-T-A-R-G-A-R-D-T-apostrophe-S, which is a juvenile form of macular degeneration, and I've had it since I was nine years old, and it caused me to have 20/400 vision in both eyes and it is not correctable with glasses or contacts. But I don't feel it impairs my ability to run competitively."

It didn't work.

"What do you see right now?"

"Can you see that man over there?"

"How do you run?"

"Have you ever fallen down?"

"Why did you start running?"

Not one question about the race.

Finally, the creature put away its pens and microphones and receded. A single figure remained, a man. I couldn't see his face, but I could feel his eyes looking at me. As I began to pull on my sweats, he approached me calmly, as if he had been patiently waiting for the media creature to leave.

"Hello, Marla, I'm Ray Flynn," he said with a touch of an Irish accent.

"Oh, hi!" I said. "I've seen you race."

I had watched Ray Flynn on one of the classic race videos that Matt had shown me. Ray had run in the 1984 Los Angeles Olympics and was Ireland's national record-holder in the mile. Now he was working as an agent, representing track and field athletes.

"You know," he said, "if you can run every race like that, the way you did today, you have a future."

Finally, here was someone who wanted to talk about the race and who didn't seem to care about my eyes. He saw me as an athlete, and that was all that mattered to him.

"I know you need to go," he said. "But let's talk again."

I'd never had an agent before. Was he suggesting he would be willing to represent me? I had a million questions. I knew Ray was not your stereotypical agent. He was no "Jerry Maguire," and I wasn't a football player saying "Show me the money." But a free pair of shoes would be nice.

Later that evening, I stood on the top platform of the awards podium and was presented with a gold medal. The U.S. national anthem played for an almost-empty stadium, but I cried anyway, thinking about how much things had changed. I had not given up, even when my body had told me to. *One year ago today you were on a stationary bike at the YMCA.* I'd cried on that bike, too.

———

Things were beginning to change. A box containing six new pairs of running shoes arrived from the ASICS company, which was interested in becoming my sponsor.

Up to then, I'd been wearing an old pair of Nike spikes that I'd ordered from a catalogue. Now I agreed to sign a contract with ASICS for six months, on one condition: that they pay Mike's way to Seville. They did more: they gave me $5,000 in travel money and offered a couple of performance bonuses if I ran well at the World Championships.

After I signed the contract, the UPS man became my best friend. He arrived not too long afterward with a half-dozen boxes full of shirts, tights, shorts, and winter gear, and it was all top quality, nicer than anything I'd ever owned before. It was Christmas in July.

Newspapers, radio stations, and magazines were leaving messages on my voice-mail. The *Today* show came to Eugene and filmed me working out for three days. I wasn't sure how to handle any of it—it was crazy and exhausting. I just wanted to get ready for the Worlds.

Finally, it was time to go. It took twenty-six hours and four flight connections to get to Seville from Eugene, including a long layover in the Munich airport, which was filled with thick cigarette smoke. But finally, we were there. Matt and I went to the hotel for the U.S. athletes, and found the dining area. As we stood in the doorway, Matt's jaw dropped.

"What?" I asked.

Matt stared around the room at all of the elite runners he read about in *Track & Field News*. The teams from Portugal and Kenya were also staying in our hotel, and the dining room was jammed with some of the most famous runners in the world, lounging over lunch in their sweats. There was Paul Tergat, the Kenyan 10,000-meter runner, who would take his second Olympic silver medal in Sydney. And Daniel Komen, the world record-holder in the 3000, also from Kenya. Rosa Mota of Portugal had won the Olympic women's marathon in '88 and the Boston Marathon twice. There was the Kenyan world record-holder in the women's marathon, Tegla Loroupe, and the three-time Boston Marathon champ, Ibrahim Hussein, yet another Kenyan.

To me, Seville was a blur of dust and heat and pollution. There was one oasis, a small park adjacent to Estadio Olimpico, with a few trees and a cool grass lawn. On the evening of my first heat in the World Championships, I went to the park and jogged for about twenty minutes, trying to relax. Then it was time to move to the warmup track.

They called the runners to check in about forty minutes before the race, and then we were quarantined in a collection of tents adjacent to the warmup area. Our bags were inspected for illegal items, and our numbers and uniforms were checked, as was the length of the spikes in our shoes.

Finally, they lined us up and we entered Estadio Olimpico on a descending ramp that took us into a dimly lit tunnel. No one spoke. But each athlete was talking to herself in her own mind, and, despite the silence, it felt like several conversations were still going on.

In the heart of the stadium, beneath the roaring crowd in the grandstands, there was a small stretch of track on which we could do strides. Then we were called into a small room where hip numbers were dispensed. The lighting in the tunnel was dull and gray, but the sound of the crowd above was so loud that the officials had to yell out our names to hand us our hip numbers.

We lined up again and marched toward the stadium entrance. As we came around a corner, the tunnel became even darker— and then, straight ahead of me, I could see light. As we walked toward it, the light changed colors, until finally it opened up, and we stepped into Estadio Olimpico itself.

It was as if Dorothy had just opened the door of her house and stepped into Oz.

It was that magnificent. I had never experienced anything like it. The stadium was shaped like a bowl, and the seats ran up very steeply, creating a wall of 60,000 people. The rim of the stadium curved inward, almost enclosing the arena. There was no direct sunlight, and no wind, just crisp national flags, hanging still and brilliant in the evening air. It was dusk.

The track was redder than any that I'd ever seen. And the grass on the infield seemed greener than any that I'd seen, too. The crowd was a wall of colors and sound. I was very thankful that my first view of this magnificent stadium was as a competitor, not as a spectator watching some race through a monocular.

Everything seemed so clear that I felt fully sighted. Perhaps it was the lighting. Or perhaps it was the adrenaline pumping through my arteries that made me hypersensitive to color, sound, and temperature. *Those press people are making a big deal out of nothing. I can see fine.*

We walked 200 meters along the shoulder of the track, still single-file, and arrived at the start. Fifteen of us took the line. Only five of us would advance to the final.

I thought for only a moment that if I did poorly, everyone would be disappointed in me, especially the press that had made so much of my disability.

But then I told myself that I was here by my own choosing and the only judgment that mattered was my own.

The race went out fast, and confusedly. Just like Dorothy, I wasn't in Eugene anymore. Everyone jockeyed for position. I have never been good off the line, and in all the jostling, I found myself in the back. The pack moved at a decent pace, but we were all clumped together, close in abilities and fitness.

The pace changed, surged, then settled. One moment I felt left behind, then the next I would suddenly run up on someone's heels, and then again the pack lurched forward. I was still near the back, and staying in touch with the middle of the pack was a constant struggle. *Maybe I'm not ready for this,* I said to myself as we approached the 800.

Just as I'd done at the Nationals, I began to question my ability. With this thought came an overwhelming sense of tiredness— almost despair. I pushed it away.

The energy I was using to run within the pack was wasteful, I decided. This pack was controlling me and I was at its mercy. I decided to try to find a rhythm, even if it was at the back. This was my only chance.

I drifted to the back, and was nearly in last place when the bell sounded.

I accelerated, and that feeling of fatigue disappeared. Suddenly, I felt fresh. I began moving up on the backstretch. I worked my way from twelfth to tenth. Just before the final turn, I moved up again and joined the front-running group of about seven athletes. We would all be fighting over those last meters for the five qualifying positions.

I could feel that the runners behind me were shutting down, turning off, as if they had already concluded that a top-five finish wasn't in them. I'd spent much of the race running wide, trying to stay clear of traffic, and as I accelerated down the backstretch I still stayed wide, passing runners who were on the inside.

As we headed into the final turn, I sensed a gap, and moved into Lane One. But the runners just ahead of me slowed down, and another runner came up on my outside. I was boxed in.

As we came off the turn, my momentum had been killed by my position and I was in sixth place. *Don't panic. Wait.* The runner on the outside moved up.

I moved out.

I passed two more runners to my inside.

I crossed the line in fourth place, but I didn't know it yet. I was still accelerating through the finish when I realized it was over. I'd qualified for the finals—and I'd run a personal best of 4:05.27, besides, with a final lap of 61 seconds. But it had felt more like a roller-coaster ride than 1500 meters.

I had experienced every possible emotion, from doubt to fatigue, to confidence and a final burst of aggression, in the space of just four minutes and five seconds.

Back at the warmup track, Mike and Matt were waiting for me. They had high-fived each other in the stands the moment I crossed the line, and now they wrapped me in hugs.

I lingered to enjoy the moment and the rest of the evening as the sun finally set and the stadium lights were illuminated. As I took one more casual lap around the track, I heard a voice say, "How'd you do, Runyan?"

It was Regina Jacobs. On this evening, we weren't competitors but teammates. Regina had just run—and won—her own semifinal heat, and now she was cooling down.

"I made it," I said. "I even ran a PR."

"What'd you run?" she asked.

I told her my time, and she congratulated me, and then we jogged for a few minutes chatting about other things.

"Isn't your birthday this weekend?" I asked her.

"Yeah, it seems I'm always in some other country on my birthday."

I went back to the hotel to rest. I felt a rush of pride, and acceptance, and achievement. Regina and I would run the World Championships final together.

The next day, I went to lunch at the hotel, in the formal dining room with its round tables covered in white tablecloths, where the world's greatest runners were gathered. I sat at a table for a while with Tegla Loroupe, one of my heroes. Then Jearl Miles-Clark sat down and congratulated me on my performance. I felt so self-conscious around her that I could hardly speak, and yet she was such a nice person and so very easy to talk to. From then on, she always said "Hello" to me, and thought to say, "Marla, it's Jearl," identifying herself. She was the only one who thought to do it, and I appreciated it.

I was proud to be in the finals, but I dreaded it, too. I began to count the hours. There shouldn't have been any pressure on me; I had already surpassed my own expectations, and everyone else's. But I knew if I didn't run well in the finals, my life would be miserable, because no matter where I finished, I'd have to live with my own worst critic, myself.

My sense of foreboding about the finals turned out to be justified. The race had the same stop-and-go surging, only worse. This time I didn't handle it well. I was passed on the outside and the inside, and I felt swallowed up by the pack, tossed back and forth by momentum changes. It was an awful feeling, like being the tail on a dog. I couldn't find a rhythm, and I didn't have anything left for a kick on my final lap. It just wasn't in my legs. I finished in tenth place with a time of 4:06.

I headed home, disappointed. But I had learned a few things, and to make a final in my first big international experience—and only my fifth 1500 ever—wasn't bad, I decided. On my first night back home in my own bed, I slept soundly.

Until the phone rang.

"Hello?" I said, trying to figure out what day it was and what country I was in.

"Marla, it's Dad." His voice sounded funny.

"Hi, Dad," I said.

"It feels good to be home, I bet." But he said it expressionlessly.

Now I sat up. Something was not right. My father sounded remote, almost formal.

"Now," he said, "are you sitting down?"

"Yes, why?" I asked, timidly. I was afraid to ask.

"Your mother . . ."

He began to cry.

Now I was crying, too.

My father explained that shortly after I had won the Pan-Am Games, my mother had gone to a doctor, and a lump had been discovered in her stomach. It was Stage Four ovarian cancer. She'd had surgery the previous Saturday, while I was in Spain, and her ovaries and part of her intestine had been removed.

Without realizing it, I'd put my hand over my mouth. Suddenly, everything moved very slowly.

"Is she okay?" I murmured, through my tears.

"We had a rough day yesterday. She's in bad shape right now."

"Can I come home?"

"We want you to come home more than anything," my father said.

I was on a plane the next day. I bought a one-way ticket and told Matt, "I don't know when I'm coming back."

My mother was at Cedars-Sinai Medical Center in Los Angeles. In addition to the ovarian cancer, she'd had multiple complications; my father had downplayed her condition on the phone. In the course of the massive abdominal surgery, her doctors had removed a large tumor, her ovaries, and a portion of her small intestine, and had scraped her diaphragm, and they'd been in danger of losing her altogether. Prior to surgery, they'd had to drain extra fluid accumulating around her lungs. She was in terrible pain. When nurses had attempted to move her for an X ray, her sutures had burst.

When I reached her bedside, she smiled and took my hand, despite her awful condition. Her voice sounded different, but her spirit was still the same. I could see her behind the ropes of tubes and the plastic bags and IV's. She had a gastronomy tube inserted into her stomach so that digestive fluids could be drained and her intestinal tract kept clear. She was being fed intravenously.

She was in the hospital for fifty-eight days. While she was there, I washed her hair, rubbed lotion on her legs, and put cold cloths on her back when it went into spasm from lying stationary for hours on end. But mostly we talked, and remembered old stories.

Every day, my father drove for ninety minutes each way to see her. Grady was there, too, of course, and he brought my mother a Walkman and tiny speakers so she could listen to music. I couldn't remember the last time the four of us had been together in one place, but now we spent almost two months in that small hospital room, dealing with a crisis that none of us was prepared for.

I stayed for five weeks. Finally, my mother improved, and I had to get back to Eugene to begin training again and to get back to my teaching job. Before I left, I had a color drawing of the Olympic Stadium in Sydney framed. I brought it to my mother, along with a large brown teddy bear in a Stars-and-Stripes sweater.

"Mom, there's the Olympic Stadium," I said. "We're all going to be there."

"I can't wait," she said.

It was the only thing I could think of to give her. A picture of the future.

9. Trials

I had begun to think of running as more than a sport; it was simply the most natural of all movements to me. Children run, without thought or persuasion. I was puzzled when someone asked me, "When did you start running?" Instead of answering, I asked, "When did you stop?" It was not a challenge for me to run every day. It was a challenge *not* to.

But I was in danger of overtraining again. Now, for every stride I was supposed to take, I took two more. One stride was to be a world-class athlete and the other was for my mother and her fight against cancer.

Running to me was cleansing and necessary; it had begun to regulate my systems, my metabolism, and even my state of mind. Any runner will tell you the physical and emotional side effects of not being able to run: they're those of an addict who can't get a fix. When I couldn't run, I felt stagnant, my head clouded with trivial tasks and my mood on edge. I felt more fatigued when I didn't run than when I did.

My experience at the World Championships had taught me that running at that level requires you to get inside yourself, I mean *really inside* your body—your mind, your heart, lungs, and muscles—and find out what you are made of. I thought I understood what it would take to make the Olympic team and to race in Sydney. I had raced against the elites, and I'd *felt* their strength and their speed. I decided that *I, and only I,* knew what it would feel like to toe the line next to a runner like Gabriela Szabo. It would just be me standing on that line. Not my coach, or Matt.

I felt that I had to do more if I wanted to be competitive in Sydney. I had a vision of myself striding around the oval in the Olympic Stadium, with my mother and father there to see it. We were all going to be there, together. But for that to happen, I had to make it happen. Me, and no one else.

So, on every ten-mile run, I ran twelve. In every fifty-mile week, I ran sixty-five. And every 400 meters that I should have run in 66 seconds, I ran in 64. In retrospect, I jeopardized my training balance and violated those all-important principles of "challenge" and "recovery" that Dick Brown had preached to me in his loft in Coburg.

I didn't care about anything but the U.S. Olympic Trials, which would be held in Sacramento, California, in July. Our apartment was a mess, but I didn't care. Anything that took my mind off running I viewed as a distraction. Holidays were a major inconvenience. I just wanted to run.

Mike Manley tried to hold me back. One day, up in Hendrix

Park after a hill session, he said, "You know, training is like the thermostat in your house. You want to get the temperature up to 72 degrees, but you won't get there any faster if you turn the dial up to 90. But you might blow out the entire system."

I didn't listen. For much of that winter, I actually ran with the marathoners in Mike's group. I became especially good friends and training partners with one of them, Liz Wilson. She could charge up a hill and back down the other side, turn around and charge back up with not so much as a glitch in her stride or a moment of hesitation to catch her breath. She just kept on going, no matter what. Nothing broke her momentum.

Sometimes at night, Matt would read to me from one of his many running books. One of them was *Train Hard, Win Easy—The Kenyan Way* by Toby Tanser. Matt read aloud an account of a typical day in the life of a Kenyan distance runner. "They get up at 6 A.M. and go for a 10K run," he said. "Then they return to camp, drink tea and eat a little before the big workout at 10:30 A.M. After that, they return for lunch and a nap. In the evenings they head out for their evening run." All of this at a 7,000-foot altitude, he added.

I wanted to duplicate that lifestyle. I decided that my life was too spoiled. I ran on fairly groomed trails in Eugene every day, and I had extra time on my hands thanks to my new contract with ASICS, negotiated by Ray Flynn. The small—but much appreciated—monthly stipend allowed me to take a hiatus from teaching. For the first time in my life, I didn't have to work and run at the same time.

I asked myself: *What makes an athlete elite?* I began to believe that I ran my best when running was my lifestyle, not just something I did from 4 to 5:30 every day—that was just going through the motions. Training was a whole way of thinking. Everything I did, every mile I ran, every hour I slept, every meal I ate had to have a purpose.

I wanted to get away. I wanted to face harsher elements and become even stronger. Liz had a friend who shared a cabin in Black Butte, Oregon, about two hours northeast of Eugene, where we could run on logging trails and hills, a much tougher terrain than Eugene's. I stayed at the cabin for two weeks with my dog, Summer, while Liz and Matt came up to train with me on alternate weekends. No telephone, e-mail, media. Just running.

I ran nearly two hundred miles in those two weeks, on paved back roads and logging trails, where the footing was rough. I slid through soft pine needles, dodged and jumped over pinecones, rocks, and fallen tree branches. One Sunday, Liz and I ran for two hours and twenty minutes on those logging trails, including nine miles straight uphill.

We measured off each quarter-mile with a bike odometer, and I marked them by tossing a handful of baking flour in the middle of the road so Matt could time our splits. We ran mile after mile, in shorts and short-sleeved shirts, gloves and hats, panting up that road while it snowed. In the distance was the snow-capped mountain of Black Butte. It was a magnificent view, and we ran in total peace and quiet—there wasn't so much as a car engine or any other racket from some man-made device. There was just the sound of our own labored breathing, and of our footsteps on the black asphalt road.

Back in Eugene, I began to think that Mike Manley was too easy on me. Sometimes, he even stood in my path to hold me back on my runs. He would insist that I run at a specific pace on a tempo run, and if I exceeded it, he blocked my way. "Too fast," he'd insist, and step in front of me on the trail. "You're supposed to run 5:30's." He'd make me rest for a few seconds. "Five . . . four . . . three . . . two . . . okay." Finally, he would step aside and let me go on.

Our work paid off. I won the national title in the indoor 3000 meters in March. Meanwhile, my training partner, Liz, finished fifth in the Olympic Trials marathon in February, and my friend Susannah Beck finished fourth.

The strength that I felt from that hard running was new to me, and it put an idea in my head. I said to Mike, "I want to run a 5000 this year. What do you think?"

"I was thinking the same thing," he said.

We agreed that I would try the 5000 in May, as a farewell to my period of endurance training. A field of elite runners came to Eugene to race in the Oregon Twilight 5000 at Hayward Field. As it turned out, four future Olympians would be in that race; with the exceptions of Regina Jacobs and Deena Drossin, the best in the country were there, including national-level 5000-runners Cheri Kenah, Elva Dryer, and Amy Rudolph. I was looking forward to it: distance runners actually invite competition, because we need good opponents to make a fast race. Otherwise, you run alone, out in front, and solely against the clock, with no pack or pacesetter to pull you along. I'd learned to value my opponents as much as I wanted to beat them.

I won. It was a strong debut: I ran 15:07.66, just one second shy of Mary Decker Slaney's stadium record, and the ninth-fastest time ever by an American. But I also knew that to be competitive at the Olympic Games, I would need to run faster, well under 15:00, in fact.

Mike and I had a decision to make once again. This time we

didn't flip a coin. Instead, we agreed that I would run both the 1500 and the 5000 at the Olympic Trials. If I qualified in both, we'd decide, based on my performance, which one to focus on for the Sydney Games.

I was getting greedy. In 1999, I had been grateful for every step I took without injury. In fact, I had developed a superstition: gratitude was my good-luck charm. But in 2000, I wanted it all.

In the week following the 5000 meters, I began to have physical problems again. I needed to recover, but I did media instead. Ray tried to keep it under control, but we scheduled three consecutive press days. The floodgates opened, and *People Magazine, Sports Illustrated for Women, Runners World, Newsweek,* ESPN, and *Oxygen Sports* arrived in town. I did four long print interviews and three photo shoots, and I spent a day with a film crew. Afterward I was drained, and slightly angry—my vision was a constant topic. I was the "blind wonder." But in my daily life as a runner, my vision was moot. I thought I had proven myself as an athlete, but we never discussed my races. Instead, I answered question after question about my eyes.

"What do you see during a race?"

"How do you keep from bumping into people?"

And one that inexplicably remained a favorite: "Have you ever fallen down?"

A photographer wanted to take photos of me running in the moonlight. "I don't think so," I said.

Finally, the crews packed up their gear and left, and I went back to training. But it immediately became clear that something wasn't right with my body. When I tried to work out with Mike a day later, my breathing was erratic and my legs were leaden.

Over the next week I had a series of puzzling symptoms, including a tingling along my spine. A Eugene physiologist named Val Starodubtsev evaluated me with a computer called Omega Waves Technology, and he prescribed rest and recovery. I followed his prescription of light jogging for a week, but for the delicate connective fascia that most runners take for granted, it was already too late.

Things came to a crisis on an easy cooldown run after a trail session with Mike. It was about a two-and-a-half-mile jog on the trail. Off I went, enjoying the sunshine. I turned with the trail through the trees, until the bridge came into view. It was a small white footbridge that I'd crossed every morning for the last two years, about ten feet long, which took all of three strides.

Suddenly, a little boy on a bike seemed to pop up out of nowhere. He was so tiny that his helmet swamped him. I stutter-stepped and dodged to the right, just missing him. I barely broke stride, and kept going as if nothing had happened. But as I veered around again to head for home, I felt something tweaky in my left knee. *Okay, that feels weird.* I took a few more strides and then stopped. I walked for a minute until the pain was gone. I leaned over and touched my shoes, stretching my hamstrings.

I started to jog again. The pain returned.

Just get home and it will be fine tomorrow.

But it wasn't. The next day, halfway through a five-mile run, the pain flared again. I didn't want to tell Mike. My first 1500-meter race of the season was only a week away, and the Prefontaine Classic was coming up as well. I could not afford time off—not *now.*

On Saturday, I tried to work out with Mike and four of his

other athletes at Lane Community College. I hated that track. It was slow. It even looked slow: a bright blue oval in the middle of a grass field, with no protection from wind, and no atmosphere. I never ran fast there. It was always a struggle.

Mike wanted me to do a series of 300s to prepare me for the upcoming 1500 meters. But it was a frustrating session—after the final 300, during an easy jog, my leg shut down.

"I'm done," I told Mike. "It's my left knee . . . on the side."

I went home and iced. That afternoon, I stretched and put on my ASICS shoes and headed out the door for an evening run. I felt a teasing pain; it was there, but not entirely disabling. *It will warm up,* I convinced myself. Those are a runner's famous last words.

The next morning, Sunday, I looked out the dew-soaked window at the rain puddling outside. I put on my shoes.

I made it two steps. The pain was worse than ever. It was not a matter of enduring it, like the day before. Now I simply . . .

Could.

Not.

Run.

"Oh, my God," I said.

I came back inside and told Matt about the pain. He tried to pinpoint the cause: was it from that tingling in my back and butt a week earlier, or an ankle turn the previous Thursday, or perhaps the sudden shift from mileage to speedwork? Or did it happen when I dodged the little boy on his bike?

I didn't know—and it didn't matter. The question now was how to fix it.

I called my friend and chiropractor, Dr. John LeGat, in a panic and left a long and fairly hysterical voice-mail on his cell phone. He was gone for the weekend, but in the meantime his assistant Brenda let us into the office and Matt hooked me up to the electric muscle-stimulation machine. I lay on a treatment table, listening to the rain on the roof, and cried. The tears were involuntary, without a sound, but as steady and uncontrollable as the rain outside.

A day later, Dr. John returned to Eugene and targeted the problem: the iliotibial band (or IT band), a long strip of connective tissue that extends from the hip to below the knee, had seized up and was inflamed. When the band is tight, it stretches like a guitar string along a bony protrusion of the femur on the side of your knee.

It was June 10. The Olympic Trials began July 14. And I couldn't run.

On Monday, it was time for retesting with Val. Afterward, he said, "You're good to go. Everything looks great." But my face did not light up. "What's wrong?" he asked.

I told him about the injury.

"There's always the pool," Val replied, trying to console me.

The pool. And the bike. I knew them too well. They represented nothing but frustration and disappointment to me.

With IT Band syndrome, any movement or bending of the knee is excruciating. Riding the bike turned out to be impossible, and I couldn't even bend my knee in the water.

I couldn't sleep at night. My world was crashing. Nothing else mattered but making the Olympic team, and as far as I was concerned, nothing else existed. I lay in bed at night while the tears poured. Matt lay next to me and just said, "I'm sorry."

"I can't believe this is happening," I would say over and over again, reaching for a roll of toilet paper to blow my nose.

On Wednesday, Dr. Stanley James, who had assisted with my knee surgery in 1996, came into his office on his day off and injected the involved area of my knee with cortisone. Dr. James was very kind and positive, and for the next three days, while I waited for the injection to work its magic, I stayed positive, too. But by Sunday, it was worse.

By now I could barely walk. I could not bend my knee at all. It was as if someone had jammed a steel spike down the side of my leg from my hip to my ankle. The spike ground into my knee if I tried to bend it, and now my ankle and calf were involved as well. It was one long chain reaction. *I need a miracle,* I thought.

I got on a plane for Colorado Springs and the Olympic Training Center to see my old friend and miracle worker, Dr. Leahy, who had worked magic on my plantar fasciitis in 1998. There were other forms of treatment I could try at the Center as well. I wasn't a big believer in traditional training-room remedies, but I was willing to try anything—and I did.

I roamed the Center looking for some kind of apparatus that I could use to simulate running. I kept a journal of my first week there:

Sunday 6/25/00
11:30 A.M.—Dr. Leahy ART hard!
P.M.—walk 30 minutes on treadmill, swim 45 minutes

Monday 6/26/00
9 A.M.—10-minute jog on treadmill, had to stop once
45 minutes on Windsprint bike, heart rate 141 average

Dr. Leahy treatment

3 P.M.—feels best ever! 45 minutes alternate
walk/jog on treadmill

Tuesday 6/27/00

9 A.M.—hard to walk, Dr. Leahy

3 P.M.—exercise impossible

Not a good day

I began to wonder why this had happened to me. Was I being punished by a higher power, or was it fate? Maybe I had asked for too much. I had to figure out why.

Dr. Mike Leahy treated athletes with deep intelligence and creativity; he wasn't just a chiropractor, but an Ironman triathlete as well, and he had served as a rocket engineer in the air force. He had a thorough knowledge of biomechanics, and ART was his creation: a method of breaking apart the adhesions that inhibited movement, thus allowing tissues to slide more freely. But Dr. Leahy knew something else, too.

One afternoon, during treatment, he informed me that several years earlier he had been diagnosed with cancer and told that he had three months to live. He had been in remission ever since, thanks in part to his strict diet of foods high in antioxidants, which kept his immune system strong. After he told me his story, I began to believe that perhaps I had suffered my injury for a larger reason: maybe I had been led to Colorado Springs so that I could learn from Dr. Leahy's cancer experience and pass it on to my mother. I went to the phone in the hallway of my dorm and called her.

"Mom, I heard something amazing today," I said.

I told her Dr. Leahy's story and gave her the name of a clinic that specialized in nutrition for patients with cancer.

"Maybe this is why I'm here," I said. "So I could learn this and tell you about it. Maybe we can go to this place together."

My mother was touched, but she didn't agree with me. While I was worried about her, she was worried about me—just like a mom. She didn't like knowing that I was hurt.

Dr. Leahy did all he could for me. He treated me every day, even on weekends. He watched me on the track to analyze my movements and tried to figure out which muscles to treat. The problem was that everything was involved, from my arch and calf to my hamstrings and lower back.

I tried every anti-inflammatory drug under the sun, with little or no success. I tried an injection of Toradol, a powerful anti-inflammatory said to have almost an anesthetic effect. I went into a treatment room, where an intern snapped his index finger against my arm searching for a vein. He poked a needle into my arm, as I stared up at the ceiling and thought, *I can't believe I am this desperate.* "Oops, I missed," the doctor said. "I'll have to try again."

It was depressing. I hated drugs—I didn't even like taking an aspirin. Running was a natural thing, not a medical thing. This was the wrong end of the spectrum.

My training had come to a complete standstill. I found it hard to believe that making the team was even still a possibility. I didn't find a cure at the Olympic Training Center or in Dr. Leahy's office—not a traditional one. But eventually, I did find something else: perspective.

It so happened that several disabled athletes were staying at the training center, preparing for the 2000 Paralympic Games. I ran into two of my former U.S. Paralympic teammates, Beth Scott and Trisha Zorn. It was a homecoming of sorts for me. All three of us were visually impaired. Beth was a B-3 like me, and Trisha was a B-2. We had a connection between us that no fully sighted person could understand. We not only laughed at each other but also at our blindness.

"Marla, come to my dorm room. I have something to show you," Beth said. "This will fix your knee."

That afternoon, the three of us sat in a tiny white-brick dorm room and watched a VCR tape of the opening ceremonies of the Barcelona Paralympics. There we were, on the screen, dressed in our red, white, and blue outfits. We called them our Domino's pizza-delivery outfits. We looked so goofy, especially with our wraparound 1980's sunglasses. We were a crew of misfits yelling and waving American flags. We laughed until my stomach hurt.

Since the injury, it felt like I kept meeting people whom I hadn't seen in years; people who had influenced my life. It was the ultimate irony—as if fate was saying "Don't forget how far you've come." I saw Adam Goucher, the kid who had shown me how to run distance. He had won the 1999 national title in the 5000, but now he was at the center battling low-back pain. One day, as I peg-legged down the steps of the dining hall, I ran into Casey Cook, my friend from the 1989 USABA Nationals. I hadn't seen him in more than a decade. Because I knew he was deaf, I took his hand and signed into it:

"Casey! It's Marla. Do you remember me?"

He handed me a small box with a microphone attached.

"Put this on," he said.

Casey had undergone surgery years earlier to have a cochlear implant placed in his inner ear, and he now had some hearing—including voices. I didn't have to sign into his hands—he could *hear* me. We sat together on a couch in the Athletes' Center and caught up on all the years that had passed. He had gone to college and to massage school. He was at the OTC to train in a tandem-cycling camp put on by the USABA.

I began to accept the possibility that the Olympics might take place without me. I had been so focused, in such a state of tunnel vision, that I saw nothing else in the world except the Olympics.

Now, that was truly *blind,* I realized.

At night, I lay in my dorm-room bunk bed and visualized the Trials. For months, I'd been visualizing. *No one ever said you need vision to visualize.* I would imagine the race: feel the pace and hear the crowd and see the streaks of color that represented uniforms all around me. Sometimes, as the vision became more and more real to me, my heart would even accelerate. Before the injury, I had but one vision, of making the Olympic team, crossing the line with Suzy Favor Hamilton and Regina Jacobs.

But now, while I was injured, a second vision began to take over. I no longer visualized finishing first, or second, or third. In fact, sometimes I wasn't in the race. Sometimes I visualized stepping off the track before the end of the first lap. I didn't like this vision, but I couldn't control it. I opened my eyes and stared at the blot on the ceiling instead, but even with my eyes open, the images continued to flit through my mind. Once, I had visualized newspaper headlines, RUNYAN MAKES TEAM. Now I envisioned a small blurb that said RUNYAN PULLS OUT DUE TO LEG INJURY.

Beth Scott suggested that I talk to a sports psychologist at the center. It was a free service, available to all the athletes.

"How is talking to someone going to help?" I said. "The only help I need is for someone to fix my leg."

But I had nothing to do, and nothing to lose. One day, I made an appointment and ventured into the Sports Psych offices. I sat down with Peter Haberl in a small room with a couch, a couple of chairs, and a box of tissues.

Oh, great, I thought, *a sob-fest. I'm not going to cry,* I told myself. I had done enough of that, and it had accomplished nothing. I was empty of tears and almost numb to the disappointment of possibly missing the Olympic Trials.

I sat down on the sofa that was obviously reserved for the patient—it was closer to the tissues. To my right was a peculiar egglike dome with a seat inside. It looked like the chair that Will Smith sat in in the movie *Men in Black.*

"What's that for?" I asked.

"It's for mental imaging," Peter explained with a very Austrian accent.

I really wasn't into this. *He's not a runner. How can he help me?* Part of me was afraid that seeing a sports psychologist was tantamount to giving up on the Olympics. Was I here to deal with my emotions? *My emotions are perfectly normal,* I thought. It was my illiotibial band that needed curing.

"So," Peter said, "tell me about yourself."

I took a deep breath and started in.

"I had a really good shot at making the Olympic team this year in the 1500 or 5000. Then I got hurt, and I haven't been able to run for four weeks."

"I see," he said.

"And the Olympic Trials are just two weeks away," I added. He nodded.

"But there's one more thing that I'm trying to deal with here, too."

"What's that?"

"I'm legally blind. I was in the Paralympics in '92 and '96, and I won. But that's not where I belong. I'm good enough to make the Olympic team. But now, with this injury, I don't know if I'll go to the Trials."

"Why won't you go to the Trials?"

"Because I don't want to go to the Trials and run poorly. Not run my best . . . not run what I know I'm capable of."

"Why not?"

"Because if I go to the Olympic Trials and fail, everyone will think it's because of my eyes, not because of my injury. They'll think, 'No way some blind girl can make the Olympic team.' "

"So, you don't want to go to the Trials because you're afraid you might fail?"

"Yes."

"But what is *fail?* What does that word mean to you?"

"It means not performing up to what I am capable of."

"And your knee is preventing you from doing that?"

"Yes!" *What was with all these questions?*

"So, let's say you go to the Trials, and you fail, as you see it, and you do not make the team because of your injury. What then?"

"Then, I'll try again in four years. And I'll know I had it in me this year."

"But what will everyone else think?"

"They'll think I couldn't make it because of my eyes."

We continued our discussion, back and forth, in a kind of mock argument.

"What if I told you I think you should stay in the Paralympics?" he said. "That you shouldn't try out for the Olympic team? That you should stay in the Paralympics because you can win lots of medals there?"

"No! I don't want to be in the Paralympics. That's not me. No. I won't go."

"Why not?"

"Because . . ." I paused. "Because, *I am an Olympian.*"

"But you haven't made an Olympic team yet. How can you call yourself an Olympian?"

"Because I just know I have that ability in me. I just know I can make the team—*could have* made the team if it wasn't for this leg. I just know it."

"But what about the others that say you weren't good enough? That you should have just stayed in the Paralympics. What about them?"

"They're wrong. I know who I am and that's all that counts."

Peter leaned back in his chair with a sense of satisfaction. It was like arguing with Arnold Schwarzenegger. It was a tough argument to win.

Peter said, "Exactly. It doesn't matter what other people think. Does it? All that matters is what you think of yourself. But you are worried about them. If you weren't, you would go to the Trials no matter what."

"Yes, I guess you're right. But if I can't run by this Saturday, I don't have a chance. It's all over."

"Why *this* Saturday? Did your coach tell you that?"

"No."

"Then who?"

"I told myself that."

"Why would you limit yourself in this way?"

I didn't have an answer.

"The fact is, we really don't know if you can make the Olympic team until the gun goes off. Right? *Marla, the future has not been written.*"

On July 4, I went home to Eugene. It was a lonely day to travel, and I was low. Everyone else was playing Frisbee and barbecuing on my country's most celebrated day—and I was giving up. I'd called my parents from Colorado Springs before I left.

"Mom," I said, "I just don't think this is going to work out. My leg isn't much better. I'm going home. I am so sorry."

"I'm so sorry for *you,*" my mom said.

I was tired of the cycle of hope and disappointment caused by my injury; the daily questions—*Can I run today? Nope. Maybe tomorrow? Maybe by Saturday?* I was weary of the emotional roller coaster, and I wanted some peace. Maybe if I made the decision to pull out of the Trials, I could find some.

But the fact remained that the Trials were still ten days away, and the team would not be chosen until then. As I sat on the plane for home, Peter's words reverberated in me: *the future has not been written.* As the plane approached Eugene, I decided to give it one last all-out effort. If I couldn't run, so be it. But at least I would know I had tried.

The next day I was in the pool, with a blue aqua-jogger float strapped around my waist. Mike sat in a chair at the edge of the pool, holding a rope tied to my jogging belt to increase the resistance. Aqua-jogging is about time, not distance, because you don't go anywhere. It's a matter of moving in one place, pedaling with your legs and thrashing your arms back and forth. Effort does not equal distance—and, for a runner, that is the most aggravating concept. It defies the purpose of exertion.

Every once in a while, Mike would release a section of rope, and I would make a little forward progress toward the other side of the pool, which would mark the end of the interval. It was grueling and tedious, but it was something.

Mike was tremendously motivating during the pool workouts, but there was something not right between us. I couldn't put my finger on it. Injuries do a funny thing to a coach and an athlete; they cause emotional stress on both sides, as I had learned from my experience with Dick Brown. The coach often feels a need to absolve himself of blame, to let the world know "It's not my fault." But I never blamed Dick or Mike. Injuries happen, and it was me who had done the running.

Fault and blame were wastes of time, especially at this point. I was more focused on making one last attempt to get ready to run at the Olympic Trials. Once again, I believed that it was all up to me, *all* up to me.

With just six days remaining before the first heats of the 1500 at the Trials, Mike and I decided that I would try to run. We discovered something interesting: if I got up on my toes in a pair of light racing flats, I could run—not for very long, but I could run, and run somewhat fast. After I stopped, my knee locked up again, and I had to go back home and ice it. But it was something.

Three days later, Mike picked me up for practice. I heard his van's horn honk from inside my apartment, and I grabbed my bag and headed outside. "Bring some ice," he yelled up at me. I turned around and grabbed an ice cup out of the freezer.

I got into the van, holding the ice cup. Also in the van was another of Mike's athletes, Kris Ihle, who had qualified for the

Olympic Trials in the 5000. I wondered if the ice was for her. Was she hurt?

"The ice cup is for you to ice your knee after the workout today," Mike said. "You'll finish before Kris, so you can ice your knee while she's still running."

"Of course I'll be done before her," I said. "Because I can only run one or two intervals."

"You're going to run four intervals today," he said. "You'll run 1000, 800, 600, 400."

Obviously, he had decided to push me through the injury.

"But Mike, I haven't been able to run more than one before my knee locks up. I don't see how I can do all four."

Mike didn't answer. We sat there in a long silence.

"Well, I'll try it," I said.

But I doubted that I could get through it. What I really wanted to do was try a 400 and see if I could get close to race-pace. It would give me confidence, something to believe in—and it would help me to determine if my IT band could tolerate a 1500-meter race.

We arrived at the track, and Kris and I began to warm up. My warmup was abbreviated, obviously. I tried to jog two laps. Nope. I stopped at one.

"I want the 1000 to be 74-second pace," Mike said.

"Mike, I think with the race so close, I'd really like to run a 400 at race-pace. You know, just to feel it?"

"You're going to run the 400—but after the other intervals," he insisted.

I knew in my heart that I would never make it to the fourth run. But I obeyed. I ran the 1000 meters at the slow pace he demanded. As we ran, I wondered whether the workout was meant for Kris. These distances and paces seemed designed to help her, not me.

As soon as we finished the 1000, my knee started to stiffen. I needed to keep going or it would lock up altogether. We took off on the 800. But this time when we crossed the finish line, my knee locked up completely, and I couldn't bend it.

"I'm done," I said. "I just wish I could have run that 400."

I limped off toward my bag and melting cup of ice and began rubbing the cup along the side of my knee.

Mike was angry. He snapped something at Kris, and then he stormed over to me.

"Get your bag. I'm taking you home."

"What about Kris?" I asked.

"I'll come back for her," he said.

I limped to his van and got in. He started up the engine and squealed out of the parking lot like an Indy 500 driver. We drove home without a word. Finally, as we pulled into the parking lot of my apartment complex, he asked if I was going to see Dr. LeGat that night for a treatment. His voice was low and tense.

"Yes, but I don't have a ride yet," I said. "Matt's in San Francisco."

"I'll pick you up," he said.

Ordinarily, Matt took me to my appointments. I didn't expect Mike to be my driver—he had never gone with me to Dr. John's before. Did he feel obliged to offer? I accepted, but uneasily. Something wasn't right here, but I couldn't quite figure out what.

"Okay," I said gently.

That night when he arrived to pick me up, Mike's anger

seemed even more red-hot than it had at the track that afternoon. It looked like he had worked himself into a state. We drove in total silence to Dr. John's office.

Dr. John put a lot of work into my leg—and he did it after hours. He was a good friend, and a good chiropractor, and I credited him with keeping me injury-free since 1998, despite my overeager training programs. I counted on him, and he was always there—so much so that I had asked him to come with me to the Trials and had bought an airline ticket for him.

When he was done working on me, I said, "Thank you."

Dr. John hugged me and said, "I'll see you in Sacramento."

Mike and I got back in the car, and again he roared the engine. *What the hell?* I thought. That was it; we obviously needed to clear the air. I waited until we pulled into the parking lot of my building. I opened the van door and the inside light went on.

"Mike, what is wrong?"

His voice was shaky and low.

"A 'thank you' would be nice," he said. "John gets a 'thank you,' and he gets paid. I don't get paid."

Now I was ten times as confused. I stared blankly in front of me and tried to decipher what this was really about.

"Mike, gosh, *thank you,*" I said.

But it had no effect. He sat behind the wheel, revving the engine, his face set. I climbed out of the van. As soon as I got inside my apartment, I called Matt in San Francisco and told him what had happened.

"Write him an e-mail and say what you need to say," he suggested. "Get it off your chest and then focus on the race."

He was right: it was three days before the Olympic Trials, and

I had to settle things and get on with preparing for the Trials. I sat down and wrote Mike an e-mail. I thanked him for the pool workouts and for the last two years of training. Then I wrote something else. I asked him to keep his anger at a distance from me. I told him that I felt I had enough cards stacked against me, and I needed all my energy for the Trials.

A day later, I got on a plane to Sacramento. There, across the aisle from me, was Dick Brown. I gave him a hug, and we chatted. I told Dick about my injury and that I had been doing the best I could with the aqua-jogging and an elliptical trainer (yet another gym machine for aerobic exercise). I explained this without panic. I no longer felt insecure or defensive or fearful about the injury. I told him I was going to will myself through the race. Dick liked my demeanor, he told me later. He thought, *This girl is gonna do it.*

In Sacramento, I flopped down on the bed and crashed. Matt, the only constant through everything, was there. I nicknamed him "The Rock." He was the mediator, the quiet reassuring neutral party who tried to keep the peace. And while all of this had been going on, he had just finished second in the *Chronicle* Marathon in San Francisco—after coaching himself.

That day, I told him, "Matt, I still haven't run even once at racepace. Nothing."

We boarded the shuttle bus and went out to the stadium so that I could try to run that single 400 that I was seeking for my peace of mind. We strolled into the stadium from the south end, where the 100-meter straightaway began. A crew was busy laying down television cables and setting up camera platforms. The stadium it-self was vast and open. If the race day was windy, I would most certainly feel it. The grandstands were a bright white and silver, and they caught the glare of the sun, which was also intensified by white walls that encircled the track, separating the fans from the athletes.

I tested the surface. It was hard and fast, typical of tracks at Olympic-quality events, most of which are Mondo, a type of syn-thetic track known for producing fast times. From a distance, it looks solid red, but up close, on your hands and knees, you can ac-tually see the interlocking patterns of the material. Mondo was a clean, hard track that would give back every ounce of force that each runner exerted on it, making it ideal for sprinters. But for the 5000- and 10,000-meter runners, its hardness would also take its toll on their legs.

"Let's try a short warmup," I said to Matt. He pressed the START button on his stopwatch, and we began an easy jog on the grass infield. We made it one lap, and then another. But on the third, I felt the knife-jab in my knee.

"How long was that?" I asked Matt.

"Six minutes and seven seconds," he said.

A 1500-meter race lasts about four minutes and change. I could only hope that my knee would hold up for that long at race-pace.

"Okay," I said, fighting back tears. "Let's try a stride. Maybe on my toes it will be different."

I laced on my lightweight running spikes and searched out a section of the track clear of cables. With every stride I felt that sharp pain.

I flopped down in the grass next to Matt. We sat there in total silence. I didn't need to say a word. He knew.

"I'm not going to cry," I said. "It won't do any good."

"I know," he said.

We gathered our stuff and got back onto the bus. As I hobbled down the aisle, a trainer asked what was wrong. I explained that I had IT Band syndrome. She said she knew a special kind of taping for the knee that might help me. I shrugged. "I'll try it," I said. I would have tried just about anything at that point. I was looking for that silver bullet anyplace I could find it. I propped my knee up, and the trainer worked on me. When she was finished, there was a tiny, crisscrossing pattern of adhesive tape along the side of my knee. It looked peculiar. She explained that it was intended to create a slight sensory block of the nerves, so that I wouldn't feel the pain. I left it on, for the hell of it.

The next morning, Matt and I headed back to the track, to see if I had improved.

"Okay," I said, trying to keep my sense of humor, "I can only jog for six minutes. So I'll warm up with just one lap, and then I'll stretch, and then I'll run a god-damned 400. And then we are going back to the hotel."

"Sounds like a plan," Matt said mildly.

I jogged. I stretched. Then I put on my spikes once more, leaned forward to stretch the backs of my legs, and said, "Ready?"

"I'm ready," Matt answered, his finger poised over his stopwatch.

I took off, on my toes, around the track. I felt rusty and fatigued. It did not feel good. It felt . . . hard. Too hard. Not how a 400 should feel just one day before the Olympic Trials.

I crossed the line. I looked at Matt. "If that was a 66, I'm in trouble," I said.

Maintaining a 66-second pace would give me a time of 4:08 in the 1500. Too slow. I figured it would take an average of 65 seconds for the entire three and three-quarters laps to make the team.

"It was a 61," Matt replied.

Where the hell did that come from? I wondered. I hadn't run a 61 in months. It was a combination of muscle memory and adrenaline, I figured. I shrugged. I grabbed a bag of ice and we climbed back onto the bus to the hotel.

I finally had my 400.

Race day arrived, hot and smoggy, and so did the countdown to the first round of the 1500. I would be in the first of three heats, along with the ever-present Regina Jacobs, and only the top two finishers would advance to the finals. Regina was a lock. That meant that I had to be second, or I was going home. While I got my crisscrossed tape-up job, I tried not to dwell on the fact that this would be my first 1500-meter race of the entire year.

As Matt, John, and Mike hovered around the warmup area, I tied the laces on my spikes and headed to the check-in area. Mike seemed distant. Even though it was 6:30 P.M., the heat was sweltering, and as the sun descended, it burned across the grass infield, intensely bright. The tension was almost as unbearable as the heat.

The gun went off, and I found a middle position within the group of twelve runners. I tried to relax and find a rhythm, but the pace was a shock to my body after swimming laps and aquajogging for five weeks. My lungs filled with the hot dry air—I hadn't breathed so hard in a long time. On the second lap, I felt internal panic. My lungs burned so badly that it felt as though I had not run in months. The pain in my chest made me virtually forget about the pain in my knee. At that moment, I had a bigger problem—not quitting.

All those miles, and hills, the long runs in the mountains, couldn't have been for nothing. *You must stay in this race,* I told myself. *There is no stopping.* But the final lap could not come soon enough.

As soon as the bell clanged, I began to move up in the pack. I found myself in fourth place. Coming off the final turn, I felt awful, miserable, like I was straining but not going anywhere. Somehow, I managed to pass two more runners and move into second, where I finished. My leg had held up.

But now both legs buckled, and I went down on my knees. My lungs were on fire. After a few seconds, I got up and went into the "mixed zone," an area for coaches and press. Ray Flynn stood there at the gate.

"Marla, you did it, you did great. You qualified."

"But I feel awful," I said, wheezing. "My lungs."

"You're just a bit rusty. You'll be okay."

My throat and lungs felt seared. I stayed under the tent, still coughing and trying to get my breath back, even after the final two heats had come and gone.

A familiar voice wafted from the warmup track.

"Good job, girl."

It was Rahn Sheffield. I grinned through my hacking.

"I feel like I just ran the mile relay for SDSU," I said.

My knee problem hadn't simply vanished. The peculiarity of the injury was that it was easier to sprint on it than to jog. The next day, when I tested it with a couple of slow ten-minute runs, both ended in pain.

On Saturday, Ray found me in the lobby of the hotel.

"Marla, there's a guy here, a doctor who works with some of our athletes. He's very good, and I think he might be able to help your knee. He's here right now in the hotel and can meet you in your room in a few minutes."

I thought about it. I knew it might bother John LeGat if I tried another treatment, but I didn't see that I had a choice. At this point, any little bit might help.

"Okay," I said and returned to my room.

Dr. Mark Scappaticci, or "Scap," as his patients called him, knocked on my door within a few minutes.

"So what's going on here?" he asked.

I started to tell him the long story of my IT Band syndrome. While I talked, he set up his massage table, and in seconds he had me on my back with my leg in his hands. I barely finished talking when he went to all the right spots, immediately. He moved my leg, lengthening the involved muscles and tissues. He worked fast and thoroughly.

"Stand up and walk around. See how that feels."

I walked to the end of the hotel hallway and back. I felt a freedom in my hip and leg that I hadn't felt in months.

"It's better," I said.

"It will take more than one treatment," he said. "When's your race?"

"Tomorrow at two," I said.

"Okay, I'll come back tomorrow morning and we'll do some more."

The next morning, Scap arrived at my door. He worked fast. Who was this guy, I wondered, who seemed to know what was wrong, and what to do? And who stormed in and out of my room in such a hurry that he had no time for small talk?

"Okay, you're all set," he said. "It's not normal, it will take more treatments, but that's all I can do today."

The phone had rung while he treated me. Matt told me that it had been John LeGat and that he was upset that I had acted without consulting him. I could only hope that he would understand that I'd done what I had to do, with the race just hours away.

I showered and put on my blue-and-white ASICS uniform. I was thin—despite the lack of running, I was a mere 113 pounds. My ribs protruded when I exhaled or stretched my arms up to the ceiling. I stood in front of the mirror and took a deep breath.

"I can do this," I said.

Matt and I left for the track.

About forty-five minutes before the 1500-meter final, I started to jog around the warmup track and then stopped. I shook my head and started walking toward my bag in the shade. The shape of a man stepped in front of me.

"You're moving much better," the voice said, and I recognized Ray's Irish accent immediately.

"Marla, I want to tell you something," he said.

I just stood there.

"You are going to make the Olympic team today."

He said it very matter-of-fact, as if he had a crystal ball and had seen into the future.

"Remember Winnipeg," he said. "Remember how that race went." The Pan-Am Games gold medal.

He reminded me that three runners would qualify for the Olympics. Regina Jacobs and Suzy Favor Hamilton were the favorites, yes, but the third spot was wide open.

"You don't need to chase Suzy or Regina. Third is just as good as first here. Hold back for as long as you can."

He was right—and he wasn't telling me anything I didn't already know, but it was reassuring to hear it from a seasoned great like Ray. With the absence of hard interval training, the race would be a disaster for me if I went out too hard. I'd go into oxygen debt too quickly. I had to be conservative, but aggressive at the same time.

I sat on a treatment table in the shade with a bag of ice on my knee. Matt and John hovered around, but no one spoke. For one moment, I considered pulling out of the race. I was so tired of it all. Tired of the pain in my knee, and tired of the tension with Mike and the arguments about which doctor was treating me.

"Final call, women's 1500 meters," a voice announced over the loudspeaker.

I got up off the table and grabbed my spikes.

"I'm gonna go do this," I said.

I went to the holding area—athletes only. Suddenly, I was alone. I sat on the aluminum bench surrounded by other bodies in colorful uniforms. I was relieved to be alone.

I began to talk to myself, focusing on the positive. *This is an opportunity. This is the Olympic Trials, and you are here. You have come this far.*

Finally, we lined up single-file for the short 200-meter walk to the start. But Regina would have none of that. She bolted into Lane One and began a stride.

Hey, I'm gonna do that too, I thought.

I took a stride down the backstretch. Other runners did the same. There was too much tension in the air. The official could not contain us.

The stands were packed; it was a sold-out crowd. I knew somewhere in that wall of color—I couldn't distinguish faces—were my mother, my father, and Grady.

I stretched. When I crossed my right leg over my left, locked my knees, and pulled up on the toes of my left foot, I could stretch the long band that plagued me. It numbed the area of pain, hopefully long enough to get myself off the line and into the race, when the adrenaline would take over and I'd forget the pain. While the commentator rattled off each runner's credentials, I continued to stretch my leg.

A familiar theme song began to play over the loudspeaker. It was the theme from *Superman*.

I smiled. I was calm. I'd come to a place of acceptance. Very simply, I would run the best race that I could—and I would accept the outcome either way.

As I stood on that line, I repeated Peter Haberl's words to myself: *The future has not been written.* Nothing had happened yet. I was still in this race.

We were called to the line.

"Runners to your marks."

The gun exploded.

The initial pace was perfect for me: Regina and Suzy avoided the lead position, which signaled that it would not be an all-out race but a slightly tactical one. Good. The pace was fast, but not overwhelmingly so.

I kept my eye on one athlete in particular, a body in blue, Shayne Culpepper. She was the most likely candidate for the third position on the team. I got right behind her and stared directly into her back. I was not going to let her out of my sight. I shadowed her.

The first two laps were a blur, as if they never happened. I just stared between Shayne's shoulder blades, and before I knew it, we were at the 800-meter mark.

A band from Stanford University began to bang on some bongo drums. The rhythm rang through the stadium. They beat the drums to our cadence, "Bong, bong, bong!" It was a natural pacesetter.

Coming down the homestretch of the third lap, someone crossed into Shayne's path. She stumbled. I jerked my hands up and gently touched her back, so I wouldn't run right into her. The collision was avoided, and we regained our stride almost immediately.

The bell clanged for the final lap. Now the race had truly begun. The crowd was on their feet. I was in sixth place.

Regina and Suzy bolted to the front. They launched into an all-out sprint for the finish, racing for the national title. I let them go—it wasn't my fight. I was racing for a spot on the Olympic team.

On the backstretch, I moved into fifth, then fourth. Just before the final turn, I said to myself, *Go get it.* I moved wide into the second lane and passed the body in blue. I entered the final turn and moved quickly back to Lane One.

An empty blanket of red track lay before me. It was the most beautiful sight I could behold. There are some advantages to being legally blind. Regina and Suzy were too far ahead for me to see them. To me, it was like I was winning.

Just meters from the invisible finish line, I began to tighten up.

I felt myself slowing. I had no idea who might be behind me, or how close. *Please don't catch me.* I crossed the line. *Was I third? Was I really third? Did I just make the Olympic team?* I couldn't see the large screen posting the order of finish.

I dragged my tired body to the side of the track, where an official was standing. I held up three fingers. "Was I third?" I asked, gasping. I wasn't sure. Perhaps there was another runner way up in front with Regina and Suzy, and I had lost sight of her.

The official said nothing, but he nodded his head ever so slightly. I was third.

I dropped my head back and raised my arms over my face and looked up into the blue, blue, blue sky. "Thank you," I said.

It was a Thank You to everyone and everything—an overwhelming emotion of gratitude. I walked toward the gate of the mixed zone, and there directly in front of me was Matt. I wrapped my arms around his neck and said, "Can you believe it? I did it!" His body was trembling. He was literally shaking.

"You ran 4:06," he said.

It was so Matt. He was the stat man, the track-and-field encyclopedia, and "The Rock," and he knew exactly what my time was.

An official ushered me back out to the track for a victory lap with Regina and Suzy. Now, for the first time, things were *exactly* as I had visualized them. Except for one thing: I was trying not to limp. Regina, now a four-time Olympian, and Suzy, on her third Olympic team, waved to the crowd. We began our victory lap.

The mixed zone was chaos. I had a press conference to attend, and I also had to report to drug testing. Officials, drug-testing chaperones, and the media all wrestled to get closest to the athletes. We were pulled in eight different directions. "Runyan, over here," a voice would say. I'd turn. Then someone else would call my name. I was pulled left and right, but I didn't care. Ray stood there at the gate, trying to look out for me. Then he said, "You know, Marla, as problems go, these are good ones to have." I laughed.

By the time I went back outdoors, the stadium was deserted. Matt was still at my side, and we began walking toward the bus.

Mike appeared. It was the first time I had seen him since the race had ended. "We need to talk," he said. "But not now. I'll let you celebrate today."

And that was it. "What was that?" I asked Matt.

"I don't know. Forget about it."

Just then, a young volunteer came up to me. "Are you Marla?" she asked.

"Yeah."

"Your mother is over there at the gate. She wants to see you."

I hadn't cried yet. Not one tear. But when I saw my mother, there was no stopping it. My parents were clinging to the side of a gate that encircled the warmup track. My mother was wearing a red, white, and blue T-shirt with a slogan that said RUN RUNYAN RUN. She did not have a strand of hair on her head because of all the chemotherapy she had endured.

I could only muster one sentence. "I did it, Mom."

"You certainly did," she said, and wrapped me in a big hug.

The next few days were a pleasant succession of congratulations, press interviews, and watching the other races at the Trials. There was just one unpleasantness left. A couple of days later, Mike came to the hotel just as Matt and I were packing to go home. He finally had his chance to say what he wanted to say. And I knew it was coming.

He began by telling me that I had run a great race. And then he said, "I'm not going to coach you anymore. You need to find a new coach. Maybe someone here in the hotel can help you."

"Okay," I responded.

This much I expected. But I was unnerved by the idea of finding a complete stranger to coach me through the Olympic Games at such short notice. Mike wasn't done talking yet, either. He had some harsh words with which to validate his decision. It was clear to me that Mike was tired, worn out. I believe he was not only tired of me, but of stresses from his other athletes as well. He said very little that actually made sense to me—except one thing: "You have lost trust in me." On this point, he was right.

I had begun to look elsewhere for answers. Still, differences aside, I had learned a lot about running from Mike, and it was sad that it would end this way.

But I realized something else, too. I came to understand that injuries, and stress, and emotions that erupted in tears or anger were a part of this game. Unforeseen circumstances were as much a part of the sport as the rewards. You had to know this going in, and you had to be prepared to deal with it. No whining or excuses. No backing out when things got rough. You set a goal and make a commitment—and sometimes the greater challenge is finding someone who will share in that commitment. I turned to "The Rock" to fill that void.

Matt and I flew home and tried to regroup. The Trials were over, but the Olympic experience was just beginning. I had a lot of planning and training left to do.

Marla Runyan

Believe it or not, my leg was still troubling me. Sure, I had just run a four-minute race, and somehow I had earned a spot on the Olympic team. But training had to resume, and quickly.

I was still injured, and I had just lost my coach. But after a few days of rest, nothing really hurt anymore. I was an Olympian.

10. Sydney

Four years for four minutes: that was what the Olympics amounted to. When I reduced it to that sort of equation; when I totaled up all the miles, all the sweat-soaked workouts, all the running shoes worn down at the heels and thrown away, all the dull aches and stabbing pains, all the injuries and the surgeries, it was preposterous. *For four minutes.* I didn't dare think of it that way.

I could only afford to think of one single step at a time—and the first step was to find a new coach. Back in Eugene, I woke up one morning and walked into the kitchen. Matt was leaning over the kitchen table, with papers spread out around him and a coffee cup at his side.

"What are you doing?" I asked.

"I'm writing your workouts," he said.

Matt had stepped into the void after my split with Mike, and he helped me regroup. Nobody knew me better: he had been in my life for over two years now, and he had watched my transformation from an injured ex-heptathlete at 136 pounds to an Olympic 1500-meter runner who now tipped the scales at just 113.

Matt actually studied my training log for fun—that's how much he loved the sport. He knew every workout I had done over the past several months; each distance, rest interval, and pace, and he was almost as well informed about my competitors.

I asked him, "Do you want to be my coach?"

Matt was the obvious choice to replace Mike, at least in the short term, and, in a way, he was already coaching me. Now he showed me what he had done: on the table, he laid out sheets of paper, a rudimentary calendar and log. He had completely organized my training schedule.

It was a painstakingly arranged plan. I could see that a lot of time and thought had gone into it: he had factored in every contingency and had designed the workouts for every single day from August 1 until the Olympic Final. They were all written out in boxes.

"We have eight weeks," he said. "But the first priority is to get the iliotibial band healthy."

"Okay," I said, relieved.

At least I had a plan.

Ray called that same morning with a plan of his own. I had to fly to New York for the *Good Morning America* show the following week, and then he had arranged for me to go to Canada to see Scap for more treatment. "You can stay there as long as you need to," he said. Then, in August, I had an appearance in Denver for the USABA, from which he had arranged for me to go to the

Olympic Training Center to see Dr. Leahy, in case I needed more treatment.

When I hung up, I felt perfectly clear. I may not have had a coach, but I was thankful to have two great friends and organizers in Matt and Ray, and I clung to them, grateful for their stability and support. It was a vast relief to know that we were all so completely focused on the same thing, with no disharmony or differing agendas.

There was a kind of peace in the single-mindedness and simplicity of training for the Olympics. After a week with Scap and a visit to Dr. Leahy, I was able to train almost fully again. Life settled into a pleasant routine of treatment and running.

The program that Matt created for me was a good one. We collaborated, and found that we made a good team. He had a difficult job: he not only had to coach me but also had to be careful not to aggravate the remnants of the IT band injury, and he had to be a comforting companion as well. It helped that I had become numb to disappointment. Each day, we'd go to the track and try a workout, and if my leg was not compliant, we simply left. There were no more tears, no fits, no anger. At this point, those would be a waste of energy. I had finally learned patience.

But one afternoon, just two days before I was scheduled to fly to Australia, a distraction came in a strange and uninvited form. I was on the track enduring a session of repeat 400's, when Matt's cell phone rang.

"This is Matt," he answered.

As I jogged past him doing a 200-meter recovery interval, I could hear tension in his voice. "Uh-huh . . . yeah . . . uh-huh."

Finally he folded up his cell phone and slipped it into his pocket without a word.

"What was that all about?" I asked.

I could sense that he was reluctant to tell me.

"Oh, some guy says he thinks he can fix your eyes."

He tried to deliver the news casually. But it was impossible. This was a thunderbolt and we both knew it.

What? I thought.

Matt made an effort to gloss over it. He gestured at his stop-watch, and the straightaway, where I was supposed to begin my next 400. "You've got fifteen seconds, better get over there."

Some guy? Out of the blue, some guy called me? About my eyes?

I didn't have time to think about it then; the workout was more important. I pushed back my thoughts until I'd finished. But then they took over.

How dare some guy call me and claim he can fix my eyes? How dare he call me in the middle of a workout?

Like I needed curing. Like there was something wrong with me. I had just made the Olympic team. I didn't think I needed to be "fixed." How dare he.

He had also called my answering machine at home and left his phone number. I listened to the message, grinding my teeth. I was furious, and more offended with each word. The voice on the machine was full of urgency—as if he wanted to hurry up and "cure me" before the Olympics. Worst of all, he made it sound as if his "cure" would help me perform better as an athlete. *This guy doesn't know what he's talking about.*

Put it aside, I told myself. It would have to wait until after the Olympics—if I ever did anything about it at all.

So why did I scribble down his number and toss it on top of the desk? It must have meant more to me than I was willing to admit.

The man called back a few days later.

"I'm looking for Marla Runyan."

"This is Marla."

I recognized his voice from my machine. I felt something cold in the pit of my stomach. I didn't want to have this conversation. Or did I? I let him talk.

There was a machine, he explained, that had been designed many years ago as a visual training device. He had adapted it for use with Stargardt's patients, and he was having some success in restoring their vision.

"One of my patients went from 20/400 to 20/60 in twelve weeks," he claimed.

"Uh-huh."

I took this with a grain of salt. Or, at least, I tried to. *Who was this guy?*

I quizzed him about his credentials. He was a doctor in North Carolina, he said. I struggled to maintain a healthy skepticism. What kind of research did he have?

There was no research validating his findings, because he couldn't obtain the funding for his study, he explained. *Uh-oh.*

"But I've been having a seventy-five-percent success rate with my Stargardt's patients," he said.

I couldn't help it. I was as interested as I was angry.

But in the next breath, his claim grew more outlandish. He told me that he had treated a shot-putter with Stargardt's and corrected his vision from 20/400 to 20/40. The shot-putter, he boasted, had improved his personal best in the shot by eight feet.

Now, this didn't sound likely. As a former heptathlete, I knew full well that visual acuity had very little to do with the mechanics of throwing. Enhanced vision would hardly translate into such a dramatic personal-best performance. This guy wanted credit where none was due.

My heart sank. *Why now?* I thought. Why did he have to do this to me, get my hopes up and then shatter them, just two days before I was to step on an airplane for Sydney?

I hung up the phone and tried to dismiss the conversation. I decided to walk to the health-food store to buy dinner.

It was no use. I couldn't get the idea of seeing again out of my mind. As I strolled to the store and back, I looked around me; at every sidewalk, every intersection, and every green tree in the park. I began to wonder what these things *really* looked like, as opposed to the hazy shapes that I barely made out.

I began to wonder *what if.*

What if some day my vision was correctable? What would I do, if I could actually see? The possibilities were endless. Medical school? Veterinary school? I would be able to drive anywhere, at any time of the day or night. I would be able to read for leisure, and see the numbers on a telephone. I would be able to run rugged mountain trails with Matt. I would be able to see his face and look into his eyes. I would be able to cross the street without thinking about it, just like everybody else. I would be able to scan a menu, find a postage stamp.

They were teasing thoughts. Almost taunting ones.

I had never really considered such things before. But now that I did, the possibilities frightened me as much as they intrigued me. How would they redefine who I was? My disability had become such a part of me that in many ways it created me and determined who I was. If I erased it, who would I be, and what would I become?

There were no answers to these questions. And suddenly, another thought seized me: this kind of thinking would get me nowhere. It would make me want things I couldn't have, and I'd resent my impairment all over again. And that would only slow me down. *Get a grip.* I had to block it out, and get on with business.

It was time to go to Australia.

Matt and I flew to Brisbane, where we would stay for two weeks in a USA Track and Field training camp. The idea was to allow the American running contingent time to acclimate to the weather and time differences of Australia.

It was a good idea: my sleep-deprived body was achy and sore upon stepping into the sub-equatorial brightness. Brisbane was a warm, friendly place, but the blazing sun took some adjusting to. It was a strange thing, to try to comprehend that we had just traveled to the other side of the globe.

Our hotel was alongside a river and a small park where we took early-morning runs. Everything seemed exotic to me, from the banyan and mangrove trees to the sounds of birds and animals rustling in the shrubs, which weren't like anything I'd heard before. I saw birds that looked something like cockatoos, but their screeches reminded me of a wild-animal park back home.

One afternoon, Matt and I ran laps around a large grass field behind the practice track. As we reached one end of the field, suddenly Matt grabbed my arm and yelled, "Watch out!"

A three-foot-long iguana was basking in the sun, directly in my path. He had blended in with the sunburned brown and yellow grass, and I would have stepped right on his back if Matt hadn't grabbed me. We definitely were not in Eugene.

The practice track was a bright blue stripe, with a small white railing where a crowd of kids and spectators lined up and asked the athletes for autographs as we filed off the USA team bus. Each morning I stopped to sign a T-shirt or two, but then I'd stalk directly to the track. I had to catch up, I reminded myself. I still felt behind in my training.

The IT band injury was completely gone, and I was one hundred percent at last. Matt timed me each day, yelling support and building confidence, and I ran some of my fastest workout times of the last two years.

Finally, the USA team flew to Sydney. Matt and I had to split up—he wasn't allowed to stay in the Olympic Village with me. Instead, he would stay with a host family nearby and commute to the Olympic Park by bus and train. The peaceful interlude in Brisbane had lulled me—now I felt the momentousness of the occasion.

I finally arrived at the Olympic Games—and getting there could only be described as "an ordeal." I spent the whole day in a variety of vehicles. Security was so tight that it made getting into the Village a major feat. First, all sixty track athletes were bussed from Brisbane to an airport on the Gold Coast. Our luggage was trucked over separately. When we landed in Sydney, all sixty of us had to reclaim our luggage—no small task since we all had identical team bags. The only way to tell the bags apart was to read the name tags, and I couldn't. Fortunately, some of my teammates helped me out.

We piled onto busses to the Village while our bags were hauled there on another truck. Now it was after midnight. We filed off the bus to find that our bags had been tossed into the middle of the street. Again, sixty Olympians scrambled around trying to identify their luggage.

An Olympic Village is not luxurious. Fans often wonder why some athletes opt to stay at hotels and forgo the atmosphere of the Village, but they don't understand just how Spartan the accommodations are. Our home for the next two weeks was a newly built and bare-bones complex of small white low-slung cinder-block townhouses. Fifteen women were assigned to one house, and sometimes up to four people shared a room, in which the only furniture was blue plastic bed-frames and some patio chairs.

There weren't enough rooms for all the athletes, so they'd brought in trailers and affixed them to the houses. I was in a trailer adjacent to the main townhouse. The first week of our stay in the Village, the temperatures at night were cool, and we froze in our beds. Team managers dispersed blankets and gave us portable heaters, which we put directly between our beds, but it was hard to get comfortable. Those blue plastic bed-frames looked like toys, something Barbie dolls might sleep in, and they were as hard as rocks. At only four percent body fat, I could feel every hard place in the mattress.

I didn't mind it, though. The Village was clean and convenient—that was all that counted. It offered a respite from the crowds and the press, which weren't allowed on the grounds. We were isolated, and I liked it that way. There was no television other than a big screen in the central area, on which coverage of the Games was shown constantly. From the streets of the Village, we could make out in the distance the various risers and curving walls of the Olympic Stadium and some smaller arenas. Once the Games had commenced, we could hear the crowds across the way, erupting at the various medal performances.

From the exterior, the Village looked like a military compound. It was sectioned off with fencing twenty feet high, and barbed wire ran on top of that—and at each end of the Village were two large gates with the highest level of security imaginable. Every day, I put my bags through a metal detector and walked through another detector. Each athlete had a credential with a bar code and a photograph, and as we entered, our bar codes were scanned and our photos examined.

The dining hall was an interesting adventure, too. It was enormous, a warehouse-sized building with a mind-boggling array of cuisines available. I filed through the buffet lines, staring into hotplates and trays, at an indistinct array of colors. There were foods from every possible country and culture available, but I couldn't tell them apart. If I wanted to know what something was, I had to ask the person to the left or right of me.

"Is that broccoli or spinach pasta?"

"Is that mashed potatoes or cauliflower?"

"Is that chicken or fish or pork?"

"What the hell is *that?*"

"Can you help me find some broccoli?" I asked a coach from the U.S. team.

Eating became so complicated that mostly I just chose broccoli and fish and salads. I thought I was eating plenty; in fact, I was certain that I'd gained weight in Australia—but I hadn't. When I stepped on a scale, it read 50 kilograms. "What is the conversion on that?" I asked one of the athletic trainers. She said that I was just 110 pounds. My previous low had been 113.

"No way," I said. "I think that's broken."

But in the Village, I weighed myself again, this time on a digital scale, and it, too, read 110. How had I gotten so low? I'm still not sure. Stress was part of it, and the injury, and my hurried attempt to prepare for the Games. Whatever the explanation, I was light. I could feel it when I jogged so easily and effortlessly on the grass in the Village.

I felt lonesome without Matt, who had to slog back and forth to the Olympic Park, fighting the crowds and bus schedules. He spent most of his time walking. He would trudge from the Olympic Park to the Village to visit me, which was a hike of about an hour. At the end of the day, he had to walk all the way back and get on another bus. He never complained.

Finding my way around the sprawling Olympic Park was not unlike starting at a new school—only magnified. It took me a few days, but I eventually got a routine down. I memorized my routes to and from all the essential places: the sports-medicine clinic, the massage area, the dining hall, the bus terminal, and the warmup track.

It was on that track each day, in the shadow of the cauldron holding the Olympic flame, that I felt the spirit of the Games most deeply. The red Mondo oval was adjacent to the largest Olympic Stadium ever built. The stadium's proportions were so big that even I could see it, and it was an architectural marvel, a handsome sailboat-like structure meant to echo the vessels that moved in and out of the city's glittering green harbor. Each day, I loped around that red track, and as I came off the first turn, there before me loomed the huge butterfly shape of the grandstands, with soaring white pylons and the Olympic flame leaping high atop it.

Each day I met Matt at the warmup track, with that huge shape of the Olympic stadium in the background. On that track, surrounded by the best athletes in the world, I had a daily sense of the occasion. Usually at a crowded track meet back in the States, there are all kinds of hangers-on and sloppy-looking wanna-be athletes.

But here they were only the best jumpers, the best throwers, and the best hurdlers. They were the elite of the elite, and it was a tremendous thing to be in that company. I never got tired of the feeling.

I dressed for the opening ceremonies, torn between reverence and a sense of the ridiculous. I was very proud to wear an American uniform, except that the attire made me look and feel like a flight attendant. I put on the obligatory red blazer, cream scarf, mid-length blue polyester skirt, and straw boater, but I couldn't make myself wear the navy-blue pumps. They felt awkward and uncomfortable on my feet—I never wear heels—so I exchanged them for a pair of running shoes. At first I carried the shoes under my arm, in case I got in trouble for breaking the dress code, but as the night wore on I ditched them.

We gathered by nation in the gymnastics stadium adjacent to the Olympic Stadium. It was a splendid thing to know that virtually every athlete at the Games was there, all dressed up by country.

Each country was called in alphabetical order, and we began the march into the Olympic Stadium. As I paraded with my fellow distance runners toward the stadium, we fell in behind the women's basketball Dream Team. They bobbed and chanted, "Who let the dogs out, who-who-who!" They were a spirited group, and they were easy to spot, since they were a foot taller than the rest of us.

As we approached the stadium, our flagbearer lifted the flag, and I could see it, waving in the evening breeze. But as we marched around the track, all I could see was a hazy ring of lights. Another distance runner, Ann Marie Lauck, narrated the festivities to me: she described the scene as Australia's great runner, Cathy Freeman, took the stage and held aloft the Olympic flame. I stared upward. At first I couldn't make out the tiny figure atop the stadium. But when Freeman lit a huge ring of fire and stood in the middle of it, I could see the giant blaze of light.

The opening ceremonies were magnificent, but they were also exhausting. The athletes spent five hours on their feet. Good thing I wasn't wearing those blue pumps.

I became totally focused on preparing for the 1500. It was a long wait for those of us who weren't scheduled to compete until the end of the Games. I didn't go to any other events. I barely watched television. I simply ate and rested and worked out.

My first heat of the 1500 wouldn't be until the Wednesday morning of the second week. Until then it was all about rest. To keep my mind off things, and to relax, I would sit in my house at the Village, my door open to the gorgeous weather and the crowd noises, while I cruised on the Internet, reading and writing e-mail on my laptop.

One afternoon, a woman appeared in the open door.

"Is Marla here?"

"She's inside," one of my housemates yelled.

I couldn't see who was speaking, of course, and even if I could have, I wouldn't have recognized her. I knew Margo Jennings only by reputation, but I'd wanted to meet her for some time. Margo was a schoolteacher from Eugene who moonlighted as the long-time personal coach of Maria Mutola of Mozambique, and their partnership had just paid off. A day or so earlier, Mutola had won the Olympic gold medal in the 800 meters.

When Mike and I had parted, I'd immediately thought of contacting her, but I didn't really know her, nor did I know much about her training philosophy or personality.

As Margo moved in front of me, I made out a smallish brunette middle-aged woman. She had a strong, up-front voice.

"I heard about your split with Mike, and I want to know if I can help you," she said.

I told her it was a welcome offer. We chatted briefly, and I explained my training up to that point and told her I was feeling good about my fitness, considering all that had happened. As we talked, she was very serious, and slightly intimidating—so much so that I almost felt I had to defend myself. But she had confidence in me, too.

"I saw Masterkova on the track yesterday," Margo said. "She looks good."

Svetlana Masterkova, the defending Olympic 1500 champion, was a favorite to win the gold medal, most observers thought—especially since Regina Jacobs had withdrawn six weeks before the Games with a respiratory infection.

"I don't know if anyone can beat her," I said.

"You can," Margo replied.

I paused. Margo had been coaching Mutola, one of the best athletes in the world, for over a decade. She did not view anyone as unbeatable, given the talent level she was used to working with.

"Well, I don't know about that," I said.

Margo raised an eyebrow. She had a better opinion of my chances than I did—something that I would come to appreciate in her. I had just met my new coach.

"If you'd like to talk about working together next year, let's meet when we get back to Eugene," she offered.

Margo and I chatted a bit more, exchanged phone numbers, and agreed to get together for coffee when the Games were over. After a few minutes she left, and I wouldn't see her again until I got back home. But what she'd said stayed with me. I didn't quite realize it yet, but Margo had put her finger on my last real vulnerability. I was finally healthy—but I didn't quite believe in myself yet.

As the first round of the 1500 approached, I was nerve-wracked. Once more, I had slightly overdone my training, and I went into the heat slightly tired, and anxious. That morning, I woke up to the sound of rain. I tried to tell myself that it was just like Eugene, as I went through my familiar pre-race ritual.

I suited up in what Matt and I jokingly called my Bat Girl outfit. The USA team uniforms were a navy blue mesh, with a red and light-blue weblike stencil pattern on the sides and on the rear of the briefs. They made us look like superheroes. One of the pole-vaulters had provoked high hilarity in our house when she stuck herself to a wall, with her legs and arms sprawled out, and said, "I'm Spiderman!"

But now as I put on the uniform, I felt exhausted. The anticipation had been draining.

As I rode the shuttle bus to the track, the rain stopped, but a slow drizzle continued to dampen the ground. At the check-in, officials held the runners in a tent where our bags were searched and inspected for labels or product logos. The International Olympic Committee was militarily strict about logos that competed with those of their loyal sponsors. Any unsanctioned logos were torn off or taped over. A woman even took a black piece of tape and covered up the small "ASICS" on my hat.

Also during the search, I was told that my small bag of acrylic replacement spikes was, for some unexplained reason, not allowed into the stadium. It was confiscated, and I was told to fill out a form in order to retrieve the bag later. Great, I thought—paperwork.

They only wanted me to write down my bib number and my name, but suddenly this task became unimaginably difficult. I picked up the pen—and my hand began literally shaking. I looked down at the paper and hurriedly and spastically scribbled something that in no way resembled a signature.

"Here," I said, and hastily shoved the paper at an official, hoping she wouldn't notice my trembling hands.

We lined up and were escorted down a spiral ramp underneath the stadium, where there was a small stretch of track. Next to the runway, a huge clock was mounted on the wall at eye level. The clock was so large that I could see the second hand ticking away. I counted the minutes. I told myself, *In sixteen minutes and thirty seconds, it will be over.*

We were led to a circle of chairs and given our hip numbers, which would display our positions on the start line. I tried to peel the large stickers from the adhesive backing. My hands were vibrating wildly. It was impossible.

"I can't do this," I said, and I handed the stickers to an official. He peeled the white paper off the backs and handed the stickers to me. I slapped them on the hips of my briefs.

Now it was just minutes before the race. We were told to drop our warmup suits into baskets and make our way out onto the track. I gazed around at the other runners. Masterkova was in my heat. I would be running against a woman who had won two gold medals in the 1996 Olympic Games and another at the 1999 World Championships. She was distinct and easy to spot: tall, almost stocky, bigger than the other runners, with a pale complexion and very blond shoulder-length hair.

It was time to enter the stadium.

It is one of the peculiarities of high-level track and field that the athletes are not allowed into the stadium until just moments before their competition. The arena is used for actual competition while all of the practicing and training is done on a warmup track. The result is that you often go into a stadium cold, with no real knowledge of what sort of surroundings or atmosphere to expect. I had never set foot in the Olympic Stadium until that moment.

As soon as we entered, I was disoriented.

Typically, the 1500-meter competitors are brought into a stadium at the 100-meter start and walked around the track to the 1500-meter start. In fact, I can't remember a time when I'd entered a track in any other way. But on this occasion, as we stepped out into the misty morning and I began to walk toward what I took to be the start, an official stood in my way, and motioned me back.

"We start here?" I said, confused.

This was backward. It was the same feeling I'd had when I got into a car in Sydney for the first time and realized that they drove on the left side of the road and that the steering wheel was on the right. The whole world seemed to have flip-flopped.

If this is the start, then the finish is where? Over there? I couldn't see it, of course. I tried to get a mental picture of the track, to map it out in my mind. There were few clues to help me. The track was symmetrical, all the way around. A solid white, unmarked containing wall bordered it, and the crowd was set back from the perimeter. I gazed upward at the soaring grandstands full of spectators. The stadium was a wide bowl, open at both ends, not as self-contained as Estadio Olimpico in Seville.

I got my bearings and stepped to the starting position.

Okay, calm down, this is only the first round. Just qualify. The top six runners from each of three heats would automatically qualify for the semifinals, as well as the six runners who posted the next-fastest times.

The gun sounded and we were off. The pace slowed almost immediately. It would be a tactical race, a jog-a-thon for the first two laps.

I ran in the middle and then drifted to the back, just to the outside of Masterkova, keeping her in my periphery. If she, too, was near the back, I figured I was safe for the time being. All that mattered was finishing in the top six and moving on to the next heat. I recalled the Pan-Am Games, and how important that final lap had been. *Position doesn't matter yet,* I told myself. The pack was all clumped together. The important thing was to try to stay as calm and relaxed as possible.

But I fought a rising anxiety. I thought, *Get UP there, right now!* But an instant later I rejected the idea. As we trotted around the monotonous oval, I kept losing my bearings. *Where are we now? Was that the backstretch, or the homestretch?* The two sides of the stadium seemed identical.

Our time for the first 800 meters was 2:20—very slow. And then things started to happen.

Right next to me, Masterkova dropped out. She just drifted into the infield and pulled up. *What?* I was puzzled. For an instant, I was a spectator in my own race again.

But in that moment, while I was wondering why the great

Masterkova had just stopped running, the pack accelerated. The other runners shot ahead and left me in their wake.

Wait! I thought. The pack had moved quickly and without warning. I had failed to react, and had fallen behind. Way behind. Now I launched a mad kick, trying to catch up. This was no time for rhythm or conservation or patience. I had blown it, and it would take all I had left to correct the mistake.

With just 200 meters to go, I was still fighting to get back into position. My kick might get me there, but, I also realized, the pack could kick just as fast and as hard. I had made a classic beginner's mistake and failed to realize that a "kick" is a relative thing. In a race of this caliber, my kick wouldn't separate me. Everybody had a kick.

I did the only thing I could: I got up on my toes and sprinted desperately for the finish line. I scrambled frantically through the pack, toward the front.

I finished seventh. One place away from qualifying automatically. But then I caught a break: my time was among the next six fastest. I had made it, barely, to the semifinals—as the second-to-last qualifier.

I was disgusted with myself. I had misjudged my opponents and my own ability. And I hadn't been paying close enough attention to the pack and had missed the dramatic pace-change. I had almost cost myself everything. *I will never, ever do that again,* I swore to myself. I hung my head, seething inside.

On the warmup track, Ray approached me.

"You were so far back," he said. "We were worried."

"Look, I made a mistake and it won't happen again," I snapped.

I had twenty-four hours to think about my narrowly averted disaster—the semifinals would not be run until the following night. The next day, the mistake gave me a sense of purpose. I had to correct it.

The next evening was an entirely different atmosphere, and an entirely different race. We were escorted and quarantined as before, and again I sat on the strip of Mondo under the stadium and stared at the big clock.

In twelve minutes and twenty-five seconds, it will be over.

I was in the first of two semifinals. In this round, the first five in each race would advance to the final, along with the two next-fastest runners. A lot less margin for error.

This time there was no rain, and the air was soft and warm. The stadium was illuminated and full to capacity, and I felt a surge of energy. My exhaustion seemed to have receded with the dead gray skies of the previous morning.

The gun sounded, and this time I took immediate control of my fate. I ran near the front, just to the outside, and off the shoulder of the leader, a nameless figure in red with whom I bumped elbows. I ran as efficiently and rhythmically as I could. Another ten runners were behind us, calmly sitting on us, while we worked at keeping the pace moving.

This time, I could sense where I was on the track, how much distance we had covered, and how much was left to run. At the 800 mark, I actually spotted the large digital clock that displayed our split time. It read "2:14." Slow, but not too bad.

I took the lead. I was tired of bumping elbows; the race seemed more laborious than it needed to be. I wanted the lead so I could relax and stop jostling. I figured that at our current pace, I could lead and yet conserve something for that final lap.

My lead only lasted a matter of seconds. My American team-mate, Suzy Favor Hamilton, came up along the outside and took over. More runners followed her. As we approached the bell lap, I counted the bodies as they passed me. *One, two, three, four . . . okay, I'm still in fifth . . . it's okay.*

Just then, a fifth opponent passed me. I had fallen from first to sixth in a matter of seconds.

So this is the Olympics.

I tried to mount something that resembled a kick.

We entered the final turn.

I was passed again. Now I was seventh.

I got up onto my toes again, and sprinted with everything in my being. I devoted every single cell and molecule to getting to that finish line.

I passed someone.

I crossed the line in sixth place—barely. I bent over. I'd run a time of 4:06.14, less than a second away from my lifetime best—and it had gotten me only sixth. The effort had felt much greater than in any race I'd run before. The Olympics, I was beginning to realize, was in a race category of its own. There was simply no experience that could have prepared me for it.

It was as though an Olympic heat had a life of its own. It was like trying to ride on the back of a boa constrictor. At one moment I was at the mercy of the pack, and struggling to stay in the race, and at another I was in the lead, and then I'd be thrown backward, trailing again and desperate to catch up. There seemed to be no consistency to it.

Now came a period of near-intolerable suspense as I watched the second semifinal. If the seventh finisher there beat my time, I was out. If my time was faster, I would be in the final.

Later, I found that the NBC-TV track commentators, Tom Hammond and Marty Liquori—who had himself made the 1968 Olympic 1500 final—had paid special attention to the pace of that seventh runner, without being completely impartial:

"Marla just ran 4:06.14; the seventh person in this race needs to run slower than that . . . the second-lap pace really lagged; we've got some people in here with big kicks who don't care if the pace is slow—and Marla Runyan doesn't care if the pace is slow! Szekely of Romania in front . . . this pace looks good for Marla . . . Szabo moving up now to qualify easily; Szekely wins it—the time . . . the time is 4:06.61—*Marla has made it!* Marla Runyan will be in the final on Sunday!"

I got my breath back, and thought about what had happened. Once again, I'd made some mistakes and been disoriented and desperate—but I had actually made it through. I was in the Olympic Final. The heats had begun with fifty athletes, and now it was down to just twelve, and I was one of them.

It was a feat that few people understood. Most spectators back home would only see the final and would remain unaware of the work and strain it had taken for those dozen runners to get there. But I knew, and so did Suzy Favor Hamilton, who had also advanced and was running superbly.

We had two days of rest between the semifinals and the Olympic 1500-meter final, which would be run on Saturday, September 30 at 8:05 P.M. I was glad for the recovery time. It gave me a chance to talk and dine with Matt. After I'd made the final, the NBC crew had called me over for a trackside interview. I said something like "I made it by the skin of my teeth. I'm going to do the best I can, and I'd really like to see Suzy come out of it with a medal. If there's anything I could do to help her, I'd do it."

In the next day or so, I heard about that from a lot of people. I thought I'd never hear the end of it. Margo Jennings was back in Eugene when she saw the interview, and she jumped right out of her chair and called my cell-phone number. I wasn't answering it, of course, but Margo left a long message.

"You can't be doing this for Suzy," she said into the phone. "You have to run this race for yourself. You can win it—*you*."

Next, I heard from Rahn Sheffield via e-mail. He pointed out that I'd been sixth in the faster semifinal. "The way I see it, you're three places out of medaling," he said. "Now go out there and kick some ass. Think medal, medal, medal, medal."

The messages were all very rousing, but I lacked the same belief in myself. Part of me said, "Let's be realistic here." I had only run 4:05, while a number of my competitors had run well under four minutes. (Suzy had run 3:57 in Oslo two months before the Games.) I had strength, but speed was a weakness. And it was my first Olympics, and in each stage of each race, I was forced to learn something new. I was the first American woman to make the 1500-meter final in her Olympic debut, and to think that I could medal seemed improbable, especially in such a tough field.

Yet when I controlled my nerves and relaxed, I seemed to make the right decisions without a lot of thought. I knew I was far from reaching my potential—it was obvious there was much more to come.

Over the next two days, I vacillated between self-doubt and confidence. Sometimes I felt mentally tough and excited for the race, and at other times I felt weak, and shaky, and scared. I was tired, but I couldn't fall asleep. It was a classic Olympic introduction. *Where do I fit into all this?* I wondered. Was it really a matter of my belief in myself, or was physiology the deciding factor? In the back of my mind, I knew that my preparation had been made far less than ideal by my injury and the break with Mike Manley. Common sense told me that running well was a function of both the physiological and the psychological.

Every now and then, I confided my doubts to Matt. "I'm afraid I don't belong here," I said. "What if I get out there and look really out of place? What if I fall off the back?"

Matt said, "You wouldn't be here if you didn't belong. When you're out there, you look like you're running easier than everybody else."

Matt reassured me. But there was a point at which I had to be alone with my thoughts and doubts, and not even he could help me.

On the morning of the Olympic final, he called me on my cell phone, a temporary luxury provided by Team USA. I was standing in line at the espresso stand in the village when the phone rang.

"Hi, it's me," Matt said. "Do you want to talk about the race?"

Matt rarely told me what to do in a race; instead, he shaped his coaching advice in the form of a belief—an expectation of what he thought I was capable of. "You're in the final, you know, and anything can happen in an Olympic final," he said. It was early in the morning. I didn't want to discuss it just then. He'd caught me off-guard.

"Look, I don't think there's much strategy to discuss," I snapped. "The best runner will win, and there isn't much I can do about it. I'll run my heart out. I'll run my best, and that's all I can do."

Sometimes his high expectations didn't sit well with me, because the pressure to succeed, the pressure not to disappoint him, was more than I could bear. I needed to know that our relationship was not conditional—not based on how I ran in a race. Any race. Even the Olympic final.

That evening, I went through my pre-race ritual for the last time: the warming up, stretching, strides, and the being quarantined in one tent or holding area after another. Although the format was the same, each Olympic race thus far had been slightly different, and so would this one be.

This was the final. This would decide the medalists—this was it. The word "pressure" is both overused and misunderstood. The thing that no one tells you about pressure is that it is not just a word—it's a state of being. When one is said to feel pressure, one actually *feels* it, in the weakening of the arms and legs, the quickening of breath, the trembling of hands, or the frantic, darting thoughts of a brain that has become suddenly and profoundly confused. There is just one sure antidote that I know of: experience.

I sat on the warmup strip of Mondo under the Olympic Stadium and went through my clock ritual for the last time. I watched the minute hand approach eight o'clock straight up. *In eleven minutes, it will be over.* My obsession with time was a way of distracting myself and of reminding myself that, no matter the outcome, life would go on.

It was a strange sensation. I had worked for so many years for this one occasion, and now that it was here, I felt a kind of slippage. It was momentous, yes, this gargantuan experience called the Olympics, but I felt a simultaneous certainty that it was just a moment in time that would pass. The pursuit of the thing, perhaps, was more important than the thing itself.

As we stepped out onto the brightly lit track, thousands of

spectators in the sold-out Stadium Australia crowd of 110,000 began to take flash pictures. It was like standing in starlight. Each competitor was introduced, and her credentials were announced. It seemed as though each runner was more decorated than the one before.

Don't listen, I told myself. *What they have run and what they will run tonight may be two very different things.* The outcome was still an unknown.

The great Gabriela Szabo was just to my left, on the inside. She was petite, and constantly jumped up and down on her toes like a nervous child. I wondered what she had to be nervous about. She was one of the favorites. Suzy Favor Hamilton was on the inside as well, also a favorite.

The gun fired—and the pack *sprinted* off the line.

For an instant, it felt as though I was in a 200-meter race without lanes. I was tangled up in a mess of feet and arms flying in every direction, and I got shoved to the back.

But in another instant, the pace quickly died. Despite that flying wedge of chaos at the start, it would be another tactical race. We were now jogging. Szabo was to my right, in the back. We completed the first 400 in a staggeringly slow time of 70 seconds. *This can't be,* I thought. At this rate, nothing would matter until the last 400 meters, and the winner would be the runner with the best short kick to the finish.

I wanted to run my race. I didn't want to sit there and then see who could kick the hardest. I wanted it to be a *race.*

I started moving up on the outside, and I took the lead. Running up front, I told myself to conserve as much oxygen as possible for that final grueling lap. I have to admit, another thought

pushed into my mind as well. For one brief instant, I allowed myself to think it. *I am leading the Olympic final.*

But as Mike Manley had once told me, "If you ever take the
lead, you had better be prepared to finish with it." No one seemed
willing to relieve me of my front-running duties. I was now the
pacesetter. My opponents were content to sit on me and wait.
And wait, and wait, for the final lap, the point at which the race
would truly begin.

I picked up the pace to 65 seconds on the second lap. Still the
pack sat in my back pocket, happy to allow the naïve American to
do all the work. But I didn't see a choice in the matter. The first
round had taught me that my kick was not as effective here as it
was in less competitive races. I lacked the 800-meter closing speed
that many of my opponents possessed. If I sat back in the pack
with the others, I might very well get left in the dust when
the surge took place. This was my only chance, I believed. So I
took it.

But by the third lap, I became disoriented again. Somehow, I
had lost my sense of where we were in the race. The track, and
the white wall, and the crowd looked so identical wherever I was
on the oval. *Do we have 600 or 400 to go?* I wondered. I had lost all
sense of where the finish line was.

Now other runners began to pass me on my right. I felt like
that annoying slow car in the fast lane. They jostled to get around
me. Finally, the bell clanged—just one lap to go. Now at least I
knew what stage of the race we were in. I had indeed misjudged the
oval; I had thought a lap and a half remained, instead of just one.

In a matter of seconds, I fell back to tenth place. By now I was
in pain, serious pain. I dug hard and deep into my chest, and ran

with whatever I could find. Lactic acid was filling my body, but I was still able to pick up my pace, just a little.

I could see the leaders—and now they were spreading thin. On the backstretch, I stared at their backs with envy. They weren't too far off—only a matter of six meters or so. It was enough, however. I couldn't catch them.

Suddenly, just 250 meters from the finish, Szabo came up on my right. *What is she doing back here?*

The crowd erupted. As we came off the turn, runners were spread out all over the track. I passed one of them again, maybe another—they were indistinct to me, I didn't know who anyone was anymore.

A fall. Someone up ahead of me and off to my left went down and rolled onto the infield.

The crowd moaned.

I hung on and powered across the finish line. I had no idea of what position I was in.

I placed my arms on my head. It had felt like a circus. A crazy, backward race.

Who had won? Who had fallen? A big screen mounted above the stadium was replaying the finish, but I couldn't see it. I walked over to the NBC crew and asked if they knew what place I had finished.

"Sixth, I think," someone said. "No, that's wrong. Eighth."

Eighth place.

It was chaos. Suddenly, my position wasn't important anymore. I felt a fist of disgust slug me in the stomach. I would never have foreseen this kind of race. Who would have anticipated it?

Just then, I saw a figure on the shoulder of the track. It was

Suzy. She was lying flat on her back. I bent over her, still trying to get my breath back.

"Suzy, what happened?" I asked. "Did you win?"

That's how confused I'd become over the last 100 meters.

Suzy shook her head from side to side, her eyes closed. No, she hadn't won. *Then what?* I wondered. Suddenly, I put it all together. *Oh, God,* I realized, *she was the one who fell.*

I bent over her. "You're going to be okay," I said, desperate to find a way to comfort her. "Suzy, don't forget what you accomplished this year. You ran the fastest time in the world. This was only one race. There will be more."

Suzy had carried enormous pressure into the race. It had taken all her effort to come back from surgery on her Achilles' tendon in '99, but she had done it. Her 3:57 earlier that season had vaulted her into position as a pre-race favorite.

She had simply run too hard too soon and had locked up 75 meters from the line. She collapsed. Later, it turned out that she may have become dehydrated and had had a slight reaction to anti-inflammatories as well.

I held Suzy's legs up with one arm and continued to talk to her, but she didn't respond. An official approached. "I can pick her up," I said. She was so light. The official said, "No, we'll get a wheelchair for her."

I kept expecting Suzy to stand up, but instead she remained limp. Her sunglasses fell off, and I picked them up and later gave them to her coach. Suzy was rolled out of the stadium, and now I was left with my own thoughts about the outcome of the race.

I was haunted by the chaos of the finish and by my decision to take the lead on the second lap. I knew everyone would question my choice. I questioned it myself. As I have said, sometimes—and perhaps more often than not—the slow races hurt more than the fast ones.

Nouria Merah-Benida of Algeria had won the gold medal in a time of 4:05.10. She'd edged Violeta Szekely of Romania by five hundredths of a second. Gabriela Szabo had come from far back to take the bronze after hurdling a British runner who'd fallen on the third lap.

Finally, I found Matt back at the warmup track.

"What the hell was that?" I asked.

"That was an Olympic final," he said.

Matt had been right: anything can happen in an Olympic final, and it did.

I was still thinking about the Olympic final on the plane going home. I had waited years for that race. Now it seemed like I might spend years thinking about it and wondering what the outcome might have been if I had made a different decision.

Taking the lead on the second lap had felt like the only choice at the time. I had convinced myself that I did not have the speed of the other girls. When the pace slowed to a jog, I rebelled. I believed that such a slow pace spelled my doom, because I would not be able to sprint the last 600 meters with my competitors. So, I ran up to the front and led. In some ways it was suicidal, but I wanted the pace to be honest. I knew they would come to get me eventually, and they did.

I will always wonder what would have happened if I had sat in the pack and kicked with the rest of the field. Maybe I could have held on for a medal. Or not.

I had to console myself with the fact that I had learned something every day, in every instant that I had spent at the Olympics. In every lap of every heat, I had gained tactical knowledge. I learned about myself, and about my potential. I learned about my competitors; that they have weaknesses and insecurities and doubts, too. I learned that I still have much more to learn and that the only way to learn it is to race internationally.

I learned that no matter how hard you train, the race is still dependent on what you believe. If I had believed differently, perhaps I could have kicked with those other runners. Somehow my motivation and confidence had wavered just a bit, and it had cost me.

Before the race, I had counted the minutes until it would be over.

Now, I count the minutes until I can have another chance.

11. The Future Has Not Been Written

When I look in the mirror, I can't see my own eyes. This is an unalterable fact. There is no miracle cure for my vision: just because I am an Olympian, life doesn't suddenly get easier. Coping is an open-ended project, much like distance running. It's a simple analogy, but apt.

Shortly after the Olympics ended, I was invited to speak to a Low Vision Symposium in Portland, where I addressed a room of seven hundred people, many of them seniors with macular degeneration. I realized that, even at 32 years old, I am still trying to educate myself, and those around me, about what I can and can't do. Each time I address the subject, my views become more crystallized. I learn more fully each day how Stargardt's disease shapes my behavior and the behavior of those around me. Here are just some of the things I've learned:

Much of the rest of the world perceives only two categories of vision: fully sighted and fully blind. Partial blindness presents a continual dilemma, both for me and for others.

I've learned how much easier life becomes when I accept my impairment and don't insist on pretending that I see things the same way that anyone else does, whether it's in a mall, on a hike, or on the track.

I've learned that, like it or not, my experience of the world is fundamentally different from yours. That's a simple fact, but it's amazing how hard I've fought it.

Take social events. I've learned that I don't like socializing in large groups. I'm trying to get better at it, but it remains a source of awkwardness for me because I can't visually recognize who is talking to me or who is around me in the room. It becomes difficult to make casual conversation when you don't know who's standing right in front of you. *I can see you, but I can't see who you are,* I want to explain. Sometimes I just fake it as well as I can. A party may never be the same pleasant experience for me that it is for others; to me, it represents work.

I've learned not to turn small tasks into epic struggles, and that being independent does not mean I can't ask for help. When you're partially sighted, there are simply certain things you can't do. It makes more sense to have somebody read something to you—to use somebody else's eyesight for a while—to help you get your job done.

I've learned that what really makes you independent is how you arrange that help. It might be hiring a reader to read your mail to you once a week or finding a personal grocery-shopper.

I go to the grocery store for myself, but sometimes, if I don't ask for help when I need it, I strain to find the right shelves, and squint at the prices. Nothing is ever easy, not even finding a can of tuna.

The cans all look the same. I stand there and go over the labels with my magnifying glass. Is it oil or water? Is it salted or unsalted? Is it albacore, or pink, or chunky white? A can of tuna could take up half the morning.

I've made two rules for myself, and I've followed them ever since. They've made life immeasurably more pleasant.

Rule one: Remember that the person I'm talking to doesn't *know* I can't see.

I remind myself of this rule in everything I do. At the grocery store, and the bank, and the sandwich shop, I constantly remind myself that the person behind the counter *can't tell.*

Which leads me to my second rule: It's not their fault.

I used to expect others to have mental telepathy. They should have realized that I couldn't see—and if they didn't, it was because they were insensitive or unobservant. I'd think, *Why is he punishing me for being blind?*

That wasn't fair.

I've learned, too, that some people want to be angry. A woman at the Low Vision Symposium told me that she often goes into her local McDonald's, where she can't see the large printed board above the counter. Each time, she asks for a printed menu, and she always gets the same response:

"Printed menus? If we have them, I don't know where they are. Hey, John, do we have printed menus?" She immediately gets resentful—and so does the guy behind the counter. Then she launches into a lecture on the American Disabilities Act and says, "You're supposed to have printed menus for people who can't see!"

When she was finished, I said, "Do you really think that's going to get you what you want? I mean, I don't think I'd be drinking a soda from that dude after I'd yelled at him."

I explained to her my view that the guy behind the counter probably doesn't know partially sighted from blind, and so he wonders why she would ask for a menu when she can't even read it.

"I know, but they're in violation of my rights," she said.

"Wait a minute," I said. "All you want is a hamburger. Let's try to figure this out, instead of getting so worked up, okay?"

I gave my new friend my two inviolable rules and advised her to invoke them whenever possible. And I added that the only reason I ever learned them was because for fifteen years I didn't follow them myself—and frustrated the hell out of everybody around me.

I'm still learning these things, just as I'm still learning about myself as an athlete, and a person. A lot has happened since I arrived home from Sydney. There was an aftermath of e-mails, phone calls, and speaking engagements, and that was the least of it. Finally things quieted down, and I had a chance to appraise all that had happened.

From time to time, I couldn't help thinking about the phone call I had received just before the Olympics from the doctor who claimed to have cured some of the symptoms of Stargardt's. The call had lingered in the back of my mind, and I couldn't help hoping that there was something to it. But in the fall, I met a doctor who was on the cutting edge of research into Stargardt's, Dr. Richard Weleber, a professor of ophthalmology at the Casey Eye Institute in Portland. We had dinner. I told him about the call. Dr. Weleber essentially invalidated everything my phone tormentor had claimed. I was disappointed, but at least I had a little peace of mind, too. To date, there is no cure for Stargardt's.

My mother was in remission during the Olympics. She and my dad couldn't get over the sight of me running on that track with the flaming cauldron atop the stadium. Their big moment came in the final, when I pulled to the head of the pack. "I looked down, and my daughter was leading in the Olympics," my father marveled.

But in the fall after we returned home, my mother's cancer returned. She embarked on a torturous new chemo regimen and had terrible reactions to it, including a lung that collapsed twice. By Christmas she wasn't able to eat and had to be fed intravenously. She's still fighting it, and she bears it all with her usual good nature, even though I know there are moments when she's low and exhausted. She remains the most life-affirming person I know.

What I have learned from my mother is the importance of attitude every day. No matter what happens, you always have a choice in how to respond. My mother told me long ago, "You can't control what happens to you, but you can control how you respond, and how you think about it. And how you feel about it." She exemplifies that. I still take every other stride for her.

Margo Jennings and I met a few times at the Allann Brothers Coffee House to talk, and we agreed to work together. She created a program that suited me perfectly: it was strictly organized, and it would curb my habit of overtraining to the point of hurting myself. "The body likes consistency," she said.

I have also learned that running saves lives. It saved mine, and Matt's. Running has the potential to alter lifestyles and priorities. I believe that many of the diseases and conditions that plague our society—hypothyroidism, Type II diabetes, obesity—are the results of a lifestyle of poor judgment. Children run. This is a fact. Yet, somewhere between puberty and adulthood, they stop running and start slouching and dragging their feet. And they sustain themselves on staples of potato chips and Coca-Cola. And the cycle continues.

Perhaps it's idealistic of me to believe that the world could be saved if only everyone started running. "I don't have the time," people say, or "I'm not a runner." There are a million excuses. But the body was made to move. Muscles, tendons, heart, and lungs were designed to be challenged and to move our bodies through our environment naturally. I believe that running is the fountain of youth. You need not look any farther than inside your own body to find a way to feel and look younger. Beauty comes from the inside out. Running doesn't require an expensive gym membership or a lot of equipment. Kenyan children run barefoot along the grass fields and unpaved roads of their villages.

Running will influence the choices you make for yourself in everyday life. You will become more selective about the foods you put in your mouth, and your body will insist upon a good night's sleep. I prefer a long morning run to a late night of "high life," and I would rather compete in a race myself than passively watch the NBA playoffs or the Super Bowl.

Basically, what it comes down to is a choice: a decision to do the opposite of what mainstream America tells you to do every day. There is no secret, no pill, no quick fix. Put away the Snackwells and the fat-free potato chips, and shop in the produce section more often. Leave your car in the garage. Move your body. Breathe. Sweat. Eat less. Drink water. A line from Matt's favorite move, *The Shawshank Redemption,* says it best: *Get busy living, or get busy dying.*

I finally made peace with my Olympic experience. I'd qualified for the team and reached the 1500 final, after only a handful of races. When I examined my performance in Sydney for its strengths and weaknesses, I decided that I truly was an endurance runner. I also decided that my real potential lies in the 5000 meters.

If I had any lingering doubts about that, they were resolved in the winter following my return home.

I flew to New York City for an exhibition challenge 5000-meter race at the uptown Armory Track and Field Center, an indoor facility known for its fast track. Racing against nothing but the clock, in a gymnasium that smelled of liniment, before a highly charged audience of two thousand high-school track-team members and some local running aficionados, I went after the American indoor record. It was only the second time I'd run the 5000.

I was extremely calm and confident going into the exhibition.

But it's a funny fact of a runner's life that as you get closer and closer to the race, your confidence diminishes. An indoor 5000 is twenty-five laps. All of a sudden, it seemed so daunting. As I warmed up, I reminded myself to keep a good attitude no matter how much it might hurt. I walked over to the pacesetters, three runners who'd been recruited to help me, and I said, "No matter what happens, if we fall off the pace, let's never think it's out of reach."

After the first two laps, we were on perfect pace. Everything felt very, very good—and then and there I knew that I was going to have the record. I held my focus: the race was so long that I refused to even look at the trackside lap-counter until we had gone ten laps.

When I came to the 3000-meter mark, I heard my time over the loudspeaker: 9:08. The three pacesetters had done their jobs and then dropped out. Now it was just a matter of how much I would break the record by. I held the pace. It felt like I had been out there a day and a half. With a lap to go, as I came to the straightaway, some guy leaned out and yelled, "Sprint now! Sprint now!" I thought, *Yeah, right, buddy. You sprint.* But I closed strong—and crossed the line with a new American record.

I broke the old record by almost 15 seconds, and my time of 15:07.33 was the world's sixth-fastest ever indoors. Lynn Jennings' previous American record of 15:22.64 had stood for ten years.

The race was exhilarating and fun—and tantalizing. It made me wonder how I'd fare in international competition, and I hoped to find out by making the World Championships team.

The record meant a great deal to me for two reasons. First, it was an indication of how my work with Margo was progressing, and it proved my potential in the 5000. Second, an Olympic medalist had set the old record. I now knew exactly what I wanted and where I was headed.

I had seen the Summer Games as an end, but in fact it was a renewal, the beginning of another four-year cycle. I've begun to work toward the 2004 Games in Athens.

I do so with a new kind of commitment and contentment: I've bought a home in Eugene, and I'm earning a real living from track for the first time in my life. I was leery of the idea of buying a house at first—it meant change, and learning another neighborhood all over again, and I was a little frightened by the prospect, especially if it meant losing any of my hard-won independence. I didn't want to rely on Matt or anyone else. But when I found my house, I knew it was the right thing.

It's a split-level wood home, on a shady green hillside, with a large picture window in the living room. Outside I can see a forest of arching pines, which soften the sunlight and are easy on my eyes. It's a short walk to the running trails, and a grocery store, and a bus stop. I've memorized the roads and footpaths.

Sometimes I've gone for hikes with Matt, and I could swear I've seen the distinctions between all the greens beneath me, the various shades of color in the trees and their outlines against the sky. The things that are most beautiful and clear to me are whole pictures, landscapes, panoramas; holistic views of something.

Late in the evenings, Matt and Summer and I like to walk to our favorite store, the Oasis, for monster cookies and green tea. On those walks, I realize that what really makes me happy is not winning medals but simply the pursuit. No matter how I try to occupy my time, I've found nothing that can replace the role that running has in my life. Nothing offers the same challenge, reward, or vision.

The ability to run every day, the freedom to move my body without pain and to feel as though I can go forever, without a finish line—this is what I see ahead.